RECHOREOGRAPHING LEARNING

This book addresses the mind-body dichotomy in movement and dance.

This book includes a description of the often-forgotten kinesthetic sense, body awareness, somatic practices, body-based way of thinking, mental imagery, nonverbal communication, human empathy, and symbol systems, what occurs in the brain during learning, and why and how movement and dance should be part of school curricula. This exploration arguers that becoming more aware of bodily sensations serves as a basis for knowing, communicating, learning, and teaching through movement and dance.

This book will be of great interest to scholars and students interested in teaching methodology and for courses in physical education, dance, and education.

Sandra Cerny Minton is Co-Coordinator of the Dance Education MA Program at UNC, a program she created and which was instituted in 2014.

Routledge Advances in Theatre & Performance Studies

This series is our home for cutting-edge, upper-level scholarly studies and edited collections. Considering theatre and performance alongside topics such as religion, politics, gender, race, ecology, and the avant-garde, titles are characterized by dynamic interventions into established subjects and innovative studies on emerging topics.

Rechoreographing Learning
Dance As a Way to Bridge the Mind-Body Divide in Education
Sandra Cerny Minton

Politics as Public Art
The Aesthetics of Political Organizing and Social Movements
Martin Zebracki and Zane McNeill

Lessons for Today from Shakespeare's Classroom
The Learning Benefits of Drama and Rhetoric in Schools
Robin Lithgow

Notelets of Filth
An *Emilia* Companion Reader
Laura Kressly, Aida Patient, and Kimberly A. Williams

Transcultural Theater
Günther Heeg

For more information about this series, please visit: www.routledge.com/Routledge-Advances-in-Theatre—Performance-Studies/book-series/RATPS

RECHOREOGRAPHING LEARNING

Dance as a Way to Bridge the Mind-Body Divide in Education

Sandra Cerny Minton

LONDON AND NEW YORK

First published 2023
by Routledge
4 Park Square, Milton Park, Abingdon, Oxon OX14 4RN

and by Routledge
605 Third Avenue, New York, NY 10158

Routledge is an imprint of the Taylor & Francis Group, an informa business

© 2023 Sandra Cerny Minton

The right of Sandra Cerny Minton to be identified as author of this work has been asserted in accordance with sections 77 and 78 of the Copyright, Designs and Patents Act 1988.

All rights reserved. No part of this book may be reprinted or reproduced or utilised in any form or by any electronic, mechanical, or other means, now known or hereafter invented, including photocopying and recording, or in any information storage or retrieval system, without permission in writing from the publishers.

Trademark notice: Product or corporate names may be trademarks or registered trademarks, and are used only for identification and explanation without intent to infringe.

British Library Cataloguing-in-Publication Data
A catalogue record for this book is available from the British Library

Library of Congress Cataloging-in-Publication Data
Names: Minton, Sandra Cerny, 1943– author.
Title: Rechoreographing learning : dance as a way to bridge the mind-body divide in education / Sandra Cerny Minton.
Description: Abingdon, Oxon ; New York, NY : Routledge, 2023. | Series: Routledge advances in theatre and performance studies | Includes bibliographical references and index.
Identifiers: LCCN 2022036943 (print) | LCCN 2022036944 (ebook) | ISBN 9781032193809 (hardback) | ISBN 9781032193830 (paperback) | ISBN 9781003258926 (ebook)
Subjects: LCSH: Dance in education. | Movement in education. | Dance—Psychological aspects. | Dance—Physiological aspects. | Mind and body.
Classification: LCC GV1588.4 .M559 2023 (print) | LCC GV1588.4 (ebook) | DDC 372.86/8—dc23/eng/20220923
LC record available at https://lccn.loc.gov/2022036943
LC ebook record available at https://lccn.loc.gov/2022036944

ISBN: 978-1-032-19380-9 (hbk)
ISBN: 978-1-032-19383-0 (pbk)
ISBN: 978-1-003-25892-6 (ebk)

DOI: 10.4324/9781003258926

Typeset in Bembo
by Apex CoVantage, LLC

FIGURE 0.1 Freidan Parker at Red Rocks Park. D025.04.0001.0007.00002. Marshal and Carolyn Durand Brooks Photography and Dance Collection, D025, The Dance Archive, Special Collections and Archives, University Libraries, University of Denver.

*This book is dedicated to Dr. Alma M. Hawkins and
Dr. Valerie Hunt, who motivated my interest in the creative
process, the mind-body connection, and beyond when I was a
student in the UCLA Dance program. I also dedicate this book
to my husband, Clarence Colburn, who has always encouraged
my creative endeavors.*

CONTENTS

Acknowledgments   xi
About the Author   xii
Preface   xiii

1   Combatting the Mind-Body Dichotomy   1
    A Discussion of the Mind-Body Dichotomy 1
    Making the Case for the Body Basis
      of Knowing—Pioneers 4
    Accessing the Body Way of Knowing 12
    Exploration Experiences 16

2   Sensory Reception and Their Contributions to
    Body Knowledge   21
    Human Sensory Systems 21
    Human Sensation and the Mind-Body Connection 26
    Applications to Learning Movement and Dance 31
    Exploration Experiences 40

3   Connections between Body, Brain, Mind, and Thinking   54
    The Body Way of Knowing 54
    The Role of Attention 70
    Mental Imagery 77
    Exploration Experiences 98

4   The Role of the Body in Interpersonal Connections
    and Communications   113
    Introduction 113

Empathy 114
Nonverbal Communication 125
Symbolic Communication 130
Exploration Experiences 142

5 The Body, Movement, Dance, and Learning 151
Popular Learning Theories 151
Creativity 173
Learning through the Arts 186
Exploration Experiences 197

6 In Conclusion 207
Further Evidence 207
Future Considerations 208
Recommendations 209
Discussion 211

Glossary 215
Index 223

ACKNOWLEDGMENTS

I would like to acknowledge the following people for their help and support in writing this book:

- Toni Duncan, MA, for reading the manuscript and providing comments, and
- Teresa Heiland, CLMA, PhD, for her help in composing the section dealing with Language of Dance, Labanotation, and Motif Notation.

ABOUT THE AUTHOR

Sandra Cerny Minton, PhD, was Dance Coordinator at the University of Northern Colorado (UNC), 1972–1998. She taught dance in the public schools at the elementary and middle school levels and presented interdisciplinary teachers' workshops face-to-face and online. Minton's Human Kinetics books include *Choreography: A Basic Approach Using Improvisation*, 4th edition (2018), and *Preventing Dance Injuries* (co-editor with John and Ruth Solomon). *Using Movement to Teach Academics: The Mind & Body As One Entity* and *Thinking with the Dancing Brain: Embodying Neuroscience* (coauthored with Rima Faber) were published by Rowman & Littlefield Education in 2008 and 2016, respectively. Minton's research, including studies of the effects of dance on creativity and self-esteem, the kinesthetic sense, body awareness, and mental imagery, has been published in juried journals. She was the 1999 National Dance Association Artist/Scholar, a 2001 Fulbright Scholar to Finland, and received the 2020 Lifetime Achievement award from the National Dance Education Organization (NDEO). Minton's MA and PhD degrees are from UCLA (dance/dance education) and Texas Woman's University (dance education/kinesiology). Her MA thesis explored involvement in improvisation experiences, and her dissertation was based on mental imagery and somatic practices. Minton has helped write the dance standards and dance curricula for the Colorado Department of Education. She is a founding member of NDEO and the Colorado Dance Education Organization (CoDEO). Minton is also on the board of the Dance Archive at the University of Denver. Currently, Minton is Co-Coordinator of the Dance Education MA Program at UNC—a program she created and which was instituted in 2014.

PREFACE

The information encompassed in this book is content the author has been thinking and writing about in one shape or form for an uncountable number of years—in fact, for her entire professional life. In the same vein, choreographers, dancers, and dance educators have realized that dance and the body provide a remarkably insightful and useful instrument for awareness about self, communication with others, interactions with the environment, and connections to cognition. In terms of one's response to the input which comes to an individual, pioneering dance educator Alma Hawkins noted that humans encounter a constant flow of sensory information from the outer world which must be brought together into meaningful relationships (5–6). Hawkins commented:

> The symbolic transformation of experience is frequently expressed through words, but not always. Sometimes we find that words are completely inadequate to express our response to some of life's encounters, especially the felt aspects of experience. In these instances, we turn to other media, such as motion, sound, or painting, as a means of expression.
>
> (6)

How and why awareness and learning can take place on the bodily level is the question explored and probed throughout this book based on the writings of many authorities from different disciplines. This question is first investigated from a historical perspective in Chapter 1 based on the mind-body dichotomy—a viewpoint which has blocked, to a certain extent, a true and thorough understanding of the bodily basis of knowing and its usefulness. The mind-body relationship is explored from both an Eastern and Western perspective as well in this chapter.

In Chapter 2, the content is focused on the human sensory systems and their relationship to the bodily way of knowing. Exteroception (stimuli coming from the environment), proprioception (input from sensors in the muscles and joints), and interoception (the ability to sense one's internal body state) are all discussed in terms of how and why they contribute to bodily knowledge. The connections between exteroception, proprioception, and interoception and dance are also explored.

Next, the question of how to tap into an awareness of the bodily way of knowing is introduced. This question is discussed from the somatic perspective and debated in terms of phenomenological, psychological, educational, and neuroscience viewpoints, followed by an introduction of why this information is pertinent to the dance education arena. Tapping into the bodily way of knowing is also based on learning to pay attention to signals from the body and how one's attention to bodily sensations can be heightened through somatic practices during the creative process and in both technique and choreography classes. The third chapter concludes by describing the relationship between body awareness and mental imagery in its various forms and their connection to and use in dance education practices.

The body way of knowing also plays an important role in interpersonal communication. Empathy is described and investigated in Chapter 4 since it is an integral factor in interpersonal communication and has bodily/neural origins. The fact that neuroscience research has shown empathy has a physical basis is presented, along with how the arts and dance are a way to encourage empathy among students. Movement and gestures are also included in this same chapter because they enable people to communicate nonverbally and make up a large portion of how humans connect. Movement and gesture are discussed based on cultural differences and why they can be considered symbolic in nature.

Chapter 5 comes full circle by demonstrating connections between well-known learning theories and dance. Relationships are drawn between dance education and Robert and Michèle Root-Berstein's theories about creativity and the thinking tools they discovered which are an integral part of the creative process. This chapter concludes with research on how and why dance can be used to develop thinking skills in students itself and through a movement/dance integrated approach.

The final chapter is included as a summary of next steps which could help promote dance as a significant educational tool and teaching strategy in the twenty-first century. It is the opinion of the author that dance education is on the brink of being discovered for the contributions it can make in the larger education world and beyond.

It is also the belief of the author that one of the reasons body, movement, and dance have not been recognized earlier for the possible contributions they can make to education is that much of what we know and create occurs below the conscious level of our thoughts. However, recent neuroscience research, as described in this book, is beginning to reveal the connection between mind and body more thoroughly. Hawkins summed up the mind-body conundrum when she wrote:

> Our mode of thought ranges from the highly conscious to the deeply unconscious. When we are functioning at the highly conscious level, we are

concerned with the outer world of reality and action. At the deeply unconscious level, our interaction with the outer world is diminished, memory traces are deeply anchored, and there is less interest in action and more concern with self-experience.

(7)

Reference

Hawkins, Alma M. *Movement from Within: A New Method for Dance Making.* a capella books, 1991.

1
COMBATTING THE MIND-BODY DICHOTOMY

A Discussion of the Mind-Body Dichotomy

While many educators stress the fact that their goal is to educate the whole person, this seems in many cases to be far from the truth, because much educational content seems to be focused on a student's mind and filling it with content, without a true interest in the body and how it might aid a teacher's goals and the teaching techniques they use. Thus, in academia, the processes of teaching and learning continue to be largely based on cognitive approaches despite the fact that holistic and embodied techniques might better serve educational goals (Rodríguez-Jiménez and Carmona 229). The foregoing educational approach is manifest in the choice of disciplines which are customarily emphasized in school curricula. For example, in a 2015 issue of the *Oxford Review of Education*, Jennifer Bleazby wrote about the relative status of certain school disciplines, indicating that mathematics and the physical sciences are often the focus of a school district's program of study, while physical education and vocational training are marginalized (Bailey 279).

Educators such as Alexia Buono who are concerned with and teach early childhood education concur, blaming the current proliferation of bullying in schools on the failure to recognize the role the body could potentially play in learning; thus, efforts to shift pedagogical practices toward a holistic bodily view need to be developed (150). "Understanding how bodily experiences afford young children's development and teachers' responses to the body in the classroom is informative in understanding the roles a school culture can have on the relationship between child development and teacher pedagogy" (Buono 150).

In reference to the influence the mind-body dichotomy has had on culture, society, and education, John Dewey, noted educator, philosopher, and psychologist, claimed, "Men are afraid . . . to recognize the most wonderful of all the structures of the vast universe—the human body" (qtd. in Buono 150). It is revealing that Dewey made the preceding statement approximately one hundred years ago.

Western Historical Perspectives on the Mind-Body Dichotomy

The educational issue that has just been noted is in part due to the pervasive mind-body duality which continues to permeate education. Everyone has a mind and body, but while the body is concrete and its actions can be observed, the mind is lacking such concrete, observable characteristics. This duality is explained in the following quotation from the writings of Gottfried Leibniz, a seventeenth-century German mathematician, philosopher, and scientist, in his attempt to explain the mind-body divide. Although he opposed the dualistic viewpoint, Leibniz explained it in the following way: "According to this dualism, the world fundamentally consists of two disparate substances: extended material substance (body) and unextended thinking substance (mind)" ("Leibniz's" *Stanford Encyclopedia*).

The mind-body question, known as the Cartesian duality, has historical underpinnings in which the mental aspects of human knowing were given precedence over those which are based on a more physical mode or bodily way of understanding. The first attempt to divide mind from body was provided by Plato, who proposed that the two entities were constituted of two different substances (Dunn 3). In fact, Plato thought the soul, if one is to think of it as synonymous with the mind, was imprisoned in the body, but did not explain how the two were connected; Aristotle did not agree and claimed the soul was the form of the body (Tan 1110). In his treatise, Robert Heinaman argued whether Aristotle could also be considered a dualist. Heinaman explained that a belief the soul exists separately from the body would qualify an individual as a dualist; however, Aristotle rejected that concept for most types of souls, particularly if he believed the soul could not exist separate from the body (84). Kenny wrote that Aristotle believed the "soul's very essence is defined by its relationship to an organic structure" (192).

The debate over the division of mind and body continued to permeate thinking during the early Christian and medieval eras. Saint Augustine believed a person's will, not their body, was the source of evil because it was the sinful soul that corrupted the body (Twietmeyer 455–56). However, Augustine often spoke about the inward and outward man; certain aspects of the soul such as the senses and sensory memory, he believed, were connected to the outward man, while the inward man included the mind and its abilities to recollect, imagine, use rational judgment and contemplate with the intellect (Kenny 420).

Later, Saint Thomas Aquinas seemed to diverge from the dualistic viewpoint when he wrote about the soul and body, asserting that "[t]he soul is more like God when united with the human body than when separated from it, because its [the soul's] nature is then more perfect"; thus, Aquinas seemed to promote one of the first instances in which there was a philosophical and religious value attributed to the body in Western thought (Twietmeyer 453–54). For Aquinas, it was the human mind which set man apart from animals, because it was the human mind which enabled man to think abstractly and make rational decisions (Kenny 435). Aquinas also determined that it was the human senses which were essential to originating and exercising the intellect, although, in contrast to current understanding of mental activity, he considered imagination to be one of the inner human senses (Kenny 435).

The modern age in thought and dualism is said to have its beginnings with the thinking of René Descartes, who separated spirit from matter (Lowney 180). In describing the mind-body dichotomy, Descartes discussed the human body's senses by stating that "things known by the intellect have a higher reality than objects of the senses" ("Rene Descartes" *Stanford Encyclopedia*). In fact, Descartes claimed that the mind was more vital than the body, which was nothing more than a machine (Buono 150). Although his attitude toward the human senses was less disparaging in later years, Descartes did focus on intellect, which he felt had "a higher reality than the objects of the senses" ("Rene Descartes" *Stanford Encyclopedia*). In the *Discourse*, Descartes described a dualism between mind and matter—a premise he used to explain his system or approach to the world (Kenny 528). However, Descartes's decision to split the human into two entities may have been based on his effort to avoid the wrath of the Catholic Church and sidestep the Church's influence on science (Pitasi 99).

Nevertheless, it is interesting to note that Spinoza, whose life span intersected with that of Descartes, seemed to adopt an opposite notion, since he believed the mind and body were parallel attributes, meaning, his "dissent stood out in a sea of conformity" (Damasio *Looking* 12). Damasio wrote that Spinoza's words were considered heretical and often banned at that time; references to his writing were customarily included only in an assault on his work (*Looking* 14).

The Eastern Perspective on the Mind-Body Dichotomy

The mind-body dichotomy as described previously seems to be a manifestation of Western thought while being relatively absent from Eastern thinking. Certainly, the main concern when considering the philosophy of the mind in the West has been the relationship between mind and the physical body (Zeuschner 69). This apparent separation seems not to exist in the East. Since the time of the Warring States, Chinese philosophy has emphasized the importance of the body. "[F]or the early Confucians, body and mind were related and sensible to each other so that one person could open up to many others and be responsive to them" (Shen 316–17). Thus, the Chinese concept of the lived body is one with one's organic body.

Christian Coseru, philosophy professor at the College of Charleston, wrote that Buddhist philosophers seem to argue that each thought is the continuation of an endless series of thoughts (13). Coseru continued:

> Buddhist philosophers did not make a radical distinction between epistemological and psychological accounts of cognition (at least not in the way that

> dominant currents in modern Western philosophy drifted away from naturalist explanations after Kant).
>
> *(13–14)*

In the previous statement, Coseru is referring to the fact that Kant, in his philosophical writings, frequently referred to the human sensory experience and intuition. Even in terms of mathematical knowledge, "Kant believed that mathematical truths were forms of synthetic *a priori* knowledge, which means they are necessary and universal, yet known through intuition" ("Imanuel Kant" Wikipedia). Thus, Kant was vexed by an issue that was central to a way of thinking twentieth-century scholars called philosophy of mind and which is related to understanding how data from the outside world reaches the brain ("Imanuel Kant" Wikipedia).

To continue with the discussion of Buddhism and the mind-body, the term *body* in Buddhism refers not only to the physical body but also to the way experiences are held in an embodied form in the mind (Sacamano and Altman 1588–89). These authors indicated that from traditional Buddhist practices, it is possible to extrapolate that experience is a literal phenomenon which is felt symbolically and inherently realized (1589). It is relevant here that there is evidence of the mind-body connection in studies of brains of Buddhist practitioners. Thaddeus Pace, professor of nursing at the University of Arizona, and his colleagues wrote that there is a reduction of cortisol secretion in the brain following prolonged Buddhist meditation (Saniotis 850).

The discussion of the mental and physical can also be extended to the Hindu experience of emotion. Based on research by another writer, two of the most important characteristics of emotions are that they are grounded and experienced in the body (Menon 44).

> In Hindu India, therefore, emotions are not separated from, and thought of, as lower than reason. Emotions are also not thought to reside in the innermost recesses of the self; introspection will not help one recognize one's emotions nor know oneself better.
>
> *(Menon 47)*

Historically, the Muslim psychological model also acknowledged the mind-body connection. For over one thousand years, Muslim physicians have understood the mind-body connection and its relationship to disease (Saniotis 854). Much more recently, a study of Muslim religious practices by Sarah Al-Rawi and Michael Fetters discussed the therapeutic qualities of prayer (Saniotis 850).

Making the Case for the Body Basis of Knowing—Pioneers

Some of the early researchers and writers dealing with the bodily basis of knowing were not dancers or physical educators. It was the belief of these individuals that the basis of man's existence in the world can be found in the body and its movements.

According to Margaret Floy Washburn, a leading American psychologist in the early twentieth century, Henri-Etienne Beaunis, a French physiologist and psychologist, wrote, "Muscle sensations enter not only into our sensations, but into perception, ideas, sentiments, emotions . . . into the whole psychic life" (qtd. in Cerny 17). Some of these convictions were especially prevalent among those who were interested in and studied human perception.

The Role of the Body and Movement in Perception

Washburn, who was best known for her experimental work in animal behavior and motor theory development, was one of the individuals who believed in the mind-body connection. Although her contributions have been somewhat overlooked, her work closely aligns with the theme of this chapter. In her book *Movement and Mental Imagery*, Washburn wrote that man "through his movements . . . takes his place in the rest of the order of nature." In fact, Washburn felt man's whole inner life can be correlated with and shown to be dependent upon body movement (Cerny 12). A photo of Margaret Flow Washburn can be seen in Figure 1.1.

FIGURE 1.1 Margaret Floy Washburn. Archives and Special Collections, Vassar College Library.

Washburn's theory of consciousness was connected to her interest in movement because she posited that consciousness arises when the senses, such as vision, create an impression of an object, and this impression is accompanied by a sense of movement either toward or away from the object. As a result, thinking becomes a derivation of the movements of different body parts. She stated:

> While consciousness exists and is not a form of movement, it has as its indispensable basis certain motor processes, and . . . the only sense in which we can explain consciousness processes is by studying the laws governing these underlying motor phenomena.
>
> *("Margaret Floy Washburn" Wikipedia)*

Paul Schilder, an Austrian psychiatrist and medical researcher, discussed the relationship between a human's inner motion in relation to perception in his attempt to explain how humans understand the outside world. In his book *Mind: Perception and Thought in Their Constructive Aspects*, he explained that tensions within one's body are the basis of larger actions which can be observed (Cerny 13). Although the initial tensions are barely observable, they comprise the skeletal and muscular tonic system which leads to larger actions in relation to objects in one's environment which can lead to learning in a variety of situations. Schilder postulated that the inner bodily tensions or motions created during perception and the resulting motor impulses were connected, but he could not explain how the two worked together (Cerny 13–14).

The Role of the Body and Movement in Symbolization and Emotion

Other scholars adopted theories related to perception in their attempt to understand human thought. Writing describing these theories can be found sprinkled throughout literature written in the twentieth century. Heinze Werner and Bernard Kaplan were two developmental psychologists who formulated a movement-based theory of perception and symbol formation. They felt that man, unlike lower organisms, is more separated from nature and the environment. This means that perception operates through a symbolic understanding of the world, which provides for man's method for knowing (Cerny 12). In their book *Symbol Formation*, Werner and Kaplan proposed that symbolic knowledge is transformed during one lifetime, because an infant initially knows the world through his or her affective sensory motor patterns. They continued that this early developmental stage is transformed into one in which objects are contemplated instead of acting in response to them, which means that the early sensory and motor patterns become internalized based on an inner schematizing activity based on the original bodily state (Cerny 12–13).

Other researchers and writers also discussed perception in terms of its relationship to emotion and how those emotions could lead to knowing. Emotion seems to have two basic functions in the perceptual process. One of these is to select whatever one is to perceive. The second is to generate the emotional reaction to the stimulus which is perceived (Cerny 15). When persons experience the world, they are emotionally motivated to choose from multiple stimuli presented to them. The motivation for such choices is based on emotions related to a particular goal at that time. David Rapaport, a Hungarian clinical psychologist, believed this response enables the individual to become more knowledgeable about objects in the environment (Cerny 15).

The second correlation with emotion noted previously, the emotional response to environmental stimuli, is thought to be generated in the living body in response to what is perceived. Joshua Rosett, former professor of neurology at Columbia University, indicated that affective states accompany perception, and emotions are remembered and closely related to the feeling and movement reactions to stimuli when they are perceived (Cerny 19). Rosett continued, "[I]n relatively quiet states of the body a certain amount of surplus energy is employed in storing experiences . . . for future use . . . and . . . this activity is largely suspended in . . . emotional states" (qtd. in Cerny 19).

Nina Bull, a significant figure in the development of psychotherapy and a pioneer in the study of the mind-body relationship, was also concerned with investigating human emotions. She designated three stages in the generation of emotions and readying the body for action. She indicated that, first, a neural readiness occurred; second, the individual assumes an activated readiness or motor attitude; and third, there is a conscious readiness in which a person adopts a mental attitude related to his or her orientation and intention (Cerny 16). Bull had the following to say about the bodily response to different feelings. She indicated that feelings occur in a continuum ranging from those that are pleasant to those which are unpleasant; the muscular reaction to pleasant feelings are much more free-flowing, spontaneous, and uninhibited than the bodily reaction to unpleasant emotions (Cerny 17).

The Role of the Body and Movement in Memory

The statement could be made that movement and the emotions generated during perception provide content for memory. Théodule-Augustin Ribot was a French realist painter and printmaker. Although he was not a scientist or psychologist, he had the following to report on the human memory process based on his experiences with mental imagery while painting. He believed mental imagery draws from memory because it is the revival of sensorimotor elements built up through perception; following an act of perception, movement residue is deposited in the human brain and muscles (Cerny 18).

Washburn also discussed the role of movement residue in the formation of memories. In brief, she explained, "those elements in the original stimulus which were not attended to cannot be recalled after an interval because not producing the proper kinesthetic excitations, they enter into no movement systems" (qtd. in Cerny 18). Bull also discussed memory in terms of the unconscious since she deemed the unconscious to be where the motor part of mental processes is conserved (Cerny 18–19).

Ribot believed emotions contribute to another aspect of human memories since the affective states accompanying perception also contribute to retained memories (Cerny 19). This sequence of processes was thought to be possible because remembered emotions were closely related to the accompanying movement reactions to perceptual stimuli (Cerny 19). Rapaport endorsed this concept since, in his opinion, memories consisted of both kinesthetic and affective components (Cerny 19), while Rosett added that experiences connected with strong emotions are remembered longer (Cerny 19).

Kurt Lewin, a German American psychologist, espoused a motivational and emotional theory of learning. Rapaport described Lewin's theory when he wrote, "[P]sychic 'tension-systems' [are] set up either by genuine physiological needs or by quasi-needs correlated to intentions," and facts which pertained to undischarged tensions were easier to remember than facts associated with discharged tensions (qtd. in Cerny 20). On this same topic, Washburn endorsed the functions of movement and emotion as a significant part of the human memory system and the ability to recall the emotion or meaning connected with a memory, which, she asserted, might revive the associated movement system (Cerny 20).

The Role of the Body and Movement in Creative Thinking

In one of his theories, Dewey endorsed the idea that the body represented a crucial component of consciousness (George 16). In her book *What is Creative Thinking?* Catherine Patrick described Dewey's philosophy of constructive thought, in which he said there was a general body disposition toward creating in a specific direction. He later described this body disposition as a felt difficulty which he believed was preparation for creative action (Cerny 21).

Harold Rugg, an American educational reformer, described a phenomenon similar to the one described by Dewey when discussing creative activity. He indicated the creative act is preceded by a body feeling or determining tendency to act or proceed in a certain direction. Rugg wrote, "These first physical movements . . . are the sources of the first flashes of meaning, for there is no 'mind' except in reactions of the body" (100). The preliminary body feelings which preceded execution of the creative act were termed felt-thoughts. Rugg explained felt-thoughts in the following way:

> While symbolization is one promising key to the locked doors of imagined conception, there are actually two means interdependent with it. The first is gesture which is the organ of feeling; the second is the verbalizing, naming process, the essence of thinking. I postulate a synthesis of the two means—gesture as *felt-thought*—as one inadequately explored key to the flash of imagined conception.

(263)

Jerome Bruner, a pioneer in cognitive and developmental psychology, concurred with Rugg when he implied that sometimes in the process of creating, the individual knows deep down what he or she wants to communicate, but that they feel they have not said it (Cerny 22).

The thinking of Eugene Gendlin, an Austrian-born American philosopher, is also relevant to the discussion of the body, movement, and creativity. Gendlin professed there was an initial body disposition in the relationship to a work being created, and that the essence of understanding and meaning was something felt or experienced (Cerny 22–23). Gendlin's concept of the body disposition, later termed the felt sense, referred to "an embodied experience of a whole situation . . . that exists before words or other symbols" (qtd. in Cornell and McGavin 30).

More Recent Commentary on the Mind-Body Connection

More recently, Andy Clark, a professor of philosophy at Edinburgh University, proposed that what we think, do, and perceive seem to be inherently intertwined; as a consequence, much of human higher cognition seems to be based on the human embodied perceptuomotor capabilities (xxvi-xxvii). "[W]hat is at issue is something to do with the separability of mind, body, and world, at least for the purposes of understanding mind as the 'locus of intelligence'" (Clark xxvii).

Daniel Siegel, a UCLA clinical professor of psychiatry and director of the Mindsight Institute, summed up the mind-body connection when he wrote, "[A] 'purely logical' mode of thinking is . . . dependent on the nonrational processing of our bodies" (29). This same author believed that neural networks extend throughout the body and send input to the brain; it is this data that forms the basis for visceral maps, provides one with gut feelings, is a source for intuition, and influences reasoning and the creation of meaning (43).

V. S. Ramachandran, the director of the Center for Brain and Cognition and a professor in the Psychology Department and Neurosciences Program at the University of California, San Diego, delved into the branch of cognitive science called embodied cognition when discussing the mind-body connection. He believed "that human thought is deeply shaped by its interconnection with the body" (143). Ramachandran continued that this notion of human thought contrasted with a classical viewpoint dominating cognitive science from the mid to late in the twentieth century that the brain was similar to a computer connected to the human body (143).

Robert Ornstein, psychologist and researcher at the Porter Neuropsychiatric Institute, University of California, San Francisco, and David Sobel, an educator, mirrored some of the previous comments. They believed that although the field of psychology has been limited by the idea that the role of the brain is to produce rational thought, it is now recognized that the brain is a large organ, producing many chemicals which keep the body out of trouble and provide stability to the organism—operations which far exceed the brain's ability to think and reason (11).

Thus, the brain's neurons do not act like the computer chips found in a computer (Ornstein and Sobel 11).

In explaining the operation of the human brain, Ramachandran pointed out that physical brain structures were important to this discussion. The mirror neurons in the brain, he argued, are crucial to being human because they are vital to our ability to understand another's point of view and empathize with each other (xv). In fact, Ramachandran claimed that the mirror neuron system may be the key to the human level of evolutionary development (xvi).

In discussing Spinoza's conception of the mind-body connection, Antonio Damasio, the chair of Neuroscience and a professor of psychology, philosophy, and neurology at the University of Southern California, noted that according to Spinoza, "*the human mind is the idea of the human body*" (*Looking* 12). Damasio added that mental processes are based on the way the brain maps the body, a connection Spinoza may have intuited at a much earlier date to produce a parallel demonstration of the mind-body connection (*Looking* 12).

The idea of a map of the body or parts of the body in the brain was also discussed by Ramachandran. In this map, "[t]he entire skin surface of the left side of the body is mapped onto a strip of cortex called the postcentral gryrus . . . running down the right side of the brain" (26). This map, which is often depicted as a man comically draped on the human brain, was originally created by Wilder Penfield, a Canadian neurosurgeon in the 1940s or 1950s. While this map is mostly accurate, some parts are not, since, for example, the map for the face is located next to the map for the hand (26). A copy of this map, also known as the homunculus, can be found on the internet by typing the words "image homunculus" into the computer search bar.

James Zull, a former professor of biology, biochemistry, and cognitive science at Case Western Reserve University, discussed the connection between human actions and the mind. He explained that responses to sensory input, although more complex in nature, are the same as reflex responses, because there is a connection between the sensation and responding action; thus, the brain's main job is "to take in sensory data and generate actions from that data" (31–32). The flow of signals moves from the back of the cortex toward the front of this same part of the brain within a fraction of a second (Zull 32). Zull concluded his discussion on this topic by saying actions performed by humans are a manifestation of thought (32).

Evidence of this same mind-body connection was also provided by Oliver Sacks, a well-known neurologist, when describing an individual who could only recognize letters by tracing their outline with one hand; therefore, it was the person's sense of muscular movement which enabled him to identify letters (59). Added evidence of the mind-body connection can be based on Sack's justification of how we see objects. He indicated we do not see objects but instead view them as shapes, contours, and boundaries (73). The relationship to the body and movement can be deducted from these properties since it is possible to form shapes with the body or trace contours and boundaries by following a pathway in space.

Norman Doidge, a psychiatrist, psychoanalyst, and researcher on faculty at Columbia University and University of Toronto, also discussed the mind-body connection in terms of human actions. He stated that the human brain converts letters and words related to thought into movements of the tongue and lips (38). In another example of this connection, Doidge suggested that during the process of writing, the brain converts words or symbols into movements performed by the fingers and hand—a connection, he perceived, could have implications for education because exercises could be performed to stimulate neurons in a possibly weak premotor brain area (38–39). While the use of such exercises is based on the proven nature of brain plasticity, they were dropped in the 1960s and deemed to be "rigid, boring and not relevant" (42).

Eric Kandel, an eminent neuroscientist and former professor of biochemistry and biophysics at Columbia University, wrote that consciousness, and therefore conscious thought, is a biological process which will eventually be explained by "molecular signaling pathways used by interacting populations of nerve cells" (*In Search* 9). The human memory process was one of Kandel's primary areas of research. In describing this process, he explained that long-term memory requires anatomical changes because the neurons involved grow new terminals following repeated practice or sensitization (*In Search* 215). Later, Kandel guessed the formation of memories was based on more than anatomical changes in the brain's neurons and surmised that the expression of human genes might also be involved (*In Search* 238).

In further developing his discussion of the mind-body connection, Damasio chose to write about the bodily basis of emotions and how they are generated. He indicated, common emotions such as sadness or embarrassment are "a complex collection of chemical and neural responses forming a distinctive pattern" (*Looking* 53). Automatic emotional responses are produced in a normal brain when an emotionally related stimulus is detected, producing temporary bodily changes and accompanying changes in parts of the brain which map the body and are the basis for thinking (*Looking* 53).

The actual interactions in the brain during thinking are beginning to be revealed through MRI brain scans. Michio Kaku, professor of theoretical physics at City College and City University of New York, explained that, to date, such brain scans have shown that thinking is not concentrated in one brain area, but instead, during thinking, electrical energy is circulated through different brain areas (23). MRI machines cannot detect the flow of electrical energy from neuron to neuron, but they can detect the flow of oxygenated blood which provides energy for neuronal activity (Kaku 23).

Summary of Information about the Mind-Body Connection and Human Thought

The following table is an effort to summarize how the mind-body connection has been described both in the past and in more current times.

TABLE 1.1 Different Authorities' Descriptions of the Basis of the Mind-Body Connection

Basis for Mind-Body Connection and Human Thought	Authorities
Whole psychic life	Beaunis
Response to sensations and perceptions	Rosett, Washburn, Werner and Kaplan, and Zull
Movement and its role	Bull, Bruner, Damasio, Dewey, Doidge, Kaku, Kandel, Ornstein and Sobel, Ramachandran, Rugg, Sacks, Washburn, and Zull
Response to the environment	Clark, Rosett, and Schilder
Involvement with emotions	Bull, Damasio, Lewin, Rappaport, Ribot, Rosett, and Washburn
Role of symbol formation and understanding	Werner and Kaplan
Relationship to memory	Kandel, Ribot, and Washburn

As can be seen from the content in Table 1.1, different authorities have described the mind-body connection in varied ways. In fact, some of the explanations overlap to a certain extent. For example, Bull, Washburn, and Damasio all discussed human emotions in this context. There were also numerous explanations in which movement and bodily actions were noted as a basis for cognition and the human thought processes.

Accessing the Body Way of Knowing

Early dance educators and somatics practitioners also focused on the connection between the body, movement, and human thought. As an introduction to this section, it is important to discuss both the thinking of the French phenomenological philosopher Maurice Merleau-Ponty and Maxine Sheets-Johnstone, a dancer, researcher, and philosopher whose work is grounded in the tactile/kinesthetic body and the phenomenology of dance.

Merleau-Ponty was known for his criticism of the Cartesian mind-body divide and for his theory of perception, in which he explained the embodied nature of human life. In his view, humans come to know their world through personal experience and the lived body, which is "the site of consciousness and subjective reality of human beings" (qtd. in Paparo 489). According to Merleau-Ponty, the lived body included the "living, breathing, acting, and thinking bodily self . . . a whole-body, context-dependent, meaning-filled activity, which is the foundation of conscious thought and reflection" (qtd. in Paparo 489). Merleau-Ponty described mind in the following way:

> Mind, the symbolic level of form that Merleau-Ponty identifies with the human, is organized not toward vital goals but by the characteristic structures

of the human world: tools, language, [and] culture. . . . These are not originally encountered things or ideas, but rather as 'significant intentions' embodied within the world. Mind or consciousness cannot be defined formally in terms of self-knowledge or representation . . . but is essentially engaged in the structures and actions of the human world and encompasses all of the diverse intentional orientations of human life.

("Maurice Merleau-Ponty" Stanford Encyclopedia*)*

Only when the body does not respond to our goals and breaks down in some way is one encouraged to explore bodily feelings (Rouhiainen 244). Nevertheless, while gaining self-understanding by paying attention to one's felt sense, it is important to realize that self-knowledge is constructed by relating to other people and the environment as well (Rouhiainen 247).

In her book *Roots of Thinking*, Sheets-Johnstone stated that a more equitable view of the body is needed than the current Western Cartesian view (16). She wrote that:

> [There is] a metaphysical dualism that diminishes the body and fails to give it its living due . . . The latter is hardly conceivable apart from both an evolutionary history and a somatology that recognize tactility and movement not simply as sensorimotor pathways but as ways of knowing the world.
>
> *(16)*

This comment indicates that humans do not simply relate to and understand the world mentally but understand it physically as well. According to Sheets-Johnstone, felt or subjective aspects of experience, or the how of experience, are anchored in the senses, particularly the tactile-kinesthetic body ("Lived Body" 48). "Moving and thinking in movement eventuate in knowledge because they eventuate in learning, *learning to move oneself effectively and efficiently in the world and learning about the world itself*" (Sheets-Johnstone "Kinesthesia" 157). In discussing consciousness, Sheets-Johnstone pointed out the kinesthetic sense and one's responses to it, and with it might be the basis of consciousness itself (Eddy *Mindful* 283).

With some slight differences from the previous interpretations, Swiss psychologist Jean Piaget attempted to reconcile the mind-body debate by discussing a parallelism which he believed existed between the two. In his studies of children's cognitive development, Piaget attempted to integrate conscious phenomena and neurological processes by conceding that there might be an equivalence between them. Thus, he proposed "an integration between the two [processes] through the progressive transformation of his psycho-physical parallelism . . . into a parallelism of deduction and experience" (qtd. in Ferrari et al. 205). Piaget's theory of cognitive development can be described as a type of embodied learning, because he emphasized the role of the body and movement in the process of acquiring knowledge early in human life as a continuity between action and thought (Marmeleira and Santos 413).

Somatics/Dance Education Pioneers and the Body Way of Knowing

One of the early educators and somatics practitioners, Australian actor and author Frederick Matthias Alexander, agreed with Dewey that the body represented a significant aspect of consciousness and the processes involved (George 16). Although the entire body is involved in the Alexander technique, the goal is to become aware of poor postural habits by tuning into kinesthetic bodily feedback through balance in the head-neck relationship (Knaster 219).

> [In the Alexander technique] . . . repeatedly experiencing (with the teacher's assistance) correct usage in motion or at rest, you sensitize your internal kinesthetic guide to be a new standard of normal against which to measure your actions . . . the intention of each lesson is . . . to recognize what you're doing. . . . When you learn to discourage . . . yourself from behaving in the habitual way, you leave your body free to act naturally . . . allowing the neuromuscular system new freedom.
>
> *(Knaster 219–20)*

Alexander training involves the process of unlearning habits that interfere with healthy neuromuscular functioning, by learning to be in the present moment, inhibiting detrimental increases in muscular tension, and psychological unease. Through use of the Alexander technique, individuals can improve their use of the total mind-body complex in present moment activities through primary control or a balanced coordination between the head, spine, rest of the body, and gravity (Davies 196).

Margaret H'Doubler, an early movement/dance educator at the University of Wisconsin, used her ideas to establish a foothold for dance in the university setting during the 1920s. She was critical of the mind-body dualism and insisted physical movements can promote learning (George 17). In her book *A Creative Art Experience*, H'Doubler noted the average person lacks kinesthetic awareness of movement and therefore is not able to tap into a primary source of self-awareness, because the "inherent relationship between thought, feeling, and action furnishes the basis and direction for . . . creative teaching and learning" (xxiii). In her approach to dance education, H'Doubler was far ahead of her times because she developed a dance movement theory based on the interplay of biology, physiology, and psychology before such connections were fully recognized (Pillinger 108).

Irmgard Bartenieff, a German American theorist, dancer, physical therapist, and dance therapy pioneer, created the Bartenieff Fundamentals of Movement, which is recognized as another system which aids participants in accessing the body way of knowing. This somatic system teaches movement efficiency by experiencing body connections through kinetic chains and spatial intention among its other components (Eddy *Mindful* 25). Bartenieff Fundamentals integrates Rudolf Laban's concepts of effort and uses descriptive language to relay the participant's inner attitude, movement quality, and inner involvement in the movements; all the efforts (space, flow, weight, and time) provide information concerning an individual's personality and state of mind (Bryl 103).

It is important to remember that the quality of movement performed is based on and connects with the attitude and mood of the mover, further endorsing the connection between mind and body. Those who use Laban movement analysis/ Bartenieff Fundamentals "analyze how a person shapes dynamically his or her inner intent and desires into the world" (Whittier 125).

The Feldenkrais Method created by Moshe Feldenkrais, a Ukrainian Israeli engineer and physicist, is another somatic system based on bodily intelligence and improving body awareness. It is the belief that improved body awareness is related to functioning as an integrated whole in the world between mind and body; it is a powerful tool for discovering where one fits in terms of social structures and relationships (Dahlberg 25). Feldenkrais's interest in exploring the body grew "in part, out of his interest in auto-suggestion, self-image and the workings of the unconscious mind" (*Mindful* Eddy 27). In the use of the Feldenkrais Method, a goal is to bring awareness to and differentiate parts of the body by integrating movement possibilities to form one's creative living experience (*Mindful* Eddy 27).

"Feldenkrais embraced phenomenological embodiment, maintaining that moving, perceiving, acting, feeling, sensing, and thinking are inseparable" (Paparo 491). A goal of the Feldenkrais Method is to produce a more fully integrated mind and body. To create his method, Feldenkrais combined information from neurology, learning theory, and psychology with his understanding of physics and mechanics to become more aware of subtle muscle movements and eliminate unnecessary muscular tension to create more efficient movement habits (Kelton 44).

Another pioneer in this area was Mabel Elsworth Todd, who promoted rational thinking, which she attributed to upright posture through her somatic system known as Ideokinesis. Todd, who was an educator at Columbia Teachers College and pioneer of the mind-body wellness, maintained that functional efficiency depends on having access to kinetic patterns which remain in the body (George 19). In her book *The Thinking Body*, Todd described the unconscious as a treasure house of the creative and a key to physiology; she advocated joining new investigations of the body by studying the unconscious (3). Todd began developing her somatic system when she sought to recover from a paralyzing accident by using mental imagery, which she believed motivated her muscles to find their natural balance and enabled her to walk again; ultimately, she learned that the images selected needed to be based on principles of biomechanical alignment and efficiently functioning muscles (Eddy *Mindful* 28–29).

It is interesting to note that many of the techniques endorsed by somatics practitioners emulate the current interest in mindfulness, which is related to the human ability to be fully present. Mindfulness techniques are available at any moment in time since the goal is to become more aware of one's mental, emotional, and physical processes. In the book *Designing the Mind: The Principles of Psychitecture*, the authors suggested using meditation to improve one's personal awareness, because it can guide one to a nonattached awareness of internal processes (30). Public educational practices do not seem at present to reflect an awareness of mindful practices in which students can connect with the living body (Buono 152).

Exploration Experiences

The point of the following exercises is to focus on the body and bring the bodily feelings or responses into consciousness. Therefore, you as the reader will be expected to describe the bodily feelings you experience after completing each exploration.

1. Lie down on the floor or on a mat on the floor with your arms at your sides and your legs straight and aligned with your hips. Close your eyes and take several deep breaths. Then, scan your body to see if you can locate places where you retain tension and see if you can let that tension go. Next, tense the part of your body where you noted tension, and then gradually release that tension. Repeat the tensing and relaxing action several times until the tension in the body part seems to relax. This exploration is based on exercises developed by Edmund Jacobson for his system known as Progressive Relaxation.
2. The following exploration is designed to bring you into the present moment through increased body awareness. When we walk, we do so automatically without thinking about it. To complete this exploration, walk forward following a straight pathway. As you walk, focus first on your head, neck, and shoulders. Do these body parts feel tense or relaxed? Next, bring your focus to your arms. Do your arms swing as you take each step, and if so, is the swinging action large, small, or somewhere in between? Finally, focus on your feet. How would you describe the amount of pressure you use each time one of your heels touches the floor, and are you pushing off with your toes at the end of each step?
3. As long as you are on the Earth, you will contend with gravity. To focus on the pull of gravity, lift one arm high above your head and then release it quickly downward without resisting gravity. Next, lift the same arm overhead, but this time as you drop your arm, resist gravity so your arm moves downward more slowly. Then, compare these two actions by describing the difference in the bodily feelings you experienced.
4. Stand with one hand flat against a wall to aid your balance and swing the leg farther from the wall repeatedly to the front and back so the fulcrum of this action is at your hip. How would you compare the downward part of the swing to the upward part of this action in terms of the bodily feelings you experienced?
5. Compare the different bodily feelings you experience in each of the following situations:

    • Walk forward in a straight pathway compared to walking on a curved pathway.

Combatting the Mind-Body Dichotomy   17

- Move your arm in a curved pathway in space so the movement is controlled, and then so it is uncontrolled or floppy. The second pathway should be one in which you change directions frequently.
- Move your arm back and forth as if you are pressing against a heavy weight, followed by moving your arm along the same pathway, but without imagining that you are trying to move a heavy weight.
- Walk forward along a straight pathway as fast as you can, and then very slowly.

6. Focus on a positive emotion and create a movement with your body. Next, focus on a negative emotion and create another movement. How would you compare the bodily feelings you experienced when performing these two actions?

FIGURE 1.2   Placement of washer on a string and how it should be held.

Source: Photograph from author's person collection.

7. Imagine that you are walking on soft, warm sand. How would your body feel in response to this image? Repeat the same exploration by imagining you are walking on crunchy leaves and, finally, that you are walking along a very slippery surface. How do your bodily feelings differ with each imagined experience?
8. Read a favorite poem and describe what it means to you in terms of the feeling communicated. What type of movement gesture would you perform to communicate this feeling?
9. The following exploration is included to help in understanding the mind-body connection:

- Tie a washer to a string that is about one foot in length.
- Hold the end of the string so the washer is suspended beneath your hand. See Figure 1.2 for an example of how to attach the washer to the string and where it should be placed in relation to your hand.
- Focus on the mental image of a circle and the washer should begin to move.
- Still the washer and next focus on a straight line. The washer should again begin to move.
- Was there a difference in the way the washer moved when you imagined the circle in comparison to imagining the straight line?
- Why do you think the washer moved? What do you believe was occurring between your brain and body?

References

Bailey, Richard. "Educating with Brain, Body and World Together." *Interchange*, vol. 51, 2020, pp. 277–91.

Bryl, Karolina. "The Three Pillars of Movement Observation and Analysis." *The Art and Science of Embodied Research Design: Concepts, Methods and Cases*, edited by Jennifer Frank Tantia, Routledge, 2021, pp. 101–12.

Buono, Alexia. "Interweaving a Mindfully Somatic Pedagogy into an Early Childhood Classroom." *Pedagogies: An International Journal*, vol. 14, no. 2, 2019, pp. 150–68.

Cerny, Sandra. *Analysis of Movement Resulting from Experiences Structured to Produce Involvement*. MA Thesis, University of California at Los Angeles, 1967.

Clark, Andy. *Supersizing the Mind: Embodiment, Action, and Cognitive Extension*. Oxford UP, 2010.

Cornell, Ann Weiser, and Barbara Mc Gavin. "The Concept of 'Felt Sense' in Embodied Knowing and Action." *The Art and Science of Embodied Research Design: Concepts, Methods and Cases*, edited by Jennifer Frank Tantia, Routledge, 2021, pp. 29–39.

Coseru, Christian. *Perceiving Reality: Consciousness, Intentionality, and Cognition in Buddhist Philosophy*. Oxford UP, 2012.

Dahlberg, Helena. "Open and Reflective Research: Methodological Reflections on the Importance of Body Awareness in Qualitative Research." *The Art and Science of Embodied Research Design: Concepts, Methods and Cases*, edited by Jennifer Frank Tantia, Routledge, 2021, pp. 19–28.

Damasio, Antonio. *Looking for Spinoza: Joy, Sorrow, and the Feeling Brain*. Harcourt, 2003.

Davies, Janet. "Alexander Technique Classes for Tertiary Music Students: Student and Teacher Evaluations of Pre- and Post-Test Audiovisual Recordings." *International Journal of Music Education*, vol. 38, no. 2, 2020, pp. 194–207.

designingthemind.org. *Designing the Mind: The Principles of Psychitecture*. Designing the Mind, LLC, 2021.

Doidge, Norman. *The Brain That Changes Itself: Stories of Personal Triumph from the Frontiers of Brain Science*. Penguin, 2007.

Dunn, Gwendolyn. "Mind and Body." (PDF) Mind and Body (researchgate.net), accessed 20 Dec. 2021.

Eddy, Martha. *Mindful Movement: The Evolution of the Somatic Arts and Conscious Action*. Intellect, 2017.

Ferrari, Michel et al. "Piaget's Framework for a Scientific Study of Consciousness." *Human Development*, vol. 44, no. 4, 2001, pp. 195–213.

George, Doran. *The Natural Body in Somatics Dance Training*. Oxford UP, 2020.

Gruber, Howard, ed. *Contemporary Approaches to Creative Thinking*. Atherton Press, 1962.

Heinaman, Robert. "Aristotle and the Mind-Body Problem." *Phronesis*, vol. 35, no. 1, 1990, pp. 83–102.

H'Doubler, Margaret. *Dance: A Creative Art Experience*. U of Wisconsin P, 1962.

"Immanuel Kant." Wikipedia, Immanuel Kant—Wikipedia, accessed 19 Dec. 2021.

Kaku, Michio. *The Future of the Mind: The Scientific Quest to Understand, Enhance, and Empower the Mind*. Doubleday, 2014.

Kandel, Eric. *In Search of Memory: The Emergence of a New Science of Mind*. Norton, 2006.

Kelton, Kathie. "Review of *Singing with Your Whole Self: A Singer's Guide to Feldenkrais Awareness through Movement* by Samuel Nelson and Elizabeth Blades." *American Music Teacher*, Oct./Nov. 2018, pp. 43–44.

Kenny, Anthony. *A New History of Western Philosophy*. Clarendon Press, 2010.

Knaster, Mirka. *Discovering the Body's Wisdom*. Bantam Books, 1996.

"Leibniz's Philosophy of Mind." *Stanford Encyclopedia of Philosophy*. Leibniz's Philosophy of Mind (Stanford Encyclopedia of Philosophy), accessed 20 Dec. 2021.

Lowney, Charles. "Rethinking the Machine Metaphor Since Descartes: On the Irreducibility of Bodies, Minds, and Meanings." *Bulletin of Science, Technology & Society*, vol. 31, no. 3, 2011, pp. 179–92.

"Margaret Floy Washburn." Margaret Floy Washburn—Wikipedia, accessed 1 Sept. 2021.

Marmeleira, José, and Graça Duarte Santos. "Do Not Neglect the Body and Action: The Emergence of Embodiment Approaches to Understanding Human Development." *Perceptual and Motor Skills*, vol. 126, no. 3, 2019, pp. 410–45.

"Maurice Merleau-Ponty." *Stanford Encyclopedia of Philosophy*. Maurice Merleau-Ponty (Stanford Encyclopedia of Philosophy), accessed 21 Dec. 2021.

Menon, Usha. "Analyzing Emotions as Culturally Constructed Scripts." *Culture & Psychology*, vol. 6, no. 1, 2000, pp. 40–50.

Ornstein, Robert, and David Sobel. *The Healing Brain: Breakthrough Discoveries About How the Brain Keeps us Healthy*. 3rd ed. Malor Books, 2009.

Paparo, Stephen. "Embodying Singing in the Choral Classroom: A Somatic Approach to Teaching and Learning." *International Journal of Music Education*, vol. 34, no. 4, 2016, pp. 488–98.

Pillinger, Barbara Baxter. "Margaret H'Doubler: Pioneer of Dance." *Quest*, vol. 32, no. 1, 1980, pp. 103–9.

Pitasi, Andrea. "Descartes, Embodiment and the Post-Human Horizon of Neurosciences." *Constructivist Foundations*, vol. 5, no. 2, 2010, pp. 1–2.

Ramachandran, V. S. *The Tell-Tale Brain: A Neuroscientist's Quest for What Makes Us Human*. Norton, 2011.

"René Descartes." *Stanford Encyclopedia of Philosophy*. René Descartes (Stanford Encyclopedia of Philosophy), accessed 20 Dec. 2021.

Rodríguez-Jiménez, Rosa-Maria, and Manuel Carmona. "Mixed Methods for Evaluating Embodied Processes in Higher Education." *The Art and Science of Embodied Research Design: Concepts, Methods and Cases*, edited by Jennifer Frank Tantia, Routledge, 2021, pp. 229–41.

Rouhiainen, Leena. "Somatic Dance as a Means of Cultivating Ethically Embodied Subjects." *Research in Dance Education*, vol. 9, no. 3, 2008, pp. 241–56.

Rugg, Harold. *Imagination*. Harper & Row, 1963.

Sacamano, James, and Jennifer Altman. "Beyond Mindfulness: Buddha Nature and the Four Postures in Psychotherapy." *Journal of Religion and Health*, vol. 55, no. 5, 2016, pp. 1585–95.

Sacks, Oliver. *The Mind's Eye*. Vintage Books, 2010.

Saniotis, Arthur. "Understanding Mind/Body Medicine from Muslim Religious Practices of Salat and Dhikr." *Journal of Religious Health*, vol. 57, 2018, pp. 849–57.

Sheets-Johnstone, Maxine. *The Roots of Thinking*. Temple UP, 1990.

———. "Kinesthesia: An Extended Critical Overview and a Beginning Phenomenology of Learning." *Continental Philosophy Review*, vol. 52, 2019, pp. 143–69.

———. "The Lived Body." *The Humanistic Psychologist*, vol. 48, no. 1, 2020, pp. 28–53.

Shen, Vincent. "Desire, Representing Process, and Translatability." *Philosophy East & West*, vol. 69, no. 2, 2019, pp. 316–36.

Siegel, Daniel. *Mindsight: The New Science of Personal Transformation*. Bantam Books, 2010.

Tan, Uner. "The Psychomotor Theory of Human Mind." *International Journal of Neuroscience*, vol. 117, 2007, pp. 1109–48.

Todd, Mabel Ellsworth. *The Thinking Body*. Dance Horizons, 1975.

Twietmeyer, Gregg. "A Theology of Inferiority: Is Christianity the Source of Kinesiology's Second-Class Status in the Academy?" *Quest*, vol. 60, no. 4, 2008, pp. 452–66.

Whittier, Cadence. "Laban Movement Analysis Approach to Classical Ballet Pedagogy." *Journal of Dance Education*, vol. 6, no. 4, 2006, pp. 124–32.

Zeuschner, Robert. "The Understanding of Mind in the Northern Line of Ch'an (Zen)." *Philosophy of East and West*, vol. 28, no. 1, 1978, pp. 69–79.

Zull, James. *From Brain to Mind: Using Neuroscience to Guide Change in Education*. Stylus, 2011.

2
SENSORY RECEPTION AND THEIR CONTRIBUTIONS TO BODY KNOWLEDGE

Human Sensory Systems

In essence, there are three overarching sensory systems which operate in conjunction with each other to produce and manage human movement directly or indirectly. According to Matthew Henley, professor of dance education at Teachers College Columbia University, these sensory systems include exteroception, proprioception, and interoception ("Sensation" 97–99).

Exteroception

Exteroception is an awareness of stimuli from the environment that can produce an action or movement response (Meehan and Carter 6). Such stimuli include those from the senses of vision, hearing, touch, smell, and taste (Henley "Sensation" 97). Some researchers believe there is a connection between exteroception and addiction—a response which is usually attributed to interoception.

Samuel DeWitt from the Center for Brain Health at the University of Texas, Dallas, and his colleagues ascertained individuals who are prone to addiction are also hypersensitive to external cues that seem relevant to oneself (376). DeWitt et al. proposed that the connection between drug addiction and exteroception might be alleviated through mindfulness training (374). Other researchers have investigated the relationship between touch and cerebral palsy—specifically, tactile disfunction in an upper limb, since such deficits seem to impact motor skills required to perform daily activities (Auld et al. 414).

Proprioception

Proprioception is an awareness of movement, shapes at joints, and one's relationship to gravity; the proprioceptors inform a person about their body's location in space and how it is moving (Henley "Sensation" 98). The proprioceptors include receptors that relay information about what is happening in the body below its surface; its receptors are found in muscles, fascia, tendons, ligaments, and joints, although some researchers think these receptors are also in the skin (Krasnow and Wilmerding 31). The proprioceptors work together with the vestibular system in the inner ear and vision to help a person balance (Krasnow and Wilmerding 30–31). The proprioceptors also work together with the receptors for the sense of touch. It would be impossible to complete even the simplest tasks important in daily life without proper proprioceptive functioning. Proprioceptors send impulses to the brain, where they are processed to determine whether to change position or stop moving; proprioceptive input is processed both unconsciously and consciously (Carter 104).

Receptors of the Proprioceptive Sensory System

Recently, a museum in the local area which specializes in the study of natural phenomena presented an exhibit on the human senses. Interestingly, there were few references to the kinesthetic or proprioceptive sense in the presentations which made up the exhibit. Dance kinesiologist Sally Fitt wrote, "The kinesthetic sense is forgotten in the traditional listing of the five senses: touch, taste, sight, hearing, and smell. It is indeed a sixth sense and intuition, and psychic phenomena should be relabeled the seventh sense" (Fitt 276).

However, there may be a good reason that the bodily sense has often been forgotten. In the case of kinesthesia, the stimulus or changes cells in a muscle undergo when the muscle expands and an individual's awareness or perception of the occurrence are described in the same way; thus, "stretching of the muscles' cells gives rise to the perception of . . . stretching!" (Pashman 36). In addition, the fact that kinesthesia is based on both an unconscious and conscious event can, at the same time, make it confusing when one attempts to understand it. Pashman summed up this conundrum in the following way:

> In the case of kinesthesia, however, both the sensation and the perception are *of the same phenomenon*, muscular stretching. Further complicating matters is that these two different kinds of events—one physical and one mental, one theoretically public and the other utterly private—are known by the same name. Correctly understood, then, kinesthesia is a double phenomenon: both an unconscious sensation of movement and a perception of that sensation.
>
> *(36)*

While earlier writers and researchers discussed the kinesthetic sense, the terms *kinesthesis* and *kinesthesia* have come to describe the conscious sensation of movement, sometimes termed *kinesthetic awareness* (Krasnow and Wilmerding 127), while *proprioception* refers to information from receptors located below the body's surface. Through the years, many movement-based abilities have been attributed to proprioceptors. Early researchers such as Gladys Scott believed this sense enabled an individual to perceive the position and motion of the whole body and its parts; determine gradations of effort; know the rate, extent, and direction of one's movements; aid dynamic and static balance; and help with duplicating movements demonstrated (Minton and Steffen 75). Other abilities attributed early on to proprioception included rhythmic abilities, perception of bodily tension, awareness of force, extent of muscular contraction, and the orientation of the body and its parts in space (Minton and Steffen 75).

More specifically, the proprioceptive receptors include the muscle spindles (fluid-filled capsules located within muscles), Golgi tendon organs (in tendons near muscles), joint receptors inside joints, and skin receptors (Minton and Faber 108 & 110). More recent research has demonstrated the muscle spindles and intrafusal fibers respond to quick and maintained stretching and changes in velocity, while the Golgi tendon organs are slow to adapt but respond to static or sustained muscle lengths and provide an accurate assessment of muscular tension (Batson "Update" 37). The joint receptors, which are also slow to respond and which were originally thought to sense joint position, do contribute to kinesthesia but have a more limited role than the muscle spindles (Schenkman et al. 214). Drawings of a muscle spindle and Golgi tendon organ can be seen in Figures 2.1 and 2.2. Finally, the skin receptors adapt rapidly, sense vibrations, and respond to touch and changes in placement and tissue damage (Batson "Update" 37).

Role of Proprioception in Somatosensory System

Proprioception is one of three parts of the somatosensory system, with each part having a distinct pathway in the spinal cord to a particular brain area. In addition to proprioception, the other two parts of this system are discriminative touch and nociception. The first of these includes light touch, along with pressure and sensitivity to vibration; it helps one describe the shape and texture of objects and aids balance (Krasnow and Wilmerding 31). The second, nociception, enables a person to sense pain or harm and includes sensitivity to temperature, itch, and tickle (Krasnow and Wilmerding 31).

Interoception

An interest in interoception has been growing as an interdisciplinary research topic due to developments in neuroscience and neuropsychology (Freedman and Mehling 66). Interoception is an ability to sense one's internal bodily state but is separate from the processing of external stimuli through vision, hearing, touch, and smell (Tsakiris and Critchley 1). Interoception is the least understood of the sensory systems but has historically been considered related to enervation of the

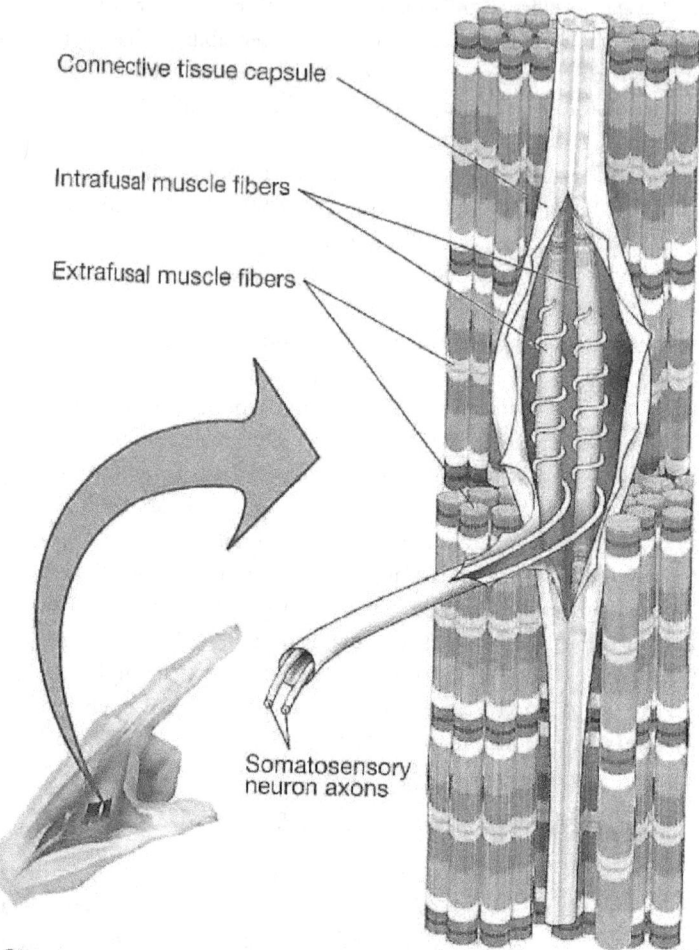

FIGURE 2.1 Muscle spindle. Schenkman Margaret, Bowman James, Gisbert Robyn, Butler Russell; *Clinical Neuroscience for Rehabilitation*, 1st ed.

Source: © 2013. Reprinted by permission of Pearson Education Inc.

viscera, such as the lungs, heart, and intestines, but is now believed to include all parts of the nervous system which control and provide feedback to maintain homeostatic balance in the body (Henley "Sensation" 99).

A broad description of interoception assigns it the role of both sensing and integrating all aspects of one's physiological state and motivational needs (Tsakiris and Critchley 1). Interceptors are located in the walls of the digestive and respiratory tracts and in the walls of the heart and blood vessels; these receptors do not mediate somatic sensations but create poorly localized sensations, such as visceral pain, thirst, hunger, excretion, and sexual feelings (Schenkman et al. 203). Similar

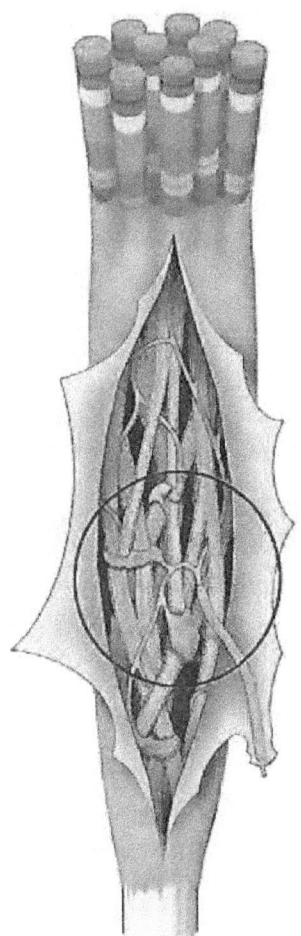

FIGURE 2.2   Golgi tendon organ. Schenkman Margaret, Bowman James, Gisbert Robyn, Butler Russell; *Clinical Neuroscience for Rehabilitation*, 1st ed.

Source: © 2013. Reprinted by permission of Pearson Education Inc.

to exteroception and proprioception, interoception is ongoing but operates below the conscious level. When interoceptive elements enter one's awareness, they can be self-reported, are close to body awareness, and can be modified by using mind-body interventions in the form of mindfulness therapies, such as yoga or the somatic therapies (Freedman and Mehling 65–66).

Sensory Integration

Stimuli reach the senses in different forms, such as light, sound, and temperature, but the human nervous system is structured to make all perceptions coherent in time and space. The integration of sensory information is based on patterns extracted by the various sensory systems from input; however, many of these patterns are similar across modalities (Haywood and Getchell 278). This means that:

> Events occur at a point in time, so the temporal properties of an event are not unique to any one modality. . . . We see a drummer strike a drum and we hear the drum's sound, but we also perceive the rhythmic pattern that existed across vision and audition.
>
> *(Haywood and Getchell 278)*

Integration of the input from the various senses begins in infancy and extends into adolescence in some cases (Haywood and Getchell 279–81). An important point is that receiving sensory information is not the same as understanding its meaning, since sensation is not the same as perception, which involves awareness along with understanding and insight.

By using sensory integration, the brain can use information from more than one sensory modality and organize it to produce an appropriate muscular response (Krasnow and Wilmerding 37). Exteroceptive sensations may include proprioceptive awareness and be related to interoceptive awareness as well. For example, when students change the tempo of a dance phrase, it "requires exteroceptive awareness and proprioceptive awareness, but the new tempo might create more excitement, anxiety, or any other emotions that are sensed through interoceptive awareness" (Henley "Sensation" 100).

Sensorimotor integration has been investigated over a hundred-year period because organized body actions depend on sensorimotor coordination (Manoel and Felicio 461). An indirect outcome of a study conducted by Manoel and Felicio indicated that young children may have difficulties performing tasks in which visual input is not associated or integrated with proprioceptive information (471).

In another study, the researchers were interested in documenting the possible effect sensory integration treatment could have on autistic children, because sensory processing difficulties are frequently reported in this population. For example, autistic children frequently display hypo- or hyperresponsiveness to external stimuli (Holland et al. 285). Some of the interventions provided autistic children in a study included sensory opportunities in the form of tactile, auditory, visual, vestibular, and proprioceptive experiences (Holland et al. 288–89).

Human Sensation and the Mind-Body Connection

The question, then, is how to describe the connection that exists between human sensory systems, cognition, and the mind. Psychologists in the late nineteenth century (Mesmer, Breuer, and Freud) and twentieth century (Reich and Perls) pioneered the connection between brain and body (Eddy *Mindful* 185). In terms of embodiment, it might be implied that perceptual and cognitive judgments are derived from and moderated by the body (Manoel and Felicio 461). "Recent theories propose that cognition is embodied in the sense that it is critically based on reinstatements of external (perception) and internal states (proprioception) as well as bodily actions that produce simulations of previous experiences" (Kiefer and Trumpp 15).

The Role of Exteroception

Of the exteroceptive senses, vision, hearing and touch operate during human cognition in a predominant way. The human body is an important reference point for human theories of meaning; for example, judgment of an object's relative size is often equated with one's ability to lift it, while understanding the height of an object or its location in space is dependent on a schematization of an upright body (Areshenkoff et al. 168).

Those who study human learning discuss learning styles or preferences in terms of modes of perception, such as visual, auditory, or tactile-kinesthetic. Visual learners prefer to process information when it is presented in the form of diagrams or pictures, auditory learners like to listen to sounds or verbal explanations, and tactile-kinesthetic learners begin learning by seeing or hearing an explanation but complete the process by touching or manipulating objects related to content to be learned.

Perceptual psychologist Rudolf Arnheim and cognitive scientist Jean Mandler believed that bodily experience, especially visuospatial experiences, play a crucial role in conceptual development (Antovic and Stamenkovic 386). It is possible to connect the bodily way of knowing with visual experiences because one can duplicate the shapes seen with shapes formed by the body and its parts. As mentioned previously, the connection between visual information can be used as a reference point for the relative size of an object, particularly when the distance from the object is taken into consideration. One can also experience depth by viewing objects in the distance—a construct which can be both seen and then experienced by the body when walking between a near and far point in space.

Hearing involves mechanical vibrations from the environment which travel through the anatomy of the ear, where they are transformed into electrical impulses; once transmitted to the brain, sounds are interpreted based on their direction, volume, and meaning (Carter 94). Auditory input can be related to the bodily way of knowing as well because it is possible to determine distance and direction from sounds as they relate to the position of one's body. Thus, sounds become louder the closer one gets to them, and it is also possible to determine in which direction to move to locate the source of a sound. Sounds have emotional connotations as well which can be connected to varying levels of tension in the body.

The touch or cutaneous receptors are located in the skin and supply the brain with information about touch, pressure, pain, heat, cold, and chemicals when the skin comes in contact with odors, acids, or other agents that can cause irritation (Krasnow and Wilmerding 126). Some of these skin receptors include Meissner's corpuscles, Pacinian corpuscles, and corpuscles of Ruffini, which respond to fine

28 Sensory Reception and Their Contributions to Body Knowledge

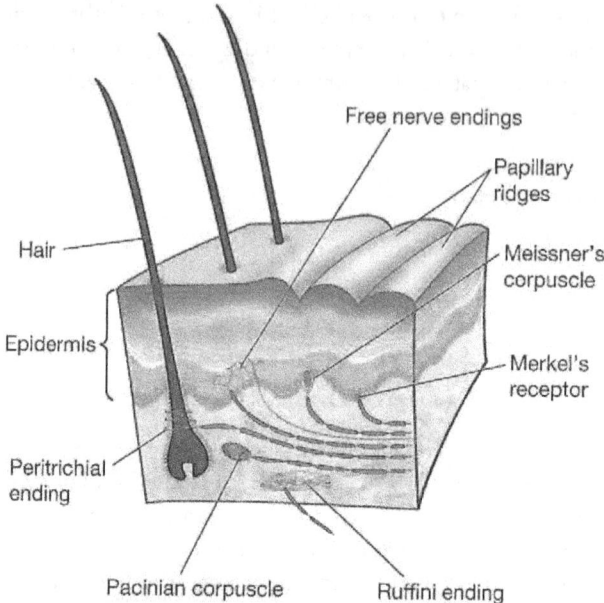

FIGURE 2.3 Different types of skin receptors. Schenkman Margaret, Bowman James, Gisbert Robyn, Butler Russell; *Clinical Neuroscience for Rehabilitation*, 1st ed.

Source: © 2013. Reprinted by permission of Pearson Education Inc.

tactile discrimination, changes in pressure, and stretching of the skin, respectively (Schenkman et al. 207–08). The most cutaneous receptors are found in the fingertips, with numerous cutaneous receptors in the palms, lips, and soles of the feet, where they contribute to postural control and locomotion (Krasnow and Wilmerding 126). Drawings of some of the cutaneous receptors can be seen in Figure 2.3.

The role of touch or a haptic presentation of content is endorsed by many educators. Individuals can use their sense of touch to distinguish between textures and determine whether an object is hard or soft. Erving Goffman and Marjorie Goodwin, who have studied human behavior, noted that tactile teaching techniques may work because the sense of touch is known to communicate intimacy and can develop cooperation and trust (Cekaite and Holm 111). It has been justified that touch is a valid form of emotional expression and can convey affection and positive feedback to the brain, while a lack of touch can increase stress and disrupt resilience. The hypothesis for the use of tactile teaching strategies is that when learners are exposed to both haptic and visual content, they will process the information more deeply than when only visual instruction is used, even when the content is initially presented through technology (Magana and Balachandran 332).

While there are various theories related to cognition, Raymond Gibbs, psychology professor and researcher at the University of California, Santa Cruz, thought that cognition is based in embodiment (Antovic and Stamenkovic 386). Gibbs clarified his theory of cognition when he said:

> [T]hroughout childhood and the rest of our lives, bodily experience plays a crucial role in conceptual development, with abstract concepts created "on demand," given the moment and the task. . . . [T]hese abstractions remain connected to original embodied experiences by means of image schematic configurations.
>
> *(qtd. in Antovic and Stamenkovic 387)*

The Role of the Proprioception

Proprioception is well-designed for developing cognitive knowledge. For example, the body or its parts can be positioned to duplicate positions and positional relationships found in concepts to be learned. In a similar way, gradations of muscular effort, the speed, direction, or extent of moving the body or a body part, and balance can copy the tension, timing, direction, size, and balance, or lack thereof, found in the content being studied.

In one study, the researchers compared two modes of teaching literacy. Under one condition, young preschool children said a target word and then wrote it with their index finger on the carpet, and under a second condition, the students said the word and traced and underlined the word with a pencil on a worksheet. The outcome was that the paired kinesthetic movements used in both conditions resulted in a higher percentage of word reading accuracy compared to the outcome of traditional teaching methods (Lozy et al. 1338).

The previous passage described that uses of movement and, consequently, proprioception to duplicate details found in content being learned can be equated with a theory called sympathetic modeling. This theory, described in his doctoral dissertation by Henrich Wolfflin, is that:

> [W]hat is seen is internally "modelled" because of an immediate, hard-wired, "sympathy." . . . His theory [operates] . . . if we think of the perceiving subject simply imagining how his own body would feel if it mimicked the form it observed. From an acquired repertoire of how various bodily postures feel, we reflexively impute such feelings to observed forms.
>
> *(qtd. in Pashman 29)*

There are historical foundations for using proprioceptive, movement-based, and embodied pedagogical approaches which endorse the mind-body connection. Dewey was one of these early educators, because he aligned his philosophy of education with student experiences and practice ("Pedagogy" 4). Dewey's philosophy developed from evolutionary naturalism, which is described in the following example. Say, there is an external prick of a thorny bush on the skin of one's leg which activates an impulse which travels to the brain; then the brain, in turn, sends another impulse back to the leg, causing one to move the leg away from the thorn ("Pedagogy" 5). However, Dewey argued that the impulse "does not begin with an external stimulus, but from a stimulus that involves the coordination among the sensory and motor actions of the learner and elements involved in their situation" (Pedagogy 5).

The following is a more recent example of embodied learning. Diana Gustafson discussed her transformative experience with embodied learning by describing it as a feminist strategy which could help women understand other ways of knowing by discovering knowledge through their bodies (55). In Gustafson's experience, the Chinese practice of *qi gong* was introduced in a course to help students examine how the body, health, illness, and healing were approached in a non-Western society (52).

The Role of the Interoception

Interoceptive awareness is still considered to be controversial according to some scientific literature, but for some, it is closely aligned with body awareness (Freedman and Mehling 66). "Interoception . . . the process of perceiving afferent signals arising from within the body including heart rate (HR) gastric signals, etc., and has been described as a mechanism crucially involved in the creation of self-awareness and selfhood" (Christensen et al. 1).

Interoception can be associated with generalized feelings of well-being or malaise (Schenkman et al. 203). The mind-body association is strengthened by the realization that interoceptive awareness can be modified by mindfulness-based therapies (Freedman and Mehling 66). Authorities on the subject of interoception, such as Erik Ceunen, Norman Farb, and Sahib Khalsa, have commented on its importance to human emotions and thinking. They indicated, "Over the past decade, the processing of interoceptive sensations has been shown to play a key role in human affect and cognition and to be of major relevance in the study of mind-body approaches to human health" (qtd. in Machorrinho et al. 88). While not yet completely proven, interoceptive signals are believed to impact cognition, attention, and perception while shaping decision-making, memory, and emotional processing (Tsakiris and Critchley 1). The ability to identify, access, understand, and respond in an appropriate way to the internal signals of interoception enables an individual to meet challenges and make adjustments (Price and Hooven 3).

In recent publications, interoception was connected with interoceptive accuracy, which has, in the past, been measured using heartbeat detection and discrimination tasks which were considered only partially objective; instead, Wolf Mehling and his colleagues developed over one hundred questionnaire items which were thought to assess sensory perceptions from inside the body as a developmental process (Freedman and Mehling 66–67). The new self-report measuring instrument, the Multidimensional Assessment of Interoceptive Awareness (MAIA), was created to measure the benefits of various somatic processes and other types of mind-body approaches (Freedman and Mehling 66). The MAIA, which includes eight scales organized into five dimensions, assesses an individual's awareness of body sensations, emotional reaction to body sensations, capacity to regulate attention, awareness of mind-body integration, and the trust attached to body sensations (Machorrinho et al 89).

It has been demonstrated that the MAIA captured changes in body awareness which individuals experienced when undergoing mind-body interventions (Freedman and Mehling 69). The studies described by Freedman and Mehling in their chapter indicated there was a connection between mindfulness training, interoceptive awareness, and the symptoms of depression (69–70). Thus, reduced depressive symptoms were

> mediated through a serial pathway, in which training-related increases in four aspects of interoceptive awareness were positively associated with the ability to decenter (the ability to view thoughts and feeling states as temporary and not related to the self), which in turn was associated with reduced symptoms of depression.
>
> *(Freedman and Mehling 70)*

Attention to interoceptive feedback is also part of some dance therapy and somatics practices. In her work, Anna Halprin addressed her students' sensations, movements, emotions, and use of imagery. Halprin asked "students to reconnect the body to its emotions, to listen to interoceptive signals, or inner impulses" (qtd. in Henley "Sensation" 99). Through Body-Mind Centering, Bonnie Bainbridge Cohen believed one can directly experience the body's anatomical systems and structures and what they embody; thus, energy embodied in the tissues can be expressed "physically through sensation, posture, movement, and body symptoms and psychologically through feelings, attitudes, and behavior" (Hartley xxxiii).

Applications to Learning Movement and Dance

The art form of dance is integrally involved with space and time—moving through and in space and along the continuum of time. The human sensory systems, including exteroception, proprioception, and interoception, all contribute to learning movement and dance in terms of these dimensions.

In terms of exteroception, the visual, auditory, and tactile senses are especially helpful, while the receptors of proprioception have a direct correlation to body awareness, movement accuracy, and the ability to correct movements associated with the techniques of multiple dance genres. The proprioceptive sensory system operates in conjunction with vision and the vestibular apparatus in the inner ear to enable humans to balance and maintain an upright posture. The emotions generated through interoception can complement or inhibit learning in a dance technique class as well. The study of motor behavior in dance is especially concerned with connecting mind and body since the senses send important information to the brain, and in its responses, the brain perceives, plans, and causes movement;

this interplay between the brain and senses takes place constantly while dancing (Krasnow and Wilmerding 2).

Exteroception and Learning in Dance

The purpose of this section is to describe some ways in which exteroception functions during the movement learning process in a dance technique class. This content will be discussed in terms of the visual, auditory, and tactile senses.

Visual Teaching Cues

Vision is an important delivery system for teaching and learning in dance technique class, but it is important to remember vision does not function in isolation in this setting, since it is tied to cooperation with other body systems. Thus, feedback from visual input supplements proprioception in the maintenance of posture and balance, which is important in learning to dance (Krasnow and Wilmerding 119). In addition, cues provided when teaching dance technique should be designed to address all learning styles—visual, auditory, and tactile-kinesthetic.

In a dance technique class, movement to be learned is traditionally modeled by the teacher and duplicated by students through visual perception; a second use of vision in learning dance technique is through error detection obtained from looking in the mirror (Brodie and Lobel 23). Since the eyes and mind work together when learning a movement sequence, students need to use their eyes to see and not just stare as a movement sequence is demonstrated; it is also helpful to really see the room, other dancers, and one's own body, but without losing kinesthetic awareness (Brodie and Lobel 27–28).

However, when dance students are in the beginning stages of learning, it is best to have them visually focus on one or two of the most prominent features of a movement phrase (Gose 35). There is also a tendency for novice dancers to view unnecessary cues, including unessential visual details, when movement is demonstrated (Kimmerle and Coté-Laurence 55).

Two types of visual input (central and peripheral) are important in learning and performing dance movements with expertise. Central vision directs dancers' movements along a pathway as they travel through space, and peripheral vision helps avoid other dancers and objects in the performance space (Krasnow and Wilmerding 120). Many movement details can be observed from a movement demonstration using central visual input. These details include the spatial aspects of movement: direction, level, size, pathway, body shapes, and position in relation to other dancers and objects in the dance space.

Another teaching technique which proved to be effective and which is partially dependent on vision is to have paired students observe each other, perform a movement phrase, and then offer suggestions (Ohlberg 3). The clothing worn by a dance teacher can also draw the students' attention to important aspects of a movement pattern, such as body line or body parts that lead an action; the elements of dance clothing might include color, zippers, waistbands, logos, or patterns and can be especially important when teaching special needs students to direct their attention (Guss-West 154).

Optical flow is a third component of the human visual system created when patterns of light are reflected on the retina; the changing angle of these patterns over time provides information about motion and position and enables one to regulate them in relation to the environment (Brodie and Lobel 24). The changing visual response to objects in the dance space can be aided by really seeing the objects or other dancers and being especially observant of their details (Brodie and Lobel 24).

The mirrors which line at least one wall of the typical dance studio have been believed beneficial by providing immediate visual feedback, and in some cases, this is true, although overuse of the mirrors can inhibit dance students from developing other sensory systems (Ohlberg 2). One researcher found that covering the dance studio mirrors resulted in a positive student response, because students could learn unrestricted by self-judgment which was caused by constant visual feedback from the mirrors (Ohlberg 5).

In another study, the researchers measured the movement accuracy and correctness of timing in twenty experienced dancers based on the efficacy of using mirrors as a teaching aid. The use of mirrors was tested under three conditions. The outcome of this study showed that when the mirrors were used only during movement demonstration and explanation, the student dancers demonstrated the best movement accuracy; when the mirrors were used only while the students practiced the movements, they displayed the best timing; and when the mirrors were used during both the demonstration and practice phase of the class, the students had the most errors in accuracy and the second-most errors in the timing of the targeted movements (Weber and Didier 1). The researchers concluded that differences in years of training may have contributed to the outcomes in this study, since the less-experienced dance students may have been distracted by the mirrors. They also proposed that accuracy with movement timing may be improved by focusing on proprioception and kinesthetic awareness and not on using mirrors (Weber and Didier 9). In light of this study, this last conclusion makes sense, because timing is not a spatially oriented movement component.

An interesting fact about vision is that it is a dominant human sensory modality and captures the attention more quickly and for a longer amount of time than other sensory input (Brodie and Lobel 24). However, since the central visual system accesses the conscious brain, it can slow reaction time and be less accurate, which results in overcontrolling movement (Brodie and Lobel 24–25).

Neuroscience investigations have revealed there are two pathways in the brain for visual perception. One, the ventral pathway, begins in the occipital brain lobe and extends to the temporal lobe and is significant in identifying an object; the other one, the dorsal pathway, also begins in the occipital lobe but extends to the parietal brain lobe and helps determine where an object is located and how it could be acted upon (Henley "Is Perception" 72). Studies have shown an increased activation in the parietal cortex of expert dancers, which could mean they are able to chunk information about movement with spatial information (Henley "Is Perception" 72).

In a final study concerned with vision, visual cues were used successfully in a dance class designed for exceptional students ages 5 to 11 with autism, Down syndrome, and intellectual issues. In this class, the cues included a visual schedule to help the students understand class transitions and various props, such as streamers, to encourage engagement. Different cards were inserted in the visual schedule to describe transitions, such as end of the warm-up or a break, as they occurred (Suppo and Swank 68). Video modeling was also used successfully in this class to bypass regression in the students' movement abilities. Thus, the students' families showed them videos between class sessions so they could practice at home. This practice enabled the students to build on skills learned in a previous class (75).

Auditory Teaching Cues

Rhythm, a component of movement, can be used as an auditory teaching cue. This is done by clapping the rhythm found in a movement phrase or duplicating the rhythm with vocal sounds. The students can then copy the rhythmic pattern as they perform the designated movement phrase. The following is an example of the use of such a teaching cue. To teach a form of Irish step dancing from the north Kerry region of Ireland, Catherine Foley sang the melodic and rhythmic structure of the tune to accompany her movement demonstration; she provided these teaching cues to illustrate the relationship between the music, rhythm, and movements in an attempt to communicate the aesthetic embodied in the dance (317).

The dance teacher can use his or her voice by supplying vocal cues that emulate the desired timing, duration, or quality found in a movement. For example, the dance teacher could speak quickly or slowly or elongate sounds verbally to match the timing of an action or the duration of time for which the movement is to be performed. It is also possible to create vocal sounds that match movement qualities. Thus, a "hmmmm" sound could indicate that a movement was to be performed using a sustained quality, while "bah bah" said with a loud voice could describe a percussive movement quality. A dance teacher can also use verbal cues such as spot to direct movement of the head when learning to turn when this skill is to be performed, although such cues should be omitted as soon as possible in the learning process to avoid sensory overload (Krasnow and Wilmerding 235).

It is also possible to use the voice to reinforce recognition of accented movements or the appropriate use of the breath (Guss-West 154–55). The music used to accompany learning a movement phrase can also emphasize the quality to be performed, as can playing a variety of small percussion instruments which produce different quality sounds. Such instruments can be used to copy the rhythmic pattern in a movement phrase as well (Krasnow and Wilmerding 234–35).

In a creative dance program designed for autistic children, the teachers found they could use vocalizations among other techniques to stimulate student engagement (Hermans 31). In the same study noted previously by Suppo and

Swank, musical cues were used; in this situation, the musical accompaniment was stopped when the students were supposed to take a break (68). While not used explicitly as a teaching cue, music-based movement therapy has helped Parkinson's patients execute actions they might find extremely challenging in other situations (McAlister 13).

Tactile Teaching Cues

Touch or hands-on work is part of many somatic practices. In the Alexander technique, the practitioner or teacher gently uses his or her hands along with verbal directions to guide clients through movements. For example, the teacher can lightly steer the client's head into its proper position on the tip of the spine (Knaster 219). In an interview, Sondra Fraleigh explained she learned about hands-on touch practices when she was certified in the Feldenkrais Method; she has since developed Contact Unwinding, in which movement is guided through contact with a student or client (Eddy *Mindful* 110).

Edward Warburton discussed touch in the context of becoming a caring dance teacher. He wrote that the sense of touch is a widely used technique to teach movement, especially to help students adjust their alignment, change neuromuscular patterns, direct focus, and prevent injuries ("Who Cares" 92). Nevertheless, there are ethical and emotional issues connected to using touch as a teaching strategy. Warburton concluded that touch should be used in the dance classroom with sensitivity and responsiveness; according to a report for the Association of Theatre Movement Educators, touch was valued when it was purposeful, useful, and gentle but should be used only after a student has given his or her permission and understands the appropriate use of touch ("Who Cares" 92).

In her article, Johanna Kirk described how she helps students be more aware of tactile sensations. She suggested having students touch props with different textures and describe these experiences with qualitative words. Some of the other exercises Kirk suggested were to explore differences between body parts that touched the floor and those that did not and to explain how clothing feels when it touches the skin; in another exploration, the same author had one partner touch the other one with light touch and then increase the pressure so they learned to distinguish between different types of touch ("Moving" 12).

Touch can be an effective teaching strategy in a dance technique class to draw the learner's attention to a particular point on the body and impart information about a more informed movement practice, but it is especially appropriate for those who have a tactile-kinesthetic learning style. However, it is important for the dance teacher to focus on exactly what he or she is trying to communicate to the student through touch, so the quality of touch used is important (Guss-West 156). The dance teacher should consider the timing, quality, pressure, direction, and intention of touch used to impart information to students (Guss-West 157).

Different uses of the fingers and hand when using touch can have varied meanings. Touching with one or two fingers serves as a focal point to draw attention to a spot on the student's body, while touching with the entire hand can supply directional information (Guss-West 157). It is also important to sustain touch for a long-enough time to enable a student to understand the information being transmitted, ask questions as to whether the meaning of tactile cues is understood, and use eye contact to assess the comfort level with use of touch (Guss-West 157).

Tactile teaching techniques have also been used successfully to teach dance to blind students. Research has shown that pedagogical techniques such as tactile modeling, along with a physical demonstration and oral description, can improve the movement skills of those who are visually impaired. Tactile modeling involves having the learner touch or run their hands over a model as he or she performs a specific movement to experience the intricacies of a targeted action. This can be done along with verbal instructions (Seham and Yeo 96–97).

Proprioception and Learning in Dance

The author's interest in kinesthesia and proprioception developed from her years teaching dance to university and elementary school students. Multiple questions arose based on these experiences, such as: What exactly is proprioception? How does it contribute to an individual's overall movement abilities? In what ways can it be used to help students learn in the dance classroom? In addition, proprioception is discussed separately here, although it is closely allied with the human sense of touch, because it operates internally rather than from an external perspective.

In answer to such questions, the author and one of her university colleagues designed a Spatial Kinesthetic Awareness Test (SKAT) for use with beginning dance students. When researching proprioception, the author discovered it is responsible for numerous human movement abilities, as noted earlier in this chapter. Thus, it was decided to limit the SKAT to measuring spatial aspects of kinesthetic abilities, including eight items using poses emphasizing body shapes and another eight items devised to focus on placement/position of body parts. *Shape* was defined as the actual shape (curved or angular) of a body part, and *placement/position* referred to the relationship between body parts (Minton and Stephen 77). The validity of the SKAT based on a correlation of judges scores for shape was .67 and .74 for placement/position. The test-retest reliability for the SKAT was .81 (Minton and Stephen 78).

Later, a study was conducted using the SKAT to evaluate changes in university students' spatial kinesthetic awareness that may have resulted from participating in a beginning or intermediate jazz or modern dance class. One hundred and fifty students completed their participation in the study (135 females and 15 males). Each student was videotaped at the beginning of the semester and toward its end, while performing the sixteen items on the SKAT, which meant attempting to accurately duplicate each item shown on a television screen (Minton and McGill "The Effects" 69). As a result, the students displayed improved overall SKAT scores on all sixteen items in six of the seven teachers' classes. Improvement at the significant level was shown for the shape component of the SKAT in five of the classes (Minton and McGill "The Effects" 70).

The author was also interested in learning about the relationship between dance teacher behaviors and students' improvement on the SKAT. The students in this quantitative study were the same students involved in the previous study (Minton and McGill "A Study" 40). The teacher behaviors studied were those in the Physical Education Teacher Assessment Instrument (PETAI), which included planned presentation (time spent presenting planned instruction), response presentation (time spent restating, emphasizing, or summarizing), monitoring (time spent observing learning environment), performance feedback (time spent providing information relative to aspects of students' performance of skill), and motivation feedback (time spent providing general responses to skill) (Minton and McGill "A Study" 50–51). The teacher behaviors were analyzed and compared by calculating the percentage of total class time that was spent engaged in each behavior (Minton and McGill "A Study" 43). The results of this study demonstrated that a higher percentage of response presentation and motivation feedback behaviors produced a positive, significant correlation with improved performance on the SKAT (Minton and McGill "A Study" 47).

Most dance students, especially beginners, are not aware of how proprioception operates. To make students more aware of proprioceptive processes, it has been suggested that students assume a specific body alignment or position using visual feedback while performing a plié and then close their eyes and attempt to maintain the same body position using their proprioceptive sense (Henley "Sensation" 99).

Many in the dance education community have discovered that external cues (the teacher's words, mirrors, and other dancers) distract dance students from focusing on the proprioceptive bodily feeling of a movement when it is performed correctly. In an article based on her research, Shantel Ehrenberg wrote that the image a dancer sees in the mirror and his or her kinesthetic awareness consistently affect each other in a type of action-reaction pattern (175). On the effectiveness of the mirror, Ehrenberg concluded that a mirror can aid self-correction and movement accuracy but can also be a negative influence by interfering with movement accuracy based on a visual image and negatively affect movement quality (182).

According to Glenna Batson, who has researched proprioception and its role in dance, proprioceptive training is an important part of a dancer's rehabilitation from injury, but there seems to be little information about the effect of targeted proprioceptive exercises on the development of a dancer's technique, except on its effect with children ("Update" 38).

One of the issues confounding the study and understanding proprioception and its relevance to teaching dance is that proprioceptive or body awareness is frequently described in relevant literature through different lenses. One lens includes the scientific or narrow study of proprioception, and the other lens emerges from more broadly based philosophical studies of proprioception and bodily awareness. The narrow lens includes studies of proprioception in relation to a specific joint, muscle, or reflex, while research that explores the body and its movements as a whole is considered broad (Barlow 41). Rachel Barlow suggested that the plethora of studies dealing with proprioception and bodily awareness in some form be situated along a continuum extending between these narrow and broad reference points (41).

Another issue which confounds understanding proprioception are the different terms associated with both the scientific and philosophical discussions; these include, among other terms, motor skills, joint position sense, and range of motion on the scientific side, and experience, expression, and perception found in dance-based philosophical discussions (Barlow 45).

Although the following two studies do not explicitly explore the relationship between proprioceptive exercises and the development of a dancer's technique, as suggested previously by Batson, they are examples of the narrower studies.

In one study, the researchers compared proprioceptive awareness in professional ballet dancers to matched controls who had no dance training. A joint-position matching task was used to assess static proprioceptive joint awareness along with another task in which participants stood with their eyes closed and were evaluated based on their static and dynamic proprioceptive awareness of center pressure variability. The latter measure was conducted using a force platform. As a result, the dancers exhibited greater proprioceptive awareness than the control subjects for the joint positioning task but not for the standing task, leading the researchers to conclude a standing task may not be sufficiently challenging for dancers when used as a measuring instrument (Kiefer et al. 126).

The aim of a second study was to assess how fatigue of the upper leg muscles affected knee joint proprioception in thirteen ballet dancers and thirteen non-dancer controls. Proprioceptive acuity was evaluated using an isokinetic dynamometer immediately before and after involvement in an isometric upper-leg muscle fatigue procedure. The outcome of this research showed that position and motion sense acuity are not affected by muscle fatigue in dancers, but motion sense is affected by fatigue in nondancers (Dieling et al. 143).

In contrast, the following two studies are examples of more broadly based dance inquiries that deal with the body sense. In the first study, the author, Susan Pashman, asked whether feeling really has a shape or form that coincides with the shape of the body or of a moving body (27). In correlating bodily movement with emotion, Pashman believed patterns of muscular tension must communicate feelings, since we can read the internal feelings of others from their facial expressions and gestures (30). In conclusion, this author resolved the connection between emotions expressed and bodily feelings based on a theory proposed by neuroscientist Antonio Damasio, in which he surmised "feeling is e-motion made conscious . . . what ends up as conscious, perceived feeling must in every case begin at the cellular level as movement, movement either toward or away from an environmental stimulus" (qtd. in Pashman 35).

In a second, more broadly based study, the researcher, Sarah Matzke, investigated how one's kinesthetic body creates knowledge of the environment and why that environment changes when participants become involved (1). In this study, the researcher wanted to understand the duet between a space and the human kinesthetic encounter with that space, and how one's experiences of a body in space shapes the understanding of a space (2–3). Sixteen dancers, aged 19 to 30, who were both students and professional dancers made up the group who would challenge or support the researcher's spatial paradigm. Through the subjects' journals and discussions, the researcher learned the following: boundaries between the body and space became fluid; multisensory experiences influenced the perception of space; sensation provided bodily awareness which the body stores as a cognitive process; participants began to think more deeply about the spaces in which they worked; and spaces are seen differently because they are related to one's being and upbringing (9–10).

Interoception and Learning in Dance

It is possible that interoception is the basis of a dancer's artistry, although this type of awareness is different from the bodily awareness gained through the somatic practices; it is interoceptive feedback that enables dancers to sensitively interpret and portray the subtleties of characters in a dance work (Henley "Sensation" 99). Portraying a character in a dance is enmeshed with the ability to tap into the emotion-generating capacity of the body.

According to the James-Lange theory of emotion, we feel an emotion because our body first feels a physical sensation, such as a rise in heart rate (Harrington 37). In an article, British psychiatry professor Hugo Critchley, who has done neuroimaging research, discussed the James-Lange theory of emotion. He wrote that according to this theory, emotion-generating stimuli cause bodily responses automatically, and different emotions are associated with a different response in the body; most important to the discussion here is that sensitivity to internal changes in the body is connected to differences in and intensity of emotional experiences (156). Although this theory of emotional generation has been challenged by some, it does provide some evidence for the connection between interoceptive experiences and human emotions.

The generation of pain is dependent on the body as well. It is a warning system which can help dancers avoid more serious injuries. Based on the neuromatrix theory, structures located in the body are responsible for generating pain. These structures include a widely spread network of neurons that form loops between the thalamus and cortex and between the cortex and the limbic or emotion-generating system in the brain. These loops are responsible for movement control and the occurrence of pain (Bellan et al. 26). The neuromatrix theory has an integral role in processing the human sense of space based on frames of reference, one of which is anatomical and has to do with the respective position of each body part (Bellan et al. 27). Since the two, the experience of pain and the body-based sense of space, are connected, spatial disruptions associated with pain can provide profound experiences (Bellan et al. 28).

In an article, Celeste Snowber explored the idea that dance and the body are a way of knowing or a form of embodied learning based on the idea that the mind and body are connected; she noted that bodily knowledge behaves like an internal GPS system (54–55). Snowber indicated that in Western societies, there has been an emphasis on the outer body as compared to the lived body, which allows one to make connections with multiple sensations around and within (55). A major value of dancing is that it can provide learners with a different way to relate to their bodies (Snowber 59).

Nevertheless, how can the process of learning in dance technique class be described? Is it more fully an inward, embodied experience or directed by input from outside the body? By investigating the process involved in learning new movement based on the students' comments, Henley and Conrad concluded that there "is a fluid and overlapping relationship between embodying and understanding . . . the two are deeply intertwined" (8). For example, one student interviewed for this article said that when learning movement, she performs it first and then slows it down so she can think about it until performing the movements becomes automatic (8). Thus, the first phase in this student's learning is fairly automatic, and therefore based in the body, followed by correcting perceived errors through a mental process. Finally, the movement material is consolidated and becomes automatic and based in the body again.

Exploration Experiences

These explorations are based on the chapter content described previously. The sections explore exteroception, including vision, hearing, and touch, and proprioception and interoception as they can be initially recognized, and in relation to their applications and use as teaching cues.

Basic Explorations with Vision

1. Select a large object that is greater in height than your total height. Then, describe the number of times your height can be used to measure the height of this object.
2. View a much smaller object and estimate whether you would be able to lift it easily or with some effort. Lift the object and describe the bodily feelings you experienced when lifting it. Repeat the same exploration with an object that is heavier or lighter than the previous object you lifted.
3. Go outside and view an object that is situated in the distance and estimate how many steps would be required to reach it. Walk toward the object and count the number of steps it took to reach it.
4. View a photo of a person in which there is a positional relationship between parts of the body. This means one or two body parts will be in a particular position or relationship to other parts of the body. Duplicate the positional relationships you see with your own body, followed by having a partner check your accuracy. You could also check your accuracy in a mirror.

5. View a different photo of a person which includes body shapes which are curved, straight, or both. Again, attempt to duplicate the body shapes with your own body, followed by checking your accuracy.
6. Select an object that has parts which are both curved and straight, followed by using one arm to copy the straight part or parts of the object. Next, use the same arm to copy the curved aspect or aspects of the same object. Describe any differences in body feelings you experienced in each part of this exploration.
7. View an object which includes straight linear parts that form an angle or angles. Attempt to duplicate at least one of these angles with a part of your body. Did you notice any difference in bodily feelings when duplicating the angles in comparison to reproducing the straight parts of the object you viewed previously?
8. This exploration is based on your central and peripheral vision. Stand in front of a mirror and perform a short movement phrase while you view your image by looking directly at it. Next, perform the same movement phrase in front of the mirror, but this time notice objects that are off to the side in the space. Describe the movement details that you noticed in each experience. Describe the objects situated off to the side in each of the two experiences. Did you discover any differences in what you noticed visually in these two experiences?

More Complex Visual Explorations

1. View a short dance movement phrase in a video. Then, attempt to duplicate the movement phrase to the best of your ability while you are positioned in front of a mirror. Did it appear you performed the movement phrase accurately?
2. Have a partner watch as you perform the same movement phrase to assess whether you performed each aspect of the phrase accurately. Then, discuss parts of the phrase that were performed accurately and those that were not.
3. Focus on parts of the movement phrase that you did not perform accurately and attempt to correct the issues. What did you need to do to correct these issues?
4. Stand in front of a mirror and watch as you perform two dance movement phrases—one that is relatively slow, and one that is fast. Next, perform the same two dance phrases without watching yourself in the mirror. Describe your bodily feelings in each experience. Were your bodily feelings the same or different?
5. View another short movement phrase in a video in two different ways. First, view the phrase without paying attention to its details, such as body shapes, changes in tempo, or transitions. Second, really see some of the details embedded in the movement phrase and describe the differences in your perceptual responses.

42 Sensory Reception and Their Contributions to Body Knowledge

6. View two videos in which the same movement is performed from the same dance genre, but in which the dancer demonstrating the movement is wearing a different type of costume or different-colored clothing. Did you notice different aspects of the movement when viewing each video? Did one type of clothing enable you to see movement details more clearly?
7. According to some of the content described earlier in this chapter, dance studio mirrors can be detrimental to learning in some respects. Describe both a positive and negative experience you have had with mirrors while learning to dance.

Basic Explorations with Hearing

1. Go outside and listen to sounds you can hear in the surrounding environment. Then, describe the direction from which each sound seems to be coming.
2. How far away would you estimate the distance of each sound is from your location?
3. Next, describe differences in the volume of the sounds you hear. For example, from my front porch, I was able to hear a plane roaring overhead, a bird chirping off to the side, a car door slam in front of me, and cars whoosh along the road behind my house. The plane was loudest, and the car sounds were quieter.
4. How would you describe the differences in quality between the various sounds?
5. How would you compare the tempo or speed of the different sounds?
6. Did any of the sounds have a rhythmic pattern? Many birds sing in a way that creates a rhythmic or repetitive pattern.
7. Did you notice changes in any of the sounds over time?

More Complex Auditory Explorations

1. Find a video of a dance movement phrase that includes changes in tempo. Create verbal cues or descriptors that are fast and slow and which could be used to describe the tempo changes in the phrase. For example, running steps are fast, although they could be followed by a slow collapse, and you could create verbal cues that mimic each tempo.
2. A phrase which involves running and a collapse would also include different movement qualities. How might you change the tone of your voice to match the different movement qualities in the phrase you selected?
3. Perhaps there are accented points in the movement phrase. Describe changes in vocal volume you might use to accentuate these movement accents.
4. Find another video of a movement phrase. Then, note the rhythmic pattern found in this phrase. Next, clap the rhythmic pattern and duplicate it vocally.
5. Create your own movement phrase and describe vocal cues you would use to aid student learning.

6. How could your breath be used throughout this movement phrase? Thus, where would you breathe in or out, and would the quality of your breathing change while performing the phrase? In what way could you use your voice to help students understand the breath qualities embodied in the phrase?
7. How might you use percussion instruments to emphasize changes of movement quality in the phrase you created? Which percussion instruments would you use to accompany different parts of the phrase?
8. Describe other accompaniment you could select to enhance the students' ability to perform your movement phrase using the desired movement quality or qualities.

Basic Explorations with Touch

1. Lie on the floor with your legs straight and your arms at your sides, followed by focusing on places where your skin touches the floor. What is the difference between your bodily feelings where your skin touches the floor and where it does not? Repeat the same exploration using a different body position.
2. Continue lying on the floor, but this time describe how your skin feels where it is touched by your clothing or dance costume. Repeat this exploration in a different body position.
3. Put three or more objects which have different textures in a paper bag. Then, put your dominant hand in the bag and touch each of the objects, followed by describing how they feel tactilely. Do the objects have a rough or smooth texture? Were they warm or cold, hard or soft?
4. Receptors in your skin also enable you to sense vibrations. Place the tips of your fingers on the side of your refrigerator when the compressor is running and you should be able to feel vibrations. Touch the outside of another electrical device and then compare any differences you noticed between the vibrations created by each device.
5. Assume a body position in which your skin is stretched. Curving your whole body in an arc over to the right side would cause the skin on the left side of your body to be stretched. Describe the bodily feeling of having stretched skin.
6. Touch the skin on your arm or a leg by using one finger, and then your entire palm. How would you describe the differences in your responses to the two types of touch?
7. Repeat the previous exploration, but this time use a light sense of touch, followed by touching using greater pressure in the following two ways. First, use one finger to experience the difference in the bodily feeling of a light touch compared with touching using greater pressure with this finger. Then use the palm of your hand to experience the difference in a light touch compared with a heavier touch.
8. Think about a piece of clothing or fabric that you enjoyed touching or stroking in the past. How would you describe this texture? Describe any feelings which come to mind that you associate with this texture.

9. Describe an experience from your past in which touch was an important and positive part of the experience.

More Complex Tactile Explorations

1. View a photo of a basic position from a specific dance genre such as an arabesque from ballet and attempt to copy this position as accurately as possible with your body. Have a partner evaluate your rendition of the position, using a gentle sense of touch to readjust the placement of parts of your body as needed.
2. View a video of a short dance phrase and reproduce it as accurately as possible while your partner watches. Next, discuss your performance of the phrase with your partner, stopping when necessary to allow your partner to use touch to adjust your placement where needed.
3. Touch can be used as an external focal point to draw a dancer's attention to the relationship between body parts. An example of this is to have your partner place two fingers on the fingertips of one arm when it is extended to the side in second position, along with putting two fingertips of their other hand on your toes when your leg is off the floor and also extended out to the same side (Guss-West 158). Was this use of touch helpful in achieving this position? If the use of touch was helpful, why do you think this was so?
4. Touch can also be used to enhance a dancer's ability to balance. This can be done by positioning two partners on opposite sides of your body. Each of the partners uses two-finger touch applied just above the wrist to your horizontally extended arms. The purpose is not to support or lead but to use touch as a focal point as you attempt to balance in a series of half-toe arabesque-like positions. This use of touch should also enable you to focus on the two touch points and better experience the energy in your arms as it flows outward horizontally from your body's center. It is recommended to repeat this exploration without the partners to help recall the bodily feelings experienced (Guss-West 158–59).
5. Five touch points can be used to encourage energy flow from the body's center and correct placement of the head in an arabesque. To do this, five helpers or partners are needed. One partner gently positions your head, two touch your fingertips on either side of your body to ensure an outward energy flow, one touches the foot of your supporting leg, and the final helper touches the toes of your extended leg (Guss-West 160–61). How would you describe the feeling of energy in your body?
6. Guss-West also used stickers on a student's body to focus attention on a body part. For instance, placing a sticker on the breastbone can create a bodily sensation and help students focus on this part of the body to change their facing quickly. Stickers on the backs of the hands can create a different sensation and help dancers channel their energy outward through the arms when the arms are held horizontally out to the side of the body (162–63).

Basic Explorations with Proprioception

1. This exercise is based on exploring gradations of muscular effort and distinguishing between them. To do this exploration, bend your arm at the elbow several times without tightening your muscles in any way. Then, perform this same action with a moderate amount of muscular resistance, and finally, with as much resistance as you can muster. Describe the difference in the bodily feelings experienced.
2. The following exploration is provided to perfect your relationship to gravity. Begin standing with your feet slightly apart and so your weight is equally distributed on each foot. Now, stand as tall as possible so your head reaches to the ceiling and your center is lifted. Next, allow your body to slump forward quickly from the waist, followed by repeating this same action slowly. What was the difference in your relationship to gravity in the two parts of this exploration?
3. To experience how timing affects your bodily sensation of an action, move one arm as quickly as possible following a curvilinear pathway in front and at the side of your body. A figure eight pathway could be used in this exploration. Repeat this exploration slowly along a similar pathway. How would you compare the bodily feelings in these two explorations?
4. The proprioceptors also enable you to sense the direction of movement of your entire body or its parts. In this exploration, you need to videotape your movements or have a partner observe your actions. Once your eyes are closed, move one arm directly forward from your shoulder, then directly to the side of your shoulder, and finally, as directly behind your body as possible. As you perform these movements, keep your arm parallel to the floor. Finally, check your videotape for directional accuracy or ask your partner whether you were able to move with accuracy in each of the three directions.
5. Repeat the previous three actions, but this time make each action larger by reaching as far as possible from the center of your body. Repeat each directional action, but make them as small as possible. Did changing the size of your actions change the bodily feeling that accompanied them?
6. This exploration also has to do with directional accuracy when you are moving your whole body. You will again need to videotape your performance or have a partner observe your movements. Now, close your eyes and attempt to walk slowly forwards, sideways, and finally, backwards, but make sure there is sufficient space around your body so you can take at least four or five steps in each direction. Again, check the videotape or with your partner to determine your directional accuracy.
7. Exploration 7 focuses on your bodily sense of placement and position. This and the following exploration are done in front of a mirror initially with your eyes closed. Stand with your feet in parallel position and put your flattened palms directly beside each ear. Each palm should be equidistant from each ear, with your palms facing your head, and your upper arms parallel to the floor (Minton and McGill "The Effects" 70). Then, open your eyes and check the positional accuracy of each body part.

46 Sensory Reception and Their Contributions to Body Knowledge

8. Your bodily sense of shape is the target in this next exploration. Again, stand in parallel position in front of a mirror with your eyes closed, and curve your upper body directly to the right side so that your head is part of the curve of your spine, your head remains with your face to the front, and your right arm is dropped straight to the floor (Minton and McGill "The Effects" 70). Again, open your eyes to check the accuracy of your body shape.
9. This exploration also focuses on your bodily sense of shape. Create three body shapes in your mind, but do not perform them. These shapes can incorporate a part or parts of your body or your whole body. Make sure the shapes do not require you to test your balance as well. Now, stand before a mirror with your eyes closed and place your body in each of the shapes you imagined. After each attempt, open your eyes to test the accuracy of each body shape.
10. Repeat the previous exploration, but this time focus on the bodily feeling that accompanies each shape. Describe and compare each of the bodily feelings you experienced.
11. Proprioception also contributes to one's orientation in space. Walk around a relatively small space while swinging your arms as you walk. Then, repeat this exploration in a large space. Did your body feel different as you walked in the two different environments? What about your bodily feelings when you were walking in the middle of the spaces as compared to walking close to the walls?
12. Based on the preceding content in this chapter, some researchers believed there is a connection between proprioception and one's sense of rhythm. Rhythms can be even or uneven. In an even rhythm, each part of the movement sequence takes up the same amount of time, while in an uneven rhythm, the parts take up a different amount of time. View the rhythms diagrammed in Figure 2.4. The top one is an even rhythm, while the middle diagram is an uneven rhythm. Try clapping each of these rhythms, and then duplicate them with your steps on the floor. Each type of rhythm should feel different in your body. How would you describe this difference?
13. Experiment with balancing on both feet and then on one foot. Then, attempt to balance in more unusual positions. For example, balance in a position in which one foot and one hand are on the floor or in which you balance on your seat with your bent legs lifted in front of your body and your arms out to the sides. How did each of these body positions challenge or not challenge your ability to balance, and how did they feel in your body?
14. Review the bodily sensations you experienced in the previous explorations and select one of these experiences. Then, see if you can perform a different movement that produces the same or a similar bodily feeling.

More Complex Proprioceptive Explorations

1. Perform a ballet adagio phrase, followed by performing a sequence of jazz movements. Then, compare the muscular effort required to perform each phrase.

Sensory Reception and Their Contributions to Body Knowledge 47

2. Try performing a modern dance side fall in a traditional manner. How would you describe your bodily feeling of gravity as you performed this dance movement? Did parts of your body seem more affected by gravity than other parts as you performed this movement? Next, try resisting gravity as you perform this action so that it is performed more slowly. Then, compare your relationship to gravity during the two experiences.
3. Describe a dance movement that is traditionally performed using a slow tempo and one that is usually performed rapidly, followed by performing each of these movements. Compare the relationship between timing and muscular effort you experienced when performing each movement.
4. View the bottom linear drawing in Figure 2.4. This drawing represents the floor pattern or pathway of two different dancers. Each of these floor patterns could be followed by performing a repetitive movement, such as a skip. Select one of the floor patterns in the diagram and attempt to follow it using a repetitive movement. Repeat this exercise using a different repetitive movement. Which rendition of the floor pattern was easiest to perform?
5. Find a photo of a dancer in which there is a positional relationship between parts of the dancer's body. Select one of the positional relationships you see in the photo and attempt to copy it with the same parts of your body. Describe any difficulties you experienced.

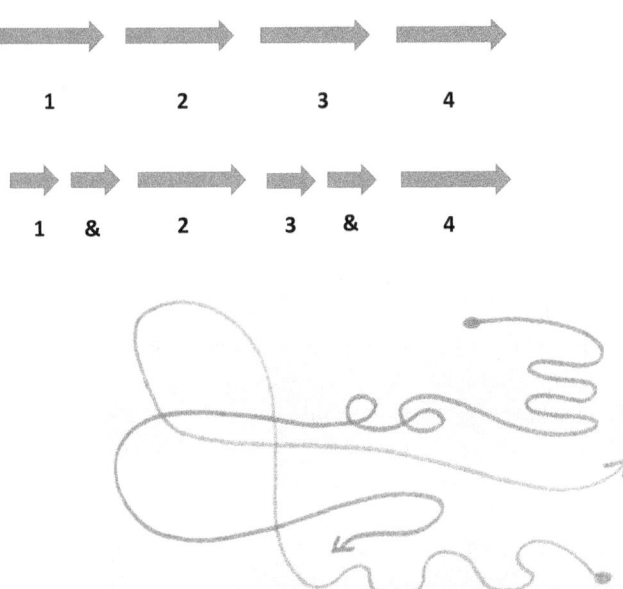

FIGURE 2.4   Even and uneven rhythmic diagrams above and floor pattern model below.

Source: Diagrams of rhythmic patterns and model of floor patterns created by author.

6. Watch a video in which a solo dancer travels throughout the stage space. Once you have sufficient knowledge of the dancer's movements, perform the entire movement sequence. How might you use your location in the space to help you remember this movement sequence? In other words, what is the relationship between your spatial location and the movements?
7. Choose a dance movement that is performed in place without moving through space and one that does travel. For example, a developpé is performed while remaining on one spot, while a tour jeté is a traveling step. Then, perform each step while in the center of your space and also next to one of the walls. How were you affected by your orientation in space when performing these two movements? Repeat this exploration with two other dance movements—one that travels and one that does not—and again compare your bodily responses.
8. Many dance movements require the ability to balance. Compare your ability to balance in the following situations:

   - A demi-plié in second position
   - Standing in second position with your knees straight
   - Performing a relevé in second position
   - Balancing in passé with the foot of the supporting leg flat on the floor
   - Balancing in passé with the support leg in relevé

In which of the previous positions was it easiest to balance? How did each position feel in your body?

Basic Explorations with Interoception

1. Lie down on the floor and close your eyes, followed by taking several deep breaths. As you lie still, bring your focus and concentration to your body. You should notice some sensations from various bodily processes, such as your gastric system or the beating of your heart. How would you describe these sensations?
2. Get off the floor and walk rapidly. Then, lie down again to see if there is any difference in your ability to observe your internal bodily processes.
3. Place your fingers gently over the inside of your wrist. You should be able to perceive the beating of your heart by connecting with your pulse. Assess your pulse under two different conditions—first, when you have been resting, and then after walking rapidly. How would you describe the differences?
4. Think about times when you felt upbeat and full of energy and other times, perhaps at the end of a day, when you were tired. How would you describe your emotional response to these two situations?
5. In the somatic system known as Body-Mind Centering, created by Bonnie Bainbridge Cohen, different organs in the body are associated with qualities of the mind. It is believed that by bringing one's awareness to a particular organ, feelings can be experienced (Hartley 196). It is postulated, for example, that

when the pancreas and gallbladder are overburdened, a situation is created which gives rise to feelings of anger and frustration (Hartley 199). Breathing is the connection between the conscious and unconscious mind, and it is thought the lungs can reflect sadness, grief, and sympathy in others (Hartley 201).

The following exploration is suggested to bring more awareness to the body's organs:

- Use an anatomy book to gain information about your body's organs and locate them in your body.
- Then, clearly visualize each of the organs in terms of their shapes and placement.
- Breathe or hiss into each organ individually to stimulate awareness and increase organ vitality.
- Explore your awareness of each organ when assuming different positions, such as sitting, lying on your front, back, and side, when positioned on your hands and knees, while standing, or in an upside-down position.
- The changes in position should be followed by whole-body actions, such as rolling or tilting. As you perform these actions, you should feel weight shifting inside your body.
- At the end of this exploration, you might like to make a drawing to capture the energies you experienced (Hartley 205–06).

6. The following exploration is also from Body-Mind Centering. It is designed to release tension in the nerves so the muscles can relax.

- Before doing this exploration, study a diagram of the spinal nerves as they branch outward from the spinal cord.
- Lie on your back and gently rock your head from side to side. This action should give you a sense of your brain, which has weight within your skull. It might help to imagine your skull as a container which is filled with water.
- Connect your sense of the brain's movements to the weight and movement of your other organs while you let your entire body roll from side to side.
- Sit and circle your head using your neck as the center pivot point but while paying attention to your brain. Then, connect with your spinal cord, feeling the connection between the brain and spinal cord.
- Increase the circling of your head so it causes your spine to curve at the same time.
- Have a partner locate the spaces between the vertebrae in your spine, and imagine the spinal nerves as they branch out into your body.
- Be aware of the energy as it flows through the spinal nerves (Hartley 264–65).

More Complex Interoceptive Explorations

1. Describe a personal experience in which you gained a sense of joy after taking a dance technique class.
2. Describe another personal experience in which you had negative feelings after taking a dance technique class. Compare the two experiences and describe why you believe you felt positive about one experience and negative about the other one.
3. Think about a time when you experienced pain while dancing. What caused you the pain, and what did you learn from this experience?
4. Discuss how you relate to the outward appearance of your body. In what way do you believe your concept of the outward appearance of your body relates to your inner bodily awareness?
5. Describe your experience of recently learning a specific movement pattern in technique class. What was your experience of learning these movements from an outer perspective? What was your experience in terms of an inner bodily experience when you learned the same movement pattern?
6. Think about two characters in books you have read who differ in terms of their personalities and how they express themselves. One of these characters should be kind and benevolent, and the other one rather mean and untrustworthy. What is your overall feeling or response to each of the characters you selected, and how would you transform your response to each character into movement? Describe the movement qualities you would use to portray each of the characters.

References

Antovic, Mihailo, and Dusan Stamenkovic. "Vision, Space, and Embodiment: Interpretation of English Idioms by Serbian Students." *Selected Papers from UK-CLA Meetings*, vol. 1, 2012, pp. 385–400.

Areshenkoff, Corson, et al. "Task-Dependent Motor Representations Evoked by Spatial Words: Implications for Embodied Accounts of Word Meaning." *Journal of Memory and Language*, vol. 92, 2017, pp. 158–69.

Auld, Megan Louise, et al. "Tactile Assessment in Children with Cerebral Palsy: A Clinimetric Review." *Physical & Occupational Therapy in Pediatrics*, vol. 31, no. 4, 2011, pp. 413–49.

Barlow, Rachel. "Proprioception in Dance: A Comparative Review of Understandings and Approaches to Research." *Research in Dance Education*, vol. 19, no. 1, 2018, pp. 39–56.

Batson, Glenna. "Update on Proprioception: Considerations for Dance Education." *Journal of Dance Medicine & Science*, vol. 13, no. 2, 2009, pp. 35–41.

Bellan, Valeria, et al. "Integrating Self-Localization, Proprioception, Pain, and Performance." *Journal of Dance Medicine & Science*, vol. 21, no. 1, 2017, pp. 26–35.

Brodie, Julie, and Elin Lobel. "More Than Just a Mirror Image: The Visual System and Other Modes of Learning and Performing Dance." *Journal of Dance Education*, vol. 8, no. 1, 2008, pp. 23–31.

Carter, Rita. *The Human Brain Book*. Dorling Kindersley Ltd., 2014.

Cekaite, Asta, and Malva Kvist Holm. "The Comforting Touch: Tactile Intimacy and Talk in Managing Children's Distress." *Research on Language and Social Interaction*, vol. 50, no. 2, 2017, pp. 109–27.

Christensen, Julia, et al. "I Can Feel My Heartbeat: Dancers Have Increased Interoceptive Accuracy." *Psychophysiology*, vol. 55, no. 4, 2017, Wiley On-Line Library.

Critchley, Hugo. "Neural Mechanisms of Autonomic, Affective, and Cognitive Integration." *The Journal of Comparative Neurology*, vol. 493, 2005, pp. 154–66.

DeWitt, et al. "The Hyper-Sentient Addict: An Exteroception Model of Addiction." *The American Journal of Drug and Alcohol Abuse*, vol. 41, no. 5, 2015, pp. 374–81.

Dieling, Simone, et al. "The Effect of Muscle Fatigue on Knee Joint Proprioception in Ballet Dancers and Non-Dancers." *Journal of Dance Medicine & Science*, vol. 18, no. 4, 2014, pp. 143–48.

Eddy, Martha. *Mindful Movement: The Evolution of the Somatic Arts and Conscious Action*. Intellect, 2017.

Ehrenberg, Shantel. "Reflections on Reflections: Mirror Use in a University Dance Training Environment." *Theatre, Dance and Performance Training*, vol. 1, no. 2, 2010, pp. 172–84.

Fitt, Sally Sevey. *Dance Kinesiology*. 2nd ed. Schirmer Books, 1996.

Foley, Catherine. "Steps, Style and Sensing the Difference: Transmission and the Re-Contextualization of Molyneaux's Traditional Set Dances within the Irish Traditional Dance Competitive Arena." *Research in Dance Education*, vol. 21, no. 3, 2020, pp. 312–27.

Freedman, Aaron, and Wolf Mehling. "Methods for Measuring Embodiment, An Instrument: The Multidimensional Assessment of Interoceptive Awareness (MAIA)." *The Art and Science of Embodied Research Design: Concepts, Methods and Cases*, edited by Jennifer Frank Tantia, Routledge, 2021, pp. 63–74.

Guss-West, Clare. *Attention and Focus in Dance: Enhancing Power, Precision, and Artistry*. Human Kinetics, 2021.

Gustafson, Diana. "Embodied Learning About Health and Healing: Involving the Body as Content and Pedagogy." *Canadian Woman Studies*, vol. 17, no. 4, 1998, pp. 52–55.

Harrington, Heather. "Female Self-Empowerment Through Dance." *Journal of Dance Education*, vol. 20, no. 1, 2020, pp. 35–43.

Hartley, Linda. *Wisdom of the Body Moving: An Introduction to Body-Mind Centering*. North Atlantic Books, 1995.

Haywood, Kathleen, and Nancy Getchell. *Life Span Motor Development*. 7th ed. Human Kinetics, 2020.

Henley, Matthew. "Is Perception of a Dance Phrase Affected by Physical Movement Training and Experience?" *Journal of Dance Education*, vol. 15, no. 1, 2014, pp. 71–82.

———. "Sensation, Perception, and Choice in the Dance Classroom." *Journal of Dance Education*, vol. 14, no. 3, 2014, pp. 95–100.

Henley, Matthew, and Robin Conrad. "I'm Not Thinking About It to Understand It, I'm Thinking About It to Do It: Students' Sensemaking Experiences from the Modern Dance Classroom." *Journal of Dance Education*, 2021, pp. 1–10.

Hermans, Carolien. "Let's Dance: Participatory Sense-Making in an Eight-Year-Old Boy with Autism." *Journal of Dance Education*, vol. 19, no. 1, 2019, pp. 23–33.

Holland, Cristin, et al. "Quantifying Therapists' Activities During Sensory Integration Treatment for Young Children with Autism." *Physical & Occupational Therapy in Pediatrics*, vol. 41, no. 3, 2021, pp. 284–99.

Kiefer, Adam, et al. "Lower-Limb Proprioceptive Awareness in Professional Ballet Dancers." *Journal of Dance Medicine & Science*, vol. 17, no. 3, 2013, pp. 126–32.

Kiefer, Markus, and Natalie Trumpp. "Embodiment Theory and Education: The Foundation of Cognition in Perception and Action." *Trends in Neuroscience and Education*, vol. 1, no. 1, 2012, pp. 15–20.

Kimmerle, Marliese, and Paulette Coté-Laurence. *Teaching Dance Skills: A Motor Learning and Development Approach*. J. Michael Ryan, 2003.

Kirk, Johanna. "Moving from the Membranes: Exploring the Integumentary System though Experiential Anatomy and Dance." *Journal of Dance Education*, vol. 17, no. 1, 2017, pp. 8–15.

Knaster, Mirka. *Discovering the Body's Wisdom*. Bantam Books, 1996.

Krasnow, Donna, and Virginia Wilmerding. *Motor Learning and Control for Dance: Principles and Practices for Performers and Teachers*. Human Kinetics, 2015.

Lozy, Erica, et al. "The Effects of Paired Kinesthetic Movements on Literacy Skills Acquisition with Preschoolers." *Journal of Applied Behavior Analysis*, vol. 53, 2020, pp. 1337–53.

Machorrinho, Joana, et al. "Multidimensional Assessment of Interoceptive Awareness: Psychometric Properties of the Portuguese Version." *Perceptual and Motor Skills*, vol. 126, no. 1, 2019, pp. 87–105.

Magana, Alejandra, and Sadhana Balachandran. "Students' Development of Representations Competance Through the Sense of Touch." *Journal of Science and Education Technology*, vol. 26, 2017, pp. 332–46.

Manoel, Edison, and Pedro Viana Felicio. "Proprioceptive-Visual Integration and Emodied Cognition: A Developmental Perspective." *Perceptual and Motor Skills*, vol. 123, no. 2, 2016, pp. 460–76.

Matzke, Sarah. "Traversing the Succession of Space to Place to Home: A Kinesthetic Comprehension of the Body as It Forms an Epistemology of Space." *Research in Dance Education*, 2021, pp. 1–11, https://doi.org/10.1080/14647893.2021.1879774.

McAlister, Brittni. *Shall We Dance: Responses of Participants to a Dance Class Designed for Parkinson's Patients*. MA Thesis, University of Northern Colorado, 2019.

Meehan, Emma, and Bernie Carter. "Moving with Pain: What Principles from Somatic Practices Can Offer to People Living with Chronic Pain." *Conceptual Analysis*, vol. 11, 2021, pp. 1–10.

Minton, Sandra, and Rima Faber. *Thinking with the Dancing Brain: Embodying Neuroscience*. Rowman & Littlefield Education, 2016.

Minton, Sandra, and Karen McGill. "The Effects of Participation in Dance Technique Classes on Student Performance on a Spatial Kinesthetic Awareness Test." *Journal of Dance Medicine & Science*, vol. 2, no. 2, 1998, pp. 68–72.

———. "A Study of the Relationship Between Teacher Behaviors and Student Performance on a Spatial Kinesthetic Awareness Test." *Dance Research Journal*, vol. 30, no. 2, 1998, pp. 39–52.

Minton, Sandra, and Jeffrey Steffen. "The Development of a Spatial Kinesthetic Awareness Measuring Instrument for Use with Beginning Dance Students." *Dance: Current Selected Research*, vol. 3, 1992, pp. 73–80.

Ohlberg, Jason. "Rethinking Technique: Considering Visual, Oral and Movement Literacy to Provide Technical Skill and Artistic Growth." *Journal of Dance Education*, vol. 21, no. 1, 2021, pp. 1–6.

Pashman, Susan. "Dancing with Damasio: Complementary Aspects of Kinesthesia, Complementary Approaches to Dance." *Journal of Aesthetic Education*, vol. 51, no. 4, 2017, pp. 26–43.

"Pedagogy in Counselor Education: Insights from John Dewey." *The Journal of Counselor Preparation and Supervision*, vol. 14, no. 1/2, 2021, pp. 1–24, https://repository.wcsu.edu/jcps/.

Price, Cynthia, and Carole Hooven. "Interoceptive Awareness Skills for Emotion Regulation: Theory and Approach of Mindful Awareness in Body-Oriented Therapy (MABT)." *Conceptual Analysis*, vol. 9, 2018, pp. 1–12.

Schenkman, Margaret, et al. *Clinical Neuroscience for Rehabilitation*. Pearson Education, 2013.

Seham, Jenny, and Anna Yeo. "Extending Our Vision: Access to Inclusive Dance Education for People with Visual Impairment." *Journal of Dance Education*, vol. 15, no. 3, 2015, pp. 91–99.

Snowber, Celeste. "Dance As a Way of Knowing." *New Directions for Adult and Continuing Education*, Summer, no. 134, 2012, pp. 53–60.

Suppo, Jennifer, and TaMara Swank. "Embracing Collaboration Through the Lens of Exceptional Needs Dance: A Mixed Methods Study." *Journal of Dance Education*, vol. 20, no. 2, 2020, p. 68.

Tsakiris, Manos, and Hugo Critchley. "Interoception Beyond Homeostasis: Affect, Cognition and Mental Health." *Philosophical Transactions Royal Society London B, Biological Science*, vol. 371, 2016, pp. 1–6.

Warburton, Edward. "Who Cares? Teaching and Learning Care in Dance." *Journal of Dance Education*, vol. 4, no. 3, 2004, pp. 88–96.

Weber, Emily, and Jennifer Didier. "Learning and Practicing Dance Phrases with and Without a Mirror: A Comparative Study." *Journal of Dance Education*, July 2021, pp. 1–11.

3
CONNECTIONS BETWEEN BODY, BRAIN, MIND, AND THINKING

The Body Way of Knowing

One of the first steps in describing the bodily way of knowing and how the body can contribute to cognition and learning is to probe the meaning of body awareness as it exists across multiple disciplines. As indicated in the following passages, there appears to be a somewhat different meaning for *body awareness*, depending on its role in a field and in studies concerned with it conducted in various fields.

Body Awareness

Occupational therapy professor Karen Hebert indicated body awareness is often associated with an enhanced ability to be aware of bodily sensations (Busch et al. 250). Those involved with perceptual and motor skills described *body awareness* as a general subjective experience of one's own body as it is related to physical stability and well-being, with the caveat that it can be modified by physiological perceptions, such as those received through the various senses; in addition, one's body awareness depends on the integration of interoceptive and exteroceptive input (Yagci et al. 842). In an article concerned with developing empathy, the educator/author associated body awareness with an enhanced ability to feel how different body parts work (Honig 2292).

In her article, physical educator Heléne Bergentoft, a secondary physical education teacher and doctoral student in sports science, offered a multifaceted description of body awareness. First, she indicated body awareness is developed through interactions with the environment and world. Second, body awareness is based on the attention paid to internal body sensations and a person's ability to recognize the relative positions of different body parts. In a third description, this author noted body awareness included both focusing on proprioceptive feedback, such as joint angles and muscular tension, and on interoceptive sensations. Finally, Bergentoft offered a more comprehensive definition of body awareness that included interoceptive systems and exteroception in terms of perception of the outside world (4).

Other researchers who work in the physical education arena discussed body awareness in terms of skill execution. Giovanna Colombetti, a professor of cognitive science, pointed out that body awareness could be either pre-reflective or reflective, depending on where the person performing the skill focused their attention (Toner et al. 303). When a person is involved with pre-reflective focus while performing a series of movements, his or her body awareness may be marginal and outwardly directed (Toner et al. 304). An example of this type of attention could be to focus on the direction in which one is moving, or the level of those movements. In reflective bodily awareness, the performer's focus is on the body or its parts and sensations which arise. Reflective body awareness comes into play when the performer is attempting to adjust some aspect of their technique or movement ability (Toner et al. 307). In conclusion, the authors of this article stated, "[S]killed performance is rarely characterized by automatic performance devoid of bodily presence but, instead, retains a keen and lucid sense of the kinesthetic sensations that accompany fluent and efficient movement execution" (Toner et al. 312).

Evidence from Somatic Practices

According to Glenna Batson and Margaret Wilson, somatics celebrates sensitivity to the body, fosters being grounded in a conscious awareness of one's own bodily experiences, and shifts the focus from the what of learning to the how (5–6). From its inception, somatics has had directed kinesthetic awareness as its focus, with the view that the body is contextual and fluid based on the outcome of movement explorations; there was and has been more interest in somatics in the process of developing awareness over the movement outcome (Batson and Wilson 6–7). Although somatics encompasses many different techniques and practices, a simple way to describe somatics is as "an experience of the self in the present moment" (Lester 31).

The aforementioned goals are pursued in somatics systems, in many instances, by engaging in conscious movement, with the purpose of amplifying oneself by awakening the kinesthetic sense; somatics can involve exploration of physical habits and behavior patterns by noticing movement elements of the body and whether the body is moving or still (Eddy *Mindful* 14). For example, breath and blood are always moving in the body, and it is possible to become sensitive to these body processes. In many instances, specific exercises or more open-ended movement explorations are used to become and be aware of one's physical sensations and the connected emotions (Eddy *Mindful* 14).

The following are examples of bringing bodily sensations to the conscious mind. By focusing on breathing while inhaling, exhaling, or holding the breath, it is possible to access feedback from one's muscles, joints, and tactile sense in the nose. Body awareness created through mindful movement found in some somatic practices can evoke emotions, create cortical connections, and activate deep brain structures. Increased body awareness can also bring one's attention to bodily tensions, blocked areas in the body, physical resistance, and movement limitations. The important point is that awareness is the first step which can lead to increased consciousness daily (Eddy *Mindful* 15).

There are different somatic systems which have many of the aforementioned body awareness outcomes as their goal. The following content is a summary of the goals of some of the earlier somatic systems in terms of body awareness.

The Alexander technique approaches body awareness by emphasizing changes in posture; it is used to improve and maintain health, reduce discomfort, and move with greater ease and clarity (Eddy *Mindful* 24). Bartenieff fundamentals teach one how to move more efficiently by creating an awareness of deep and superficial kinetic chains, breathing, core support, rotation of joints while moving, shifting weight effectively, and having a clear intention when moving through space (Eddy *Mindful* 25). In Gerda Alexander's Eutony (GAE), participants strive to balance muscle tone in their bodies among other goals; GAE can teach deep body awareness and increase sensitivity to the relationship between oneself and the outside environment as an individual gains more proprioceptive awareness (Eddy *Mindful* 25–26). Finally, in Awareness through Movement and Functional Integration of the Feldenkrais Method, the emphasis is on bringing awareness to differentiating between body parts and integrating the many ways in which one can move the body to create a unified life experience; in this latter somatic system, participants are taught to bring their awareness to often subtle feedback from carefully structured movement sequences in a class environment or one-to-one sessions (Eddy *Mindful* 27).

Body Awareness and Somatic Practices—Non-Western Influences

It would be remiss to discuss somatics and its role in creating awareness of one's body without including information about how Asian and African movement practices create an awareness of bodily sensations and how they influenced developments in the somatics arena. In particular, the somatics pioneers of the first two generations were influenced by practices found in their own cultures as well as from cultures outside their own (Eddy *Mindful* 86).

> There were significant influences from eastern cultures [on somatics]—examples include concepts such as the use of breath tantamount within yoga practice (as in the work of Ida Rolf), the grounding in tai chi and chi kung (as in the work of Irmgard Bartenieff), the reflexive responses of judo (as in the work of Feldenkrais), and the autonomic responses in Katsugen Undo (as in the work of Bonnie Bainbridge Cohen).
>
> *(Eddy* Mindful *86)*

African movement and dance practices have also been influential in the development of somatics, although their influence is less direct than the influences of

Asian movement practices. Nevertheless, the connection between African dance and somatics is significant. This is true, because African dance has played a prominent role in African culture in the form of rituals, healing practices, group and community identity, and establishing connections with the ancestors (Eddy *Mindful* 96). The connection between African dance and healing practices is especially noteworthy in this context.

Brenda Dixon Gottschild insisted postmodern dancers erased the influence of Black culture on their art form (George 6). In his book about the natural body and its relationship to somatics, Doran George, formerly of the UCLA World Arts and Culture faculty, noted that somatics practitioners appropriated and acknowledged their debt to traditions from Eastern cultures yet ignored acknowledging contributions from African cultures (6).

While African and Eastern movement practices and their influence on the development of somatics in the West can be acknowledged, there is a primary difference in how the information and content is delivered and the extent to which it is used (Eddy *Mindful* 85). For example, Eastern movement practices, such as those named previously, and African dance are an inherent and integral part of each of their respective cultures, whereas the Western practice of somatics, although becoming more widely disseminated, has been introduced and layered onto an already-existing cultural milieu.

Body Awareness and Somatic Practices—Various Applications

Musicians have benefited from somatics training, particularly those who perform while in a seated position. The issue when in this position is that the torso often feels cut off from the lower body, which limits how musicians respond to the music while performing (Johnson 18). Somatics practitioners have recommended exercises away from an instrument to create an awareness of the body and wake up the musician's kinesthetic sense. One exercise recommended was based on the Aston paradigm, in which the musician tunes into the body to discover a neutral seated position in which the body is positioned at a midpoint between being slumped forward and having the back arched. This means the pelvis is centered and the spine has settled into balance with gravity. Tuning into the breath was also recommended in this article, along with closing the eyes and focusing on the piano's keys to feel vibrations from sounds with one's fingertips. This last exploration was followed by checking the breathing after the sound died away (Johnson 18–19).

A study was conducted to explore whether Feldenkrais's Awareness through Movement could be used to improve the physical functioning and balance of people with intellectual disabilities (ID), since physical problems seem to appear in this population earlier than in their nondisabled peers; in this study, thirty-two middle-aged participants with ID were randomly assigned to the treatment group who received Feldenkrais training, and the control, who received no movement training and assessed pre- and post with the Short Physical Performance Battery (SPPB) (Torres-Unda et al. 104 & 106). The SPPB includes three tasks: walking speed, the chair rise test (rise from the chair as quickly as possible), and standing balance, in which a score between 0 and 4 is assigned, with a higher value representing the best performance (106–07). Although the control group subjects performed better on the SPPB than those who received the Feldenkrais training at the beginning of the study, by the end of the study, the reverse was true (109).

Another premise is that bodily engagement can be taught using somatic education techniques. Korthagen, Rogers, and Raider-Roth, who are involved with teacher training, believed there is a relationship between a teacher's sensations and intentions on the internal side and their actions on the external side which could affect their presence while teaching (Lachance et al. 29). The authors conducted a study with student teachers in which they participated in body awareness somatics workshops which provided combined techniques to promote vitality and relaxation (Lachance et al. 30). The outcome of the somatics intervention was that the student teachers reported changes in their self-relationship while teaching or became aware of their lack of presence; in their words, they "became sensitized to the presence of the self as a body in the environment while teaching" (Lachance et al. 30).

Allyson Neal did a study in which she attempted to synthesize the results of other research completed to assess the effect of somatic interventions to improve self-regulation in children and adolescents who have suffered trauma. Some of the interventions used in these studies included mindfulness training, yoga, breathing exercises, and self-regulation behaviors; mindfulness emphasizes the present moment and can be achieved by focusing on one's awareness of bodily sensations, among other techniques (173). Neal described studies in which mindfulness training improved self-regulation, self-esteem, positive thinking, and produced calmness (173).

Body awareness/somatic techniques have also been used to reduce post-disaster psychological symptoms, or PTSD. In one study, the researchers wanted to know whether somatic intervention techniques could be used to reduce such symptoms. This study was completed using social service workers who were involved in post-disaster relief following hurricanes Katrina and Rita. Ninety-one of the workers in this study received treatment, which included Somatic Experiencing (SE), in which individuals focus on their perceived body sensations. These workers were compared with a matched comparison group of fifty-one other workers who did not receive the somatic intervention training (Leitch et al. 9). At the end of the study, the researchers discovered both groups' PTSD symptoms became worse, although these symptoms worsened significantly less in the treatment group; at a later follow-up, both groups displayed decreased PTSD symptoms, with the treatment group showing a more significant decrease (Leitch et al. 15).

Body Awareness and Somatic Practices in Dance

Glenna Batson explained how improved postural control could be modified and retrained using somatics techniques. For example, Ideokinesis concepts can be applied in this context by visualizing the whole or part of a movement, while Alexander procedures can be used to limit movement range along with paying particular attention to sensations experienced during movement ("Improving" 9).

The Alexander technique was used by a ballet instructor in combination with the neuromuscular re-education work of Irene Dowd, who is on the faculty at Julliard, where students learn by doing in her kinesthetic anatomy classes. The ballet teacher in this study pointed out that the somatic applications provided the students with an internal authority and autonomy; outcome assessments were based on class observations which were conducted three times during an eight-month period, along with student and teacher interviews (Berg 148–49). To facilitate a somatic approach to ballet class content, the teacher provided suggestions about how the movements being learned should feel in the body, along with an image-based vocabulary related to targeted anatomical concepts and use of tactile corrections (Berg 150–51). One of the students responded to the teaching strategies by saying she developed an internal focus which enabled her to better deal with her structural issues, another believed the class techniques prevented injuries, and a third said she now had improved alignment and control (Berg 155). A photo of Dowd can be seen in Figure 3.1.

The use of dance science and somatic teaching interventions was the focus of a modern dance class in which six students learned two contrasting dance phrases based on spinal movements. The students learned the movement phrases from videos performed by an expert dancer and were videotaped as they performed each phrase at the beginning of the study and again eight weeks later (Andersen 166). In the intervening eight weeks, the students participated in a training workshop which included somatic and dance science content. The somatic content was based on Bartenieff fundamentals, Feldenkrais work, body scans, and the Pilates pelvic clock, while the science instruction consisted of viewing anatomical illustrations, descriptions of spinal actions, and practicing movement exercises, such as weight shifting and balancing (Andersen 167). The students also participated in an entry-and-exit questionnaire and interview.

The outcome of the aforementioned study showed the students displayed both overall skill improvement and partial improvement, indicating learning varies among individuals (Andersen 164). In terms of body awareness, one student reported she was better able to integrate concepts taught in the class into her own movement and could now understand how to perform movements rather than simply looking at what a movement is; another student learned how to use her spine effectively to avoid possible injury and reported greater ability to sense different parts of her body (Andersen 169).

Another dance teacher, Lauren Kearns, also combined approaches from several somatic practices to teach her advanced-level dance students. Some of the specific teaching strategies included the constructive rest position from Ideokinesis, pelvic clock from Pilates, and three Bartenieff explorations in which the students focused on internal and external hip rotation (36–38). Anatomically based mental imagery, focused inhaling and exhaling, and placement of fingers on body parts to accentuate bodily sensations were also part of the teaching strategies connected with the Pilates pelvic clock (Kearns 37–38). The author indicated that after she had integrated the somatic theories into her class, the students displayed significant improvements in the way they approached movement and demonstrated an

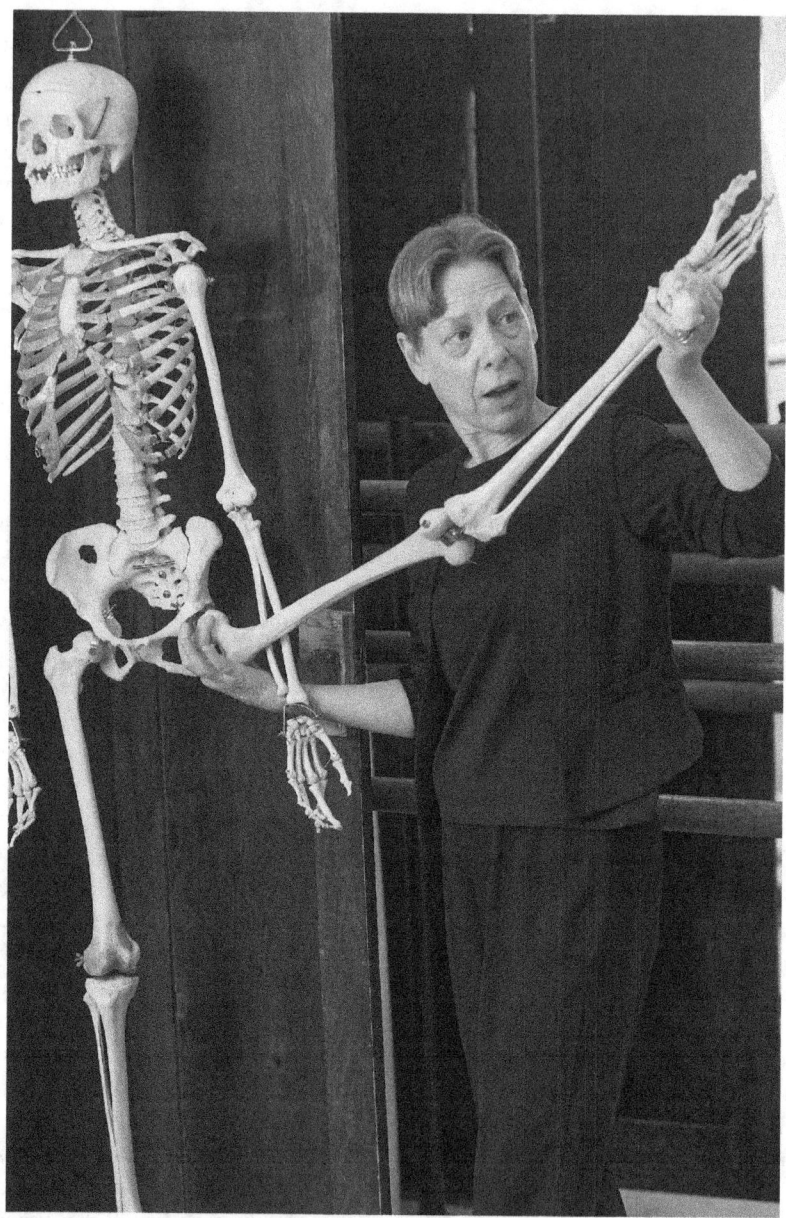

FIGURE 3.1   Irene Dowd with skeleton used for teaching anatomy.
Source: Photo by Jim Lafferty.

increased mindfulness and expressiveness in the classroom, during rehearsals, and when onstage (Kearns 39).

In another study, two professional dancers commented on their ability to make connections between their customary way of performing dance movements and performing those movements after integrating Alexander technique concepts in their performance of the movements (Fortin and Girard 126). While both dancers admitted that it was easier to apply the Alexander concepts to ballet over modern dance, the primary challenge was the frustration they experienced between performing movements using their habitual body sensations and the new sensations experienced while integrating Alexander technique concepts into the performance of typical dance movements (Fortin and Girard 129–30). There is a photo of Alexander working with a young client in Figure 3.2.

FIGURE 3.2   F. Matthias Alexander with young client.

Source: © 2022 The Society of Teachers of Alexander Technique, London.

A somewhat-different application was recommended as a way somatics made contributions to dance training. In this situation, a learning paradigm was suggested "in which augmented body awareness in the context of 'spaced,' or 'distributed' practice could be one somatic strategy that dancers could use in learning and refinement of skilled coordination" (Batson and Schwartz 53). In the Feldenkrais Method, learning is said to occur when the body is at rest; thus, research was conducted in which dance students were asked to experience thirty minutes in which they moved and rested in equal amounts of time, although the students could apportion the time at rest within the time frame in any way they desired. The students were also asked to reflect on their experience following each session (Batson and Schwartz 52). These reflections revealed rest provided information about how the dancers learned; when similar somatic interventions were used by a different teacher in technique class, he noticed the students seemed more in control of their bodies and it appeared the teacher was not forcing them to move (Batson and Schwartz 53).

In her article, Donna Dragon, a dance professor at Bridgewater State University, recommended using somatics teaching strategies which incorporate student-centered delivery methods rather than a teacher-centered pedagogical approach. In a student-centered approach, the focus is on helping the students explore and understand the somatic class content in a holistic manner. In comparison, a teacher-centered approach involves delivering a series of movements or exercises which the students are expected to copy precisely—an approach which perpetuates authoritarian dance teaching methods from the past (30).

Connecting Body Awareness, Mind, and Thinking

The connection between mind and body was aptly described by Maxine Sheets-Johnstone when she challenged some of the previous descriptions of the mind-body connection, self, and consciousness by writing:

> [P]ursuit of validating a self and a pre-reflective self-consciousness fail to accord with the spatio-temporal and kinesthetic nature of the lived body . . . in essence, the descriptions short circuit the lived body's spatio-temporal presence anchored in tactile-kinesthetic-affective realties.
>
> *(Sheets-Johnstone "Lived Body" 28)*

If one considers the self as concurrent with or related to mind, Sheets-Johnstone appears to be drawing connections between mind and body by asserting that mind is dependent on and integrally connected to the body based on bodily sensory modalities. Later in her article, Sheets-Johnstone clarified the spatial and temporal aspects of her theories and emphasized the importance of the connection between consciousness and the body. She noted:

> [T]he felt on-going presence that constitutes the lived body's experienced hereness is not simply a spatial presence, but a spatio-temporal presence

foundationally grounded in the tactile-kinesthetic body. . . . The absence of kinesthesia and more broadly, the tactile-kinesthetic-affective body, in such a "stream of consciousness" are absences that may well be likened to "an absence of the body below the neck."

(Sheets-Johnstone "Lived Body" 50)

The Phenomenological Perspective

According to Merleau-Ponty, the body is innately connected to the world and to itself because it can never be considered only as an object or subject; there is a simultaneous and mutual relationship between the two (Bailey 281).

Many writers besides Maxine Sheets-Johnstone have added to the phenomenological discussion concerning the mind-body connection. Mari Sorri, a ceramic artist, challenged the mind-body dichotomy by stating that when making her artistic creations, her body often knows more about how to interpret her creative process than her mind (15). To bolster her argument about the mind-body connection, Sorri cited a theory of cognition promoted by Michael Polanyi, a Hungarian British polymath who made contributions to philosophy, in which he maintained human cognition is bodily in nature because it is produced through a type of absorption which is not, and perhaps cannot be, articulated by the knower (Sorri 15).

Sorri furthered her argument by elaborating on Polanyi's belief that all human activity takes place on a continuum between activities performed by the body and those that are conceptual; purely bodily activities are nonverbal, and conceptual thoughts are usually verbal (Sorri 16). Finally, this same author explained Polanyi's distinction about bodily and conceptual activities in more detail by discussing explicit and tacit knowledge; explicit knowledge can be articulated conceptually, while tacit knowledge cannot be fully described (17).

In another article, the author Glenn Hartelius described somatic phenomenology as "studying body-located sensate markers of psychological process[es] within the lived experience of the body" (87). Based on his work, this author thought certain phenomenological markers could be correlated with specific mental processes in the effort to improve the ability to focus when an individual is taught how to describe them as a body-felt skill (88). The author described phenomenological markers as emotional signals that may or may not be consciously recognized but which originate as neuroanatomical processes (89).

In discussing the mind-body issue, author Julie Cheville, professor of literacy education at Rutgers University, pursued a more all-encompassing discussion by suggesting theories of embodied cognition should represent the human body both as an object of one's culture and yet also a subject of cognition (86). This author's quest to resolve the relationship between mind and body was to create a theoretical framework that "reconciles culture, corporeality and cognition" (90). "To fully confront the longstanding dichotomy of mind and body, however, embodied cognition must document how the human body, despite its condition as an object of culture, exerts subjective influence on the mind" (Cheville 91).

In conclusion, Cheville asserted that a theory of embodied cognition should consider the human body in terms of both cultural influences and subjective experiences with one's body (101). She also recommended a better understanding of this issue could be achieved by improving communication between disciplines concerned with connections between mind and body so they could better inform each other about their discoveries (102). This conclusion was correlated with Damasio's belief that we know little about the mind-body relationship (Cheville 102)—a lack of knowledge which could profit from greater interdisciplinary communication on this topic.

The Psychological Perspective

Michel Ferrari, a Swiss neurologist and professor of neurology at Leiden University, and his coauthors examined the origins of consciousness using Piaget's theories. Although there are many interpretations of consciousness, for Piaget *consciousness* involved a subjective awareness that is not a given but instead is constructed; it was an active process that goes beyond exposure to the environment, requiring deliberate action (Ferrari et al. 196–97). The preceding comment can be relevant here if consciousness is considered to be one with mind or the content of the mind which can be discussed verbally. The parallel nature of Piaget's understanding of the mind-body relationship was described previously in Chapter 1 of this book.

When discussing the felt sense concept, developed by Gendlin over fifty years ago, researchers Cornell and McGavin pointed out that although the content in the felt-sensory experience is ultimately acknowledged by the mind, the body is a key component; it is something which is more than thought and can be experienced at the body level (31). The felt sense is not the same as an emotion or thought; it is truly meaningful and "is *experiencing forming itself*, and can be sensed" (Cornell and McGavin 31).

The process involved in Gestalt psychotherapy provides other evidence for the connection between mind and body. In this approach to the therapeutic process, practitioners believe the body holds a history of adjustments a person has made in his or her life based on muscular tensions held in the body; by addressing one's bodily responses first, Gestalt therapists believe they can bring past experiences into conscious awareness (Grossman 76–77). The hypothesis on which Gestalt therapy is based is that if a client becomes more sensitive to somatic sensations, resistances are reduced and the client becomes more responsive to the present (Grossman 84).

The Educational Perspective

Unfortunately, the Cartesian dualism continues to inhabit education in different ways. Marek Tamm, professor of cultural history, said that initially, the emphasis was on the mind but there seems to be a recent interest in the body—an interest which has not totally displaced the interest in the mind (Herman and Hofmann 448). However, the nature of the mind-body dichotomy is beginning to change, and "as a result, distinctions between body/matter and mind have come to fade and their rivalry has made place for notions of entanglement, assemblage and hybridity" (Herman and Hofmann 449). Herman and Hofmann indicated that a broader and more accurate interpretation of the mind-body discussion could create alternative views on the body and mind as they function in education (451).

On a more concrete level, other research has indicated there are important implications for the embodied perspective as it applies to teaching and learning. Thus, students can change their thinking and how they feel and behave by making changes in their breathing or posture (Bailey 281). Furthermore, once the distinction between inside and outside of the body is negated, one recognizes mind is situated in a world of the brain, body, objects, and other people (Bailey 287).

The instructional method is one of the most fundamental concepts related to effective learning in education because "the method of presentation directly and substantially influences students' accumulation and retention of knowledge" (Sullivan 129). Cognitive psychological research has shown that hand gestures appear to provide for an embodied effect along with verbal information and that the teacher's use of gestures surpassed presentation of items on a screen in terms of content remembered (Sullivan 130). In their research, other psychologists found that if the instructor's gestures matched pictures presented to students, the students quickly responded to the picture by incorporating information from the instructor's gestures into a mental model based on the instructor's message (Sullivan 137).

In light of the aforementioned educational research, several other investigators discovered that when letters were presented to subjects, the premotor brain areas were activated. The reasoning behind this discovery was that these are the same brain areas involved in writing the letters. "This activation of mirror neurons in the left premotor cortex may give students the feeling of familiarity with a word, and therefore help them remember it in a recognition task" (qtd. in Sullivan 135).

The body-based teaching methods described in the preceding text included altering students' breathing and posture and the teacher's use of hand gestures. An additional physically based teaching strategy is having students learn by doing, which could provide a more student-centered form of instruction. However, it seems that manually based teaching methods have been, in many instances, subverted by a preference for teacher-centered delivery or manual learning strategies in which student discovery and problem-solving are absent (Hutt 549–50).

In a historical summary of manual training methods used in US schools, Sébastien-Akira Alix noted that manual training classes (woodworking classes for boys and sewing for girls) enjoyed considerable support during the nation's Progressive era, especially in the Northeast and Midwest (494). This craze was due largely to the beliefs of Progressive reformers, such as John Dewey and James Stout, who believed in a new body-mind education that might produce a revolution in American education (494). This author concluded by saying:

> "[L]earning by doing" thus appears to have worked against the principle of making pupils "the sun about which the appliances of education revolve." . . .

When translated into everyday school practices, this new or progressive, education indeed assumed an unexpected form: the children's body and hands were considered "agents of the mind" only to the extent they fostered instructional, social and gendered goals set by adults.

(495)

The Neuroscience Perspective

Neuroscientist Antonio Damasio explained that the brain and body are customarily thought of as separate structures, and the idea that it is the entire organism which interacts with the environment is often disregarded; however, when we use our exteroceptive senses, both the body and brain participate, interacting with the environment (*Descartes' Error* 224). Damasio continued:

> Perceiving the environment . . . is not just a matter of having the brain receive direct signals from a given stimulus. . . . The organism actively modifies itself so that the interfacing can take place as well as possible.
>
> *(Descartes' Error 225)*

While many believe the mind-body issue might best be solved through analytic philosophy, Antonio and Hanna Damasio disagreed, since they prefer to focus instead on "biological scaffolding without which the body certainly cannot be present in the mind" (15). Communication between mind and body, these authors indicated, is dependent on chemical and neural signals sent by the body to the brain (16). Second, the brain represents states in the body as they occur, but it can also modify these representations, and most important, the brain can stimulate body states (16). The previous two authors acknowledged that understanding how the body and brain communicate has deep implications for the comprehension of consciousness and social behavior (16).

Damasio and Damasio continued that communication between the body and the brain does not go only in one direction from body to the brain but actually occurs from the brain to the body as well (16). An example of the first type of communication is the fact that chemicals in the body send messages to the brain, for example, about the contraction and dilation of smooth muscles or concerning the amount of oxygen in bodily regions (17). An example of the brain-to-body communication occurs through nerves and chemical channels to initiate muscular contraction or to release hormones to regulate viscera (17). The point is that the body and brain are occupied in a constant interaction; the most remarkable aspect of these processes is their constant interplay primarily below the conscious level (Damasio and Damasio 17–18).

Later in the same article, the authors explained there is another network linking mind and body. "[I]n certain circumstances, as an emotion unfolds, the brain rapidly constructs maps of the body comparable to those that would result were the body actually changed by that emotion" (18). These emotionally based body loops function as a type of warning system and are triggered by the brain's mirror neurons, which play a role in enabling one to understand the actions of others by putting one in a comparable state in preparation for reacting (Damasio and Damasio 19–20). A final point the authors made is, feeling an emotion is both mental and physical, but the difference for the feeling-based body-mind connection is that feelings are based on a state in the living organism (21).

Noted neuroscientist Eric Kandel agreed with Antonio and Hanna Damasio's explanation of the biological basis of emotion. Kandel, who specialized in psychiatry during his medical training, wrote that the human state of depression occurs when a complex neural circuit becomes disorganized. Professor Helen Mayberg and others have used brain scanning to identify components of this circuit; two components include parts of the brain which mediate unconscious and motor responses to emotional stress, and a second brain area which brings self-awareness and interpersonal experiences together (Kandel "New Science"). These two brain areas, Kandel continued, connect to brain areas responsible for sleep, appetite, libido, emotions, memory, and executive function ("New Science"). Kandel conceded that although the understanding of the biological basis of mental disorders has been slow to evolve, research using brain scanning techniques has shown they have a bodily basis; the new science of mind is rooted in the idea that mind and brain are inseparable ("New Science").

In the 1970s, cognitive psychology and neuroscience merged, resulting in cognitive neuroscience, which introduced biological methods for exploring mental processes (Kandel *In Search* 7). In his book, Kandel explained his concept of a new science of the mind as a molecular biology of cognition. This new science, he stated, "has allowed us to explore on the molecular level such mental processes as how we think, feel, learn, and remember" (8). Although the bodily basis of mind may be disturbing to some, Kandel indicated that consciousness is actually a biological process based on molecular signaling pathways used by nerve cells (*In Search* 8–9). Kandel noted that the new science of the mind will address philosophical questions concerning the mind that some have struggled with for centuries (*In Search* 9). Thus, consciousness will be explained in detail eventually (Kandel *In Search* 8–9).

Neuroscientist V. S. Ramachandran turned to the discipline of embodied cognition to help explain how human thinking is shaped by interconnections with the body and by the human processes of sensation and movement (143). Much of Ramachandran's concept of the mind-body connection is tied to his knowledge of the human brain's mirror neuron system. In one example, he described how humans manage to translate facial expressions they see into emotions based on responses from the mirror neurons (143). In a second example, Ramachandran explained humans can view an action performed by another person which, in turn, leads to a very small but measurable increase in action readiness in the muscles of the viewer; thus, the muscles of the viewer simulate the perceived action (142).

Ramachandran's explanation of body image appears to illustrate the connection between mind and body as well since the brain records an innate body image;

when a person's visual or somatic sensory input does not match their body image, disharmony can ensue, disrupting an individual's sense of unity (254). In expanding on the concept of body image and a person's sense of unity, Ramachandran suggested "there is a genetically specified mechanism that allows a template of one's body image . . . to become transcribed into limbic [brain] circuitry" (258).

Connecting Body Awareness, Mind, and Thinking in Dance

What has come to be known as 4E Cognition is redefining what it means to think, especially the way in which thinking is connected to and explained in dance (Henley "Thinking" 130). Henley wrote:

> [W]e, dance educators, can still fall prey to the trap of communicating implicit messages to our students that "dancing" happens in one part of class—when we are bending, twisting, jumping, and shaking—and "thinking about dance" happens in another part of the class—when we are talking and writing.
>
> *("Thinking" 129).*

In light of the previous quotation, 4E Cognition, which has emerged from and is still connected to phenomenological philosophy and cognitive science, redefines the functioning of mind in relation to the body and action (Henley "Thinking" 130). The term *4E Cognition*, originally attributed to philosopher and cognitive scientist Shaun Gallagher, refers to four overlapping domains of thinking described in *The Oxford Handbook of 4E Cognition* as embodied, embedded, extended, and enactive (Henley "Thinking" 130). Psychology professor Raymond Gibbs defined *embodied cognition* as the idea that mental percepts, which are usually thought to occur in the mind, are, in truth, dependent on the body (Henley "Thinking" 130). Scholars Albert Newen, Francisco Varela, and others contended that in embedded and extended cognition, the spatial range of cognition is based on how the body interacts with the environment, while enactive cognition refers to how an individual's actions can modify the environment (Henley "Thinking" 130).

An example of how an individual can interact with aspects of the environment was provided in an article by Ojeya Cruz Banks in which he explained how dancers think with and through the music when performing African dance; in the dances, performers need to remain alert, supple, and responsive to the music (181). When training, his teachers encouraged Cruz Banks to think in terms of how the mind, body, and music connect; in fact, in African dance, the performers see themselves as part of the percussion ensemble (181). "How musicality is taught in African/African diaspora dance styles elucidates [an] intersubjective learning process" (Cruz Banks 176). According to Cruz Banks, the interconnected learning process described by Cruz Banks relates to aspects of 4E Cognition.

When connected to dance, writing can be considered embodied language. Alexandra Bradshaw-Yerby explained that embodied writing is a process which connects dancing and writing and is based on using improvised movement as indispensable and pre-verbal to enact literary devices such as alliteration through motion, sensation, and spatial relationships (193). In one embodied writing exercise, students were instructed to freely write about a memory based on their senses, improvise in movement based on the same memory, and freewrite again; in another exercise, the students touched a piece of fruit, such as a strawberry, and then freewrote and danced about their sensory response (Bradshaw-Yerby 194). In terms of 4E Cognition, writing when connected with improvisation makes the writing more authentic and personal and can be a foundation for self-realized content (Bradshaw-Yerby 195).

Miriam Giguere sought to examine how the social nature of dance can influence perception, mental imagery, and cognitive function from a 4E perspective ("Social Nature" 132). Giguere pointed out that the body and social interactions have long been ignored as contributing to cognition; however, mental states are based on an interplay between internal and external factors ("Social Nature" 133). Giguere discovered students fulfilled various fluid roles as they worked creatively—facilitator/organizer, compliant follower, naysayer, or loner ("Social Nature" 135). Examples of thinking connected with these roles was explained in the following way. The facilitator/organizer would propose a choreographic idea, attempting to have the group try it out; the compliant follower respected the facilitator/organizer's instructions, the naysayer rejected ideas or provided negative feedback, and the loner would present an idea he or she developed independently (Giguere "Social Nature" 135). The literature on 4E Cognition which Giguere reviewed presented cognition as a social act, with the conclusion that group process could be a tool for developing cognition (Giguere "Social Nature" 135).

Lindsay Lindberg et al. discussed movement improvisation as a tool which can be used to support embodied interactions, especially in making sense of settings which are outside the dance studio (2). In this study, the authors/researchers were concerned with using an enactive approach in which cognition is an active accomplishment grounded between a willing individual and their surroundings (2). In a ninety-minute workshop, the researchers used design-based research to learn how novice dancers engaged with improvisation in a museum environment as a tool for making sense of input; improvisation experiences involved responding to external stimuli, in conjunction with a partner, in response to a selected artwork, and through scaffolded experiences beginning with pedestrian movements (Lindberg et al. 4–5).

Based on video analysis in the previous study, the researchers concluded that the students used their bodies to make sense of the artwork, which is evidence of dance as embodied, enactive cognition (6–7). For example, in one instance, a student stood in front of a painting to observe it, followed by improvising movements in response to the painting, and then, prompted by a see-and-move game, changed those movements (Lindberg et al. 8). The students' improvisational experiences in the art museum demonstrated the students engaged with themselves and their surroundings as examples of how dancing is thinking (Lindberg et al. 9).

In his article, Christian Kronsted also discussed improvisation from the viewpoint of enactive cognition based on affordances or interactional possibilities presented to an organism; when one acts on affordances, more affordances are, in turn, presented (169). Kronsted believed that teaching students how to be good improvisational dancers means teaching them how to perceive the environment, which produces an affordance-action cycle (170). Kronsted's suggestions for teaching improvisation as an enactive practice included paying attention to the possibilities, using exercises that break movement habits, listening more carefully to the music, steering attention to the novel, or changing the improvisational environment (172–73).

The Role of Attention

Recognizing and describing one's bodily sensations requires paying attention or attending to them on the mental level. Otherwise, such sensations would remain beyond one's conscious realm and escape recognition and subsequent description. Thus, there is a symbiotic relationship between attention and body awareness.

In discussing embodiment and awareness, Susan Grossman, a Gestalt clinical social worker, wrote, "Attention is focused awareness" (76). Such focused awareness can be achieved by calling a subject's attention to a body part which is targeted for achieving increased awareness (76–77). Sports scientist Gabriele Wulf noted that much work has been conducted in sports psychology which emphasizes the importance of attentional focus in learning movement and perfecting one's performance (Mattes 258). Since attention is a concentrated mental activity, prominent American philosopher, historian, and psychologist William James explained attention requires selecting one stream of thought out of a multitude of ideas occurring simultaneously in the brain (Krasnow and Wilmerding 98).

However, there are different types of attention. First, attention is divisible, which means one can separate their attention between different types of input. Second, one's attention can shift from one type of input to another. Third, it is possible to sustain one's attention, but at the same time, attention is limited by the number or types of input to which one can attend (Krasnow and Wilmerding 98). In addition, attention can be controlled or automatic. Controlled attention is willful and serial, meaning, each part of the attentional process takes place in sequence; automatic processing of input is fast and not under control of one's will, because it takes place without conscious thought (Krasnow and Wilmerding 99).

Nevertheless, attention involves much more than concentrating on a single aspect of the input or stimulus. "It involves the process of filtering through the potential surrounding stimuli in any given moment . . . and deliberately attending only to those that support the demands of the task at hand" (Guss-West 9–10). For example, as you read this text, numerous other stimuli can be seen and heard from the surrounding environment and must be filtered out to give priority to the content on this page.

Attention and Focus in Eastern Movement Practices

The previous information attempted to establish a connection between mind and body during the processes of attending to or paying attention, but how is the divide between mind and body and attention approached in Eastern movement practices?

Eastern movement practices are developed from three foundations: alignment and posture, energy and breath, and attention and focus (Guss-West 52). The first of these foundations is outwardly directed and prevalent in Western movement practices, but the second and third are less recognized in the West and require attending to the inner work involved in learning how to move successfully and fully (Guss-West 53).

The role of breath in Eastern movement practices is to produce a quantity of oxygen in the body which has an impact on one's quantity and quality of energy (Guss-West 53). Eastern movement practices also differentiate between the in-breath and out-breath. The in-breath is a moment of replenishing one's potential and expanding the body's cavities, while the out-breath is the moment when one expels toxins from within the body and oxygen flows from the lungs throughout the body to provide energy and power (Guss-West 55–56). Examples of paying attention to use of breath in Eastern movement practices follow.

The word *yoga* comes from the Sanskrit *yug*, which means yoke, and refers to joining the self with a universal spirit or cosmic consciousness (Knaster 345). In 1920, a form of yoga was introduced in the United States in which the mind and breath were used to direct one's attention and energy to the spinal cord, which is the approximate location of the body's chakras, or energy centers (Eddy *Mindful* 88). In yoga, breath regulation, or *pranayama*, slows the breath while expanding lung capacity and respiration and helps regulate flow in body channels (Knaster 346).

The breath and energy are also important to the practice of tai chi chuan, which evolved from a Chinese form of martial arts. In tai chi, the emphasis is on moving from one of the prescribed postures to another without holding the body in a rigid manner; the point is to flow from one posture to the next without interruption (Knaster 336). The use of breath in tai chi is based on the principle of storing and delivering energy noted previously.

Chi kung is a third Eastern movement practice which has been followed in China over the last five thousand years; it means to work with the chi or vital energy in the body (Eddy *Mindful* 92). Chi kung "focuses on the inner working of the moving body—on developing awareness and attention, on the use of conscious breath, and promoting optimum energy flow and fluid movement for maximum efficiency" (Guss-West 46). Guss-West also pointed out that the chi kung movement family incorporates a continuous and circular movement flow and energy; one of the goals is to bring attention to bodily tensions, which can block energy flow (48 & 52).

Based on the previous discussion and as a modern dancer and practitioner of yoga, the author has always believed that breath or breathing forms a connection between mind and body. According to Rosalba Courtney, DO and PhD, who conducts courses in Integrative Breathing Therapy, knowing how to breathe forms "a bridge linking mind and body. It's a powerful anchor for mindfulness. It's a tool for training stress resilience, a way of knowing ourselves more deeply and a pathway for treating ourselves more kindly" ("Breath, Mind Body").

Attention and Focus in Somatics

Various somatic systems also provide evidence for using attention to focus on the connection between mind and body. Martha Eddy noted, "When the body is experienced from within, a myriad of physical and mental conundrums can be revealed. In some cases, these mysteries are solved, and in most cases, learning transpires" (*Mindful* 18). Somatic practitioners often ask guiding questions to help clients pay attention to sensations which arise from within the body (Eddy *Mindful* 131).

In Laban Movement Analysis/Bartenieff Fundamentals of Movement, clients are taught to pay attention to how they initiate movement and to the spatial intention of their movements (Eddy *Mindful* 25). In this system, movement is identified as a form of language which is both expressive and functional; students are taught to pay attention to four movement categories, which include body, effort, shape, and space (Whittier 125). According to Richard Strozzi-Heckler, who has spent considerable time and effort researching and teaching somatics, these four movement categories display a person's inner intent and outward desires (Whittier 125). In terms of the movement in this somatic system, *body* refers to connectivity, actions, and phrasing; *effort* describes the use of energy and dynamics; *shape* includes how the body and its parts are shaped; and *space* reveals spatial pulls, pathways, and zones (Whittier 125).

When using the Feldenkrais Method, careful attention is paid to mindful movement practices. In this somatic method, *function* refers to an interaction of an individual or self with the outside world or environment (Mattes 260). In the Feldenkrais work, students' attention is focused on sensory information which accompanies a series of movements, with the goal of selecting easier, more efficient, and effective movement patterns (Mattes 261). Feldenkrais teachers make a point of not directing the student's movements toward a specific outcome but to one which is more spontaneous and functional (Mattes 263). In this method, students are taught carefully designed movement sequences and systematically practice their ability to pay attention and respond to subtle bodily feedback (Eddy *Mindful* 27).

Body-Mind Centering (BMC), created by Bonnie Bainbridge Cohen, is focused on drawing the student's attention to the physiological body systems to provide a route to achieving different movement qualities and various ways to connect with the mind; this somatic system works because humans can pay attention to their inner and outer functions (Eddy "Practical Application" 87).

In terms of attention, practitioners of the aforementioned somatic system believe "[w]hat is being differentiated is the state of mind that calls upon a particular resource in the body that, in turn, influences the meaning or nature of an action"; specific principles of BMC call one's sensory attention to different body systems, such as the skeletal, muscle, or nervous systems, or the body's organs (Eddy "Practical Application" 87). Thus, to focus on the skeletal system, a student could initiate a kick by activating the femur while paying close attention to the bodily sensations that arise from the hip joint, which also provides a sense of the shape and form of this action. To focus on the muscles, the student would need to pay attention to the hip flexor muscles to gain a feeling for the power and force of the kick. When initiating the same action from the intestines, the student would need to focus their attention more deeply, to deliver a less-specific, more feeling-based response (Eddy "Practical Application" 87).

Attention and Focus in the Creative Process

Creativity is involved with generating new ideas and products and, as such, is important to the ongoing, positive continuity of civilized cultures. Doing creative work requires the ability to control one's attention, or otherwise, the creative problem or issue would remain unsolved. The study of creativity and attention, however, is complicated by the fact that there are many forms of creativity, such as those which are artistic, scientific, or technical; in addition, creativity cannot be limited to the figural or verbal modes, since creative endeavors such as dancing are neither figural, like a painting, or verbal, as in writing (Lunke and Meier 2).

British American psychologist Raymond Cattell thought investigating the creativity-attentional relationship also required sifting through cognitive theories on creativity and the relationship between general intelligence and creativity (Frith et al. 139). Neuroscience scholar Mathias Benedek and his colleagues noted it is thought the brain's executive control processes and the processes of attention are believed to be the basis for creativity, because they help maintain and update information in working memory so that effort and behavior toward the goal can be completed (Frith et al. 140).

The outcome of one study on artistic creativity and cognition was that "[t]he divergent figural creative test correlated positively with attention whereas the verbal test did not . . . [which] lead [the researchers] to hypothesize a domain specific positive relation between divergent figural creativity and attention" (Lunke and Meier 10). According to the results of a second study, executive attention control emerged as an important factor, producing a strong relationship between fluid intelligence and divergent thinking, whereas mind wandering was not significant in predicting divergent thinking performance (Frith et al 147). Fluid intelligence refers to the reasoning ability to generate, transform, and manipulate new input in real time.

While beyond the scope of the current discussion, it appears that being able to maintain one's attention plays an important role in the ability to complete a creative project, although the details of that relationship seem to be determined by the form of testing (figural or verbal) used in a study and the type of thinking involved.

Attention and Focus in Dance

Attention, or the ability to pay attention, is important in all phases of dance education. Learning in dance technique class means focusing one's attention on the visual patterning of the movements demonstrated, along with being attuned to the overall bodily feelings that accompany the correct performance of those movements. Attention is important as well during the creative choreographic process to enable the choreographer to select movements or movement sequences which fit his or her concept of the work being created.

Attention and Focus in Technical Dance Training

In a study of attention in dance technique classes, Catherine Seago discovered the students had a limited awareness of the role attention could play in their dance learning experiences (258). When learning in dance technique class, attentional focus can involve internal or external focus. When using internal focus, the mover concentrates on specific components of the movement task, while external focus means concentrating on the effects of the movements performed (Krasnow and Wilmerding 108).

Sports coach Greg Dea explained internal and external focus in the following way: internal attentional focus involves focusing on parts versus focusing on patterns when using external focus (Guss-West 23). "An external focus approach highlights patterns of movement and overcomes the challenges inherent in trying to consciously coordinate and control many moving parts" (Guss-West 23–24). When using an external focus, attention is directed outside of oneself and to the movement outcome, while an internal focus involves attending to the mechanics of one's own movements in a part of the body (Guss-West 23).

An internal focus is more useful for a novice when they are first learning a movement, to help them notice details, but could be detrimental to a more advanced mover and interfere with performing the movements in an automatic or habitual manner (Krasnow and Wilmerding 109). The advantages of using an external attentional focus when learning and performing movement are that muscular activity is more efficient and extraneous movements are reduced, movements become more fluid, and movement becomes more automatic to permit multitasking (Guss-West 24–25). In the outcome of her study on attentional focus, Seago seemed to agree (258). In another article, Rebecca Gose pointed out that a more advanced dancer usually performs parts of a movement sequence automatically which requires little conscious attention and provides more time to pay attention to other aspects of the movements, such as subtle artistic phrasing (36).

An example of internal attentional focus when performing a crawl in swimming is to push backwards, while an external attentional focus could be initiated by pushing backwards on the surrounding water (Guss-West 25). The following is another dance example of external attentional focus versus an internal focus. In this case, the targeted movement is to balance in fifth position while the feet are in relevé. An externally focused teaching cue would be to push the floor away, and an internal focused cue is to squeeze the legs together (Guss-West 31).

The following is an added example of external and internal attentional focus in the performance of a port de bras. In this instance, external focus could be to imagine expanding one's wings while feeling the wind between the tips of the feathers, while an internal focus would be to suggest opening the arms like wings and keep the fingers soft (Guss-West 36). Nevertheless, even though dancers of all skill levels can benefit from the use of externally focused imagery in technique class, the ability to use it successfully is a learned ability (Guss-West 152).

When switching from using internal focus versus external focus, it might feel as though there is a loss of conscious control. Using internal attentional focus does not allow the dancer to be present as they are dancing, because the effort is directed toward thinking and controlling the movements, whereas an external focus relies on the body's wisdom and allows for fast, reflexive actions, constant adjustments, and efficient use of one's muscles (Guss-West 41).

While external attentional focus appears to be the most productive and efficient method in the dance technique teaching process, the issue remains that dance teachers need to help students learn to selectively focus on input that will be most helpful to their learning process. In her study of students' attentional practices in undergraduate technique classes, Seago was interested in exploring factors that influenced students' attentional choices and the effectiveness of those choices. One outcome of this study was that exploring uses of attention through different means, such as those which are verbal or visual or based on imagery and relationships, enabled the students to have an increased awareness of the role of attention in their learning process; this researcher also learned that improvisational experiences helped the students learn about the importance of attention (252).

Rachel Rimmer also endorsed the idea of using exploration or improvisation as a teaching strategy in dance technique classes, although its use in such classes has been largely unexplored (143). Rimmer pointed out that the purpose of using improvisation in this setting is that such work enables students to pay attention or engage with movement at a deeper level; the outcome of this approach was that the students took ownership of the movement materials (144–45).

Several students in Seago's study reported they could experiment with attention when there was less going on, allowing them to stop and think about on which content to focus (253). Thus, the students were learning to focus on their role in creating learning for themselves. There was also a realization among the students that it was more effective to shift one's attention away from the look of the movements to the bodily feeling of the movement, while shifting attention from the end goal helped the students make choices about the movement process (Seago 254–55).

Attention and Focus During Dance Making

It is evident that a choreographer pays attention to many aspects of the choreographic craft during the process of making a dance. However, the discussion here is limited to the act of creating movements that will eventually be shaped into a fully formed work. During this process, the choreographer's attention or focus is extremely important, especially if the choreographer is attempting to express a specific intent in the piece. Diana Green explained that dances created without an intent in mind can wander aimlessly without thought or attention as to why the piece is being created (*Choreographing* 7).

Thus, most dances begin with an inspiration related to an intent, to which the choreographer responds and which is combined with memories and the choreographer's imagination during the creative movement improvisation process (Minton *Choreography* 3–4). The ability to focus on an inspiration can guide movement selection to be included in a piece throughout the creative process and determine the movements included in a work. To provide a simplistic example, if the inspiration is a series of geometric shapes painted in bright colors, the movements created will most likely have a sharp, angular quality in contrast to softer movements based on an inspiration which contains rounded shapes and is light blue.

In considering attention or focus during the improvisation process, Jacqueline Smith-Autard indicated "there are moments when a movement feels right and fits the composer's image"; this means the choreographer selects movements, particularly the initial movements in a work, based on feeling and intuition (39–40). In her choreography book based on creating from within, Green wrote that a choreographer comes in touch with their intent through the process of improvisation since it enables the dancer to react in the moment without thinking (*Choreographing* 23). She suggested that during an improvisation involving organic dance form, there is a need to pay attention to the kinesthetic feeling of the movements which arise and focus on where the movements need to go next (263).

Fiona Bannon and Carole Kirk proposed that choreographing a dance begins by paying attention to the feel of an idea (289). Kerry Chappell, who has investigated creativity as it relates to dance education, indicated creating involves paying attention to the embodied and physical elements of creativity (Watson et al. 155). Nevertheless, Watson et al. acknowledged that little research has been done on the embodied elements of creative work, although such investigations might extend the body of creativity research (155).

In terms of attention, the aforementioned researchers felt paying attention to the embodied elements or feel of an idea could be described in relationship to openness or the ability to try something new (Watson et al. 158–59). One of the subjects in the previous study commented that during the creative process, she needed to go inside and become reflective; another subject claimed part of her creative choreographic process was the conscious or unconscious recall of previously learned movements (Watson et al. 160). While working on group creative projects, some subjects felt they picked up or paid attention to movement ideas from others in their group (Watson et al. 161). In this same article, other subjects discussed improvisation as a form of letting movement arise spontaneously (163), along with taking the time and space to allow unknown movement possibilities to emerge (167).

Mental Imagery

Eric Franklin, who has done extensive work with imagery, described the power of mental imagery by explaining that what goes on in one's mind, including one's thoughts, mental pictures, states of attention, and instances of intuition, has a great capacity to affect the development of one's movement skills and many other abilities as well (xii).

"One of the most remarkable capacities of the mind is its ability to simulate sensations, actions, and other types of experience" (Moran et al. 224). This means imagery occurs when a person can report the experience of perceiving in the absence of the pertinent sensory input (Kosslyn et al. *The Case* 3). Stephen Kosslyn and his colleagues explained:

> [A] mental image occurs when a representation of the type created during the initial phases of perception is present, but the stimulus is not actually being perceived; such representations preserve the perceptible properties of the stimulus and ultimately give rise to the subjective experience of perception.
> (*The Case* 4)

Imagery differs from an afterimage because it can be prolonged, can be brought to mind voluntarily, and is an integral part of memory, problem-solving, creativity, emotion, and comprehension in languages (Kosslyn et al. *The Case* 4). When most people discuss imagery, they think of visual imagery or being able to focus on pictures in the mind, but *imagery* can refer to any perceptual modality, including auditory, and tactile-kinesthetic imagery. Engaging in the use of imagery is an introspective process—one of looking within (Kosslyn et al. *The Case* 4). As such, imagery can provide connections between mind and body. New neuroimaging technologies, such as positron emission tomography (PET) and functional magnetic resonance imaging (fMRI), now allow the theoretical aspects of imagery to be tested in humans, demonstrating that imagery and perception in the same modality engage much the same neural mechanisms (Kosslyn et al. "Neural Foundations" 635).

While imagery and its uses have been discounted by some, recent research in the neurosciences has proven its existence based on functioning of and changes in brain activity. Motor imagery is usually described as visual or kinesthetic—in the first instance, the individual produces a visual image of the targeted movement—while kinesthetic imagery refers to being able to generate the bodily sensation of the movement (Mokienko et al. 483). However, there is some confusion about the term *motor imagery* since some authorities use the term *motor imagery* while others prefer *kinesthetic imagery*, *movement imagery*, or some combination of these terms (Moran et al. 225). Research on motor imagery is important because it allows researchers to study the relationship between consciousness and action (Moran et al. 226).

Brain imaging technologies have enabled an exploration of the biological basis of mental imagery (Seiler et al. 422). Thus, movement imagery has been linked to conscious activation of brain areas responsible for preparation and execution of the targeted movement, although activation is usually weaker under the imagined condition (Mokienko et al. 483). It has also been discovered that motor imagery is a function of experience, as it interacts with genetic (biological) variability from person to person, is based on efficiency in recruiting neural networks of the brain, and can involve more than one brain area (Seiler et al. 421).

In addition, fMRI studies suggested that visual and kinesthetic imagery recruit some similar brain areas, but also some areas of the brain which are unique to each imagery modality (Seiler et al. 422). Seiler et al. added that the type of movement imagined is related to the resulting form of neural activation in the brain, meaning, that such research should be based on imagining the same movements from study to study (423). In another fMRI study, the researchers found that modality-specific brain networks were composed of brain areas involved with processing respective types of sensory information, although imagery connected with auditory input led to a relative deactivation in brain areas connected with visual imagery, and vice versa (Zvyagintsev et al. 1421).

Types of Imagery

Early on, psychologist Allan Paivio proposed that imagery served both cognitive and motivational functions based on imagery content; the Sport Imagery Questionnaire (SIQ) was designed by Paivio based on five imagery categories (Overby and Dunn 10). Two categories in the SIQ are related to cognitive imagery functions and include cognitive general imagery, which has to do with choreography and improvisation, and cognitive-specific imagery, which is connected to specific dance skills, such as performing a rond de jambe correctly; other categories in the SIQ are based on motivation and include motivation general-mastery, associated with mental toughness, control, and confidence; motivation general-arousal, connected with arousal and relaxation in the performance and competition arena; and motivation specific imagery, which is related to being able to perform with skill and expression (Overby and Dunn 10). Several researchers studied imagery use in forty-two professional ballet dancers based on the previous five described categories in the SIQ and found the dancers used both the cognitive and motivational functions of imagery (Fish et al. 3).

Psychologists Nordin and Cummings conducted research to analyze dancers' imagery use; as a result, they created the Dance Imagery Questionnaire (DIQ) to assess the frequency dancers engage in different types of imagery (87). One thousand sixty-eight male and female dancers who participated in twenty-five dance forms at the beginning to professional levels participated in this study (85). This research confirmed that dancers engage in four imagery types: technique, role and movement quality, mastery, and goals (Nordin and Cummings 91). The researchers concluded that the DIQ can measure the frequency of image use, with the dancers engaging in technique imagery most frequently and mastery imagery least, and with more experienced dancers engaging in all types of imagery more frequently (Nordin and Cummings 95).

After considering multiple sources, Vicky Fisher proposed an imagery model that differentiates between image types and image use; she indicated the "what" aspect of an image refers to both the image content, the sensory modalities involved, and the perspective from which the first two components are experienced (254). To clarify, sensory modality refers to the type of sensation imagined, image content to its subject matter, and perspective to whether the subject perceives the image as internal or external (Fisher 255). In terms of the function of the image, Fisher noted three primary roles or functions for an image; these were its physical, affective, or cognitive functions (260). The physical function has to do with the impact the image has on the body or on movement; the affective function pertains to one's emotions and awareness of self in relation to the image; and the cognitive function is related to the memory and meaning of the image (Fisher 260). The aim of the aforementioned framework "is to help dancers, dance teachers and choreographers make more strategic and effective use of imagery" (Fisher 265)

More recently, many types of mental imagery have been discussed, but their descriptions and names can be confusing at times, as indicated previously. Mental practice is one type of imagery used by both athletes and dancers alike. *Mental practice* usually refers to rehearsing a movement skill or movement sequence without executing it physically; it can mean reviewing movement procedures or visualizing movement details (Krasnow and Wilmerding 268). When mental practice is used, the neural pathways from the brain to appropriate muscles are activated, but the activation level is not great enough to cause the muscles to move, while the brain areas associated with the imagined movements are also activated (Krasnow and Wilmerding 270).

Imagery can be external or internal. When using external imagery, the mover imagines movements that occur outside the body. This type of imagery is similar to imagine viewing a video of a moving body. When using internal imagery, the mover imagines the movement being performed by one's own body, and the sensations of the movements and its visual appearance are experienced (Krasnow and Wilmerding 271).

Visual imagery refers to imagining a visual representation of movements, while *kinesthetic imagery* refers to the bodily sensation experienced when the movement is performed, especially when it is performed correctly. Imagining seeing an endless series of clouds as one moves forward is an example of a visual image, but moving as if you were stepping on clouds represents a kinesthetic image. It is interesting that in a study connecting visual imagery to listening to music, visual imagery was found to be important as an intermediate aspect of consciousness (Vroegh 1).

Direct imagery is a representation nonverbally of a movement, such as imagining you are an arrow flying through space as you perform the movement (Krasnow and Wilmerding 271). Indirect or metaphoric imagery involves using an external object or idea to serve as a suggestion for the desired manner a movement should

FIGURE 3.3 Imagining a wave.

Source: © Eric Franklin. *Dance Imagery for Technique and Performance*. Human Kinetics, 2014, p. 91.

be performed (Minton "Assessment" 280). According to Franklin, metaphoric imagery is a type of comparison; it involves using one object to describe another (31). A tree swaying in the wind can be used to envision the body as an anatomical structure which can absorb force because it has some give (Franklin 18). Figure 3.3 of a wave is an example of another metaphoric image created by Franklin.

Images, known as lines-of-movement imagery, describe the spatial orientation of a movement or its direction in relation to other body parts; global images create an overall feeling state, and anatomical imagery incorporates specific anatomical terms but is presented indirectly (Krasnow and Wilmerding 271). To imagine a string that connects your hip to your toes as you kick your leg forward is an example of a line-of-movement image, while imagining you are in the arctic, cold, to be able to move in a confined and restricted way is a global image. An example of an anatomical image would be to imagine releasing the tendons of the quadriceps muscle at the hip to initiate a leg extension and attain the proper ninety-degree position; this approach should allow the psoas muscle to provide the proper impetus to initiate the extension (Solomon 113). The terms used to describe mental imagery overlap in some circumstances. For example, indirect or metaphoric images can incorporate both visual and kinesthetic properties, as in the example of the cloud-based image noted previously.

The concept of the body image is a final way to describe and discuss mental imagery. It is a concept that has permeated psychological literature for many years.

The body image refers to the picture one forms of their own body in their mind (Schilder 11). The body image is also associated with bodily sensations from one's own body (Delinsky 280). However, the body image can be affected by many different factors, including one's stage in life, culture, family, and interpersonal relationships (Cash and Smolak 7).

Disturbances in the body image are the core issue of concern in eating disorders, such as anorexia and bulimia. Anorexia nervosa is characterized by a refusal to maintain a normal weight, a fear of gaining weight, and a disturbance in the way one's weight or shape is experienced (Delinsky 280). While most information about disturbances in body image have been associated with girls and women, there has been a realization recently that body image issues are also found among males, although such issues are related to muscularity rather than to the perceived percentage of body fat present in one's body (McCreary 198). Maintaining a healthy body image is dependent on having discussions which reinforce such an image and using strategies based on good nutrition and safe conditioning habits (Krasnow and Wilmerding 218).

Table 3.1 includes a summary of imagery in terms of the name, description, category (type or use), and an example of the image.

Uses of Imagery

Imagery has had a long history based on its use in memory systems, religious practices, healing and shamanic practices, psychotherapy, sports, and of course, dance (Franklin 4). Imagery can be used to teach movement and perfect movement skills, but it can also be used in relaxation exercises and by somatic practitioners to develop body awareness. In addition, images help when remembering long movement sequences, motivate a higher level of performance, aid in perfecting the artistic aspects of movement, and can be used as part of a healing intervention (Krasnow and Wilmerding 275).

Theoretical Basis for Use of Imagery

There are various theories which attempt to explain why the different forms of mental imagery can be effective and how they work. In the case of mental training or mental rehearsal, the models explaining its operation are differentiated based on whether the effects are the result of neuromuscular processes or central mechanisms in the form of symbolic codes or programs (Schack 133). A new explanation for the effect of mental rehearsal has been described in the perceptual-cognitive hypothesis which proposed that strong representation units are linked to perceptual representations, such as kinesthetic, visual, or acoustic effect codes, and because these representations have a spatiotemporal structure, they can be directly translated into movement (Schack 133). In addition, it is proposed that mental rehearsal internally activates and serves as a stabilizing influence on the representation system (Schack 133).

TABLE 3.1 Categorization of Imagery Based on Type or Use, along with Descriptions and Examples

Imagery Name	Description	Categorized by Type or Use	Example
visual	seeing still or moving pictures in the mind	type	visualizing a circle in the mind
auditory	imagining sounds	type	hearing a bird call in your mind
tactile-kinesthetic	feeling/body sensation	type	imagining moving arm forcefully
spatial	location in space	type	imagining moving forward
motor	imagining movement	type	imagining moving based on specific body feeling
cognitive general	related to choreographing or improvising	use	using mental images to create movement
cognitive specific	related to performance of specific dance skill	use	using mental images to improve performance of codified movement
motivation general-mastery	associated with mental toughness, confidence	use	using mental image to enhance confidence during performance
motivation general-arousal	connected to arousal and/or relaxation during performance	use	using mental image as calming influence preceding performance
motivation specific	ability to perform with skill and expression	use	using mental image to perfect skill and projection
mental practice	rehearsing movement skill without performing it	type	seeing oneself perform a particular movement or sequence in their mind
external	imagine movements outside the body	type	imagining moving like a tree bending in the wind
internal	imagine one's body moving in a specific way	type	imagining moving one's body using a particular quality
direct	imagine moving like a particular object	type	imagining moving one arm like an arrow flying through space
indirect or metaphoric	using an external object as a movement suggestion	type	imagining moving like a flowing river
lines-of-movement	spatial orientation or direction of movement	type	imagining moving one leg to the side of body
global	overall body feeling	type	imagining the whole body feeling relaxed
anatomical	uses specific anatomical terms	type	imagining head of femur turning in hip socket to achieve outward rotation
body image	picture in mind of own body	type	imagining shape of specific body parts in negative or positive way

Visual images are a mental picture assembled from bits of sensory information that are integrated together; images convey the physical structure of forms found in experiences and when visual areas of the brain are engaged (Zull 112–13). As such, visualizing is related to memory; an image is generated by a pattern of electrical energy, but this pattern is different for every visual experience (Zull 114). The physical experience of touch works in much the same way as visual imagery formation because the sensory data generated during touch generates neuron firing patterns in the brain which can be imagined (Zull 114). However, the other senses of hearing, smell, and taste can also generate imagery, but the process is more indirect. "The sound, taste, or smell of things trigger our memory of real objects in the world, but do not generate the image themselves"; thus, the memory produces the same neuron firing pattern but does not create an image of the object which produced the smell or taste (Zull 115).

Research by Muriel Roth and her colleagues demonstrated there is considerable overlap between brain networks involved with imagined actions and those that are active when an action is performed; thus, many of the same sensorimotor regions of the brain are activated when thinking about and planning an action as when one performs the same movement because they are part of the physical act (Jeannerod 104). In addition, the fact that the same brain networks are activated when experiencing an image of an action and during performance of the same action seems to mitigate the idea that thought is distinct from the body (Fisher 253).

Nonmovement Imagery Applications

Imagery has been used for many years as a relaxation technique. In one study, the researcher compared the effectiveness of mindfulness meditation training to the use of guided imagery relaxation for depressed patients and learned that both treatment groups of subjects displayed a significant decrease in symptoms. The researcher postulated that the guided imagery allowed the participants to disengage from their symptoms by focusing on the imagery (Costa and Barnhofer 416–17).

It is understood that mental imagery has an important role in producing anxiety in adults, but several researchers were interested in learning whether imagery also plays a role in creating adolescent anxiety. As a result, researchers learned that imagery was an important component in adolescent anxiety disorders (Ghita et al. 556). In another study, imagery was used to ease anxiety in children with chronic illnesses. In this study, chronically ill children were able to identify a happy place, like a theme park or vacation spot, as their imagery strategy; the researchers discovered such imagery strategies could be combined with positive self-talk and relaxation and that the children were able to personalize their coping strategies (Nabors et al. 2708 & 2715).

Mental imagery has also been used to treat addiction. In a fourth study, the researchers were interested in learning how imagery might be used to treat cocaine addiction. The outcome of this study was that a reduction in cocaine use was connected to employing self-guided imagery with positive themes, while mental imagery, which simulated increased cocaine use, did not reduce the subjects' cravings (Lowry et al. 2418).

In another study, mental imagery in the form of motor imagery was investigated in children between the ages of 5 and 9 years. Marc Jeannerod, a cognitive science expert, and Theo Mulder, who, with his colleagues, has researched the role of imagery in learning movement, described motor imagery as the capacity to mentally rehearse a motor action without performing the movements (Guilbert et al. 622). The goal of a study by Jessica Guilbert and her colleagues was to determine whether motor imagery refinement in children was related to their increased ability to integrate proprioceptive input with visual and auditory input (621). The researchers concluded that motor imagery refinement is partially related to the children's ability to integrate proprioceptive input with other sensory information. (Guilbert et al. 621–22).

Imagery has also been used to improve the ability of older adults to learn a new route to a location. Learning a route is an important spatial ability which appears to decline with age (Carbone et al. 1568). Elena Carbone and her colleagues investigated the benefit of teaching both older and younger adults an imagery strategy when they were learning a new route. Two conditions were used in this study—some practiced learning the new route using an imagery strategy, and the others engaged in alternative activities before learning the same route without receiving any advice on how they could approach this task (Carbone et al. 1568). The imagery strategy tested was based on being able to visualize their path and mentally recall landmarks and their location along the route; the outcome was that those subjects who used the imagery strategy had a better ability to recall landmarks on the route regardless of their age (1568–69).

Imagery Applications in Somatics

Perhaps the most overt and readily identifiable use of imagery in somatics began with the work of Mabel Todd. As mentioned in Chapter 1, in her efforts to heal from an accident, and later to teach improved posture to her students, Todd developed imagery which could be related to having an anatomically balanced body (Eddy *Mindful* 28). One such image was to imagine you have a dinosaur's tail dragging from the end of your spine while attempting to run away from it; another of Todd's images described visualizing your head as it reaches upward to a hook in the sky while you are hanging by your hair (Todd 211). Todd believed daily anxieties and emotions produced muscular tensions, which could be seen in unbalanced postural accommodations (288), and the images she designed were a way to create a more balanced body.

Todd's work was further developed by Lulu Sweigard, whose goal was to find balance by concentrating on a picture which could produce neuromuscular responses through the least effort; this approach, known as Ideokinesis, contrasted with imposing fixed or correct positions on the body which were thought to be correct (Eddy *Mindful* 28). Sweigard wrote that one of the greatest impediments to motor learning was to emphasize volitional muscular effort during the learning process, because such an emphasis becomes a handicap; rather, the teacher should stress which movements are to be performed, not how they are to be performed, because the human nervous system takes care of the how (169). The belief was that the use of voluntary muscular control when learning movement interferes with automatic responses which coordinate with sensory input, alerting the nervous system to make needed changes and produce appropriate neuromuscular patterns (Sweigard 169). Sweigard used many visual images when working with her students, one of which can be seen in the drawing in Figure 3.4. When using this image, students were instructed to imagine watching while the hip pockets on the back of the pelvis moved around to the front to stimulate narrowing at the front and widening at the back of the pelvis.

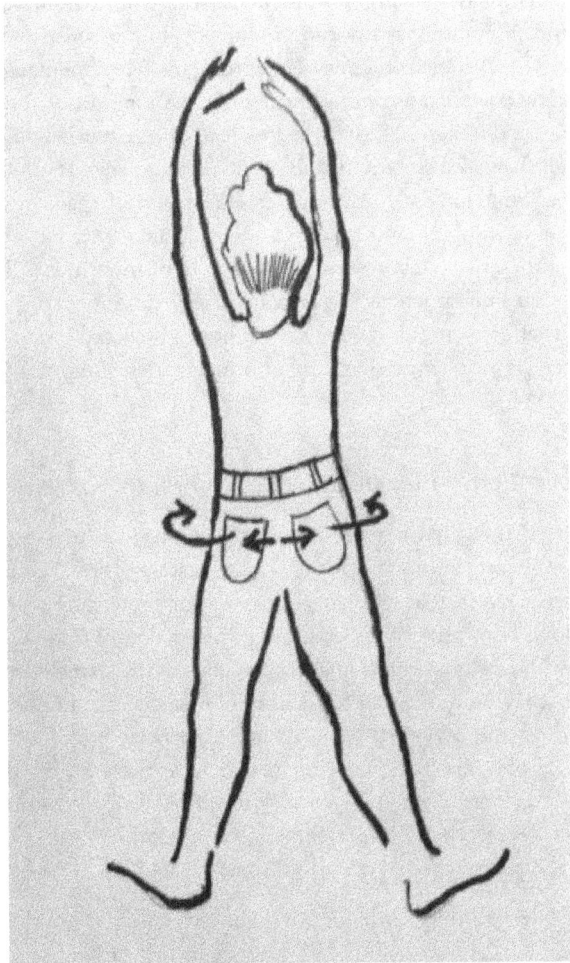

FIGURE 3.4 Image of hip pockets located on back of pelvis.

Source: Drawing by author based on Figure 12 in Sweigard, Lulu. *Human Movement Potential: Its Ideokinetic Facilitation.* Dodd, Mead & Company, 1974, p. 239.

In devising what became known as the Alexander technique, Alexander learned to re-educate the somatic bodily sensations he experienced between his head, neck, and back to bring them back into alignment, since previously his faulty sensory habits had led to an incorrect felt sense of alignment. "The underlying sense of this is that there is an organic congruence to the body that if maintained, will enable a fluency and flow to movement" (Stuart 317). In correcting one's alignment, the Alexander teacher helps a student inhibit the action that feels right in the body but is not (Stuart 318). Due to the emphasis on the felt sense in correcting body alignment, the Alexander technique relies on kinesthetic imagery.

Kinesthetic imagery also seems to be foundational to the Feldenkrais Method. Both Feldenkrais' Awareness through Movement and Functional Integration somatic systems emphasize bringing the client's awareness to differentiating parts of the body and integrating many movement possibilities into one's experience (Eddy *Mindful* 27). When using Awareness through Movement techniques, the practitioner guides participants through structured explorations involving thinking, sensing, moving, and imagining; options are created for experiencing new ways of moving through increased sensitivity and improved efficiency (Fonow, et al. 118).

In Bartenieff Fundamentals, movements take place in space with the whole or part of the body moving and by using a particular quality or effort; a change in intent will automatically alter these three aspects of movement (Bales 73). The fact that Bartenieff Fundamentals is integrally involved with both space and effort indicates that its effectiveness is dependent on both visual and kinesthetic imagery, although *imagery* is not expressively mentioned in descriptions of this somatic system.

Imagery Applications in Teaching Dance Technique

Franklin indicated there has been a shift in the interest in imagery in the dance world and it is now just gaining acceptance (1). Kinesiologist Marie-Claude Durand and her colleagues stated that it has been known for some time that athletes who use imagery along with physical practice are more successful (Franklin 1). As such, one's definition and description of imagery depend on the frame of reference used; choreographers may be more interested in how imagery can improve their dancers' performance, while a theory-oriented individual may prefer a more scientific definition. In addition, one's skill in using imagery affects the outcome (Franklin 4). Franklin continued that "*[i]magery is a multi-perspective, multisensory mental representation of movement, future or past scenario, or motivational state*" (4).

According to Lynette Overby and Jan Dunn:

> Dance imagery is the deliberate use of the senses to rehearse or envision a particular outcome mentally, in the absence of, or in combination with, overt physical movement. The images may be constructed of real or metaphorical movements, objects, events, or processes.
>
> *(9)*

The applications and use of imagery in dance are similar to its use in sports and exercise science; however, due to aesthetic and theatrical factors, some applications are unique to dance (Overby and Dunn 10). Franklin noted five benefits for the use of imagery related to dance technique: First, there are motor-specific images, a form of mental rehearsal, which can be used to improve the coordination of specific movements. Second, motor-general or biological imagery is used to improve biomechanical functioning but is not tied to a specific movement sequence. Third, imagery has long been used to improve alignment. Fourth, imagery can aid flexibility, and fifth, some images can be used to improve expression (10).

According to Katherine Pavlik and Sanna Nordin-Bates, imagery use by dancers can be categorized based on who uses dance-based imagery; the conclusion here is varied, but it appears imagery is used in dance by many types of individuals—young children, university students, professionals, and recreational dancers (53). Like some of those cited previously, these two authors believed imagery in dance can be categorized based on the type of imagery used and why it is being used (55–56). Finally, imagery was discussed in this article based on when and where it is used and the sensory modalities involved (57). The article also included information about the creation of imagery and differences in imaging ability (58–59).

There has been much research done on how imagery has been used by dancers and dance educators. In particular, the effectiveness of mental practice has been found to be useful in learning and performing movement skills and has been investigated using three experimental conditions: physical practice, mental practice without physical practice, and by combining physical and mental practice in one study. Recent reviews have continued to show mental imagery has a positive effect when it is used together with physical practice (Overby and Dunn 10).

Katy Carey and her colleagues were interested in the effect of movement expertise on motor imagery and the effect of mental rehearsal on actions without performing the movements (1). Eighteen female ballet and modern dancers, including six dancers at each of three levels of expertise, took part in this study; a short videotaped tendu movement sequence which was novel to all subjects was the targeted material to be learned (Carey et al. 5). To assess the subjects' imagery abilities, two mental imagery questionnaires were given before the actual study; these were the Test of Ability in Movement Imagery (TAMI) and the Subjective Movement Imagery Questionnaire 3 (MIQ-3) (5–6). Tobii eye-tracking glasses were used to record pupil dilation, which is an index of attention and mental effort (6). The outcome of this study showed (1) there was no significant difference in imagery ability between dancers with different levels of movement expertise, and (2) during the imagined condition, beginning and intermediate dancers may need to generate more mental effort to generate a motor image than do expert dancers (7 & 9).

Overby and her colleagues were interested in comparing imagery used by dance teachers, figure skating coaches, and soccer coaches. As a basis for this research, forty-nine subjects (thirty-five females and fourteen males) were given an imagery use questionnaire to determine any differences in imagery use between the three groups (Overby et al. 323 & 327). All three groups of subjects reported they used imagery while teaching or coaching; the dance teachers and soccer coaches indicated they used more internal than external imagery, but the figure skating coaches reported using both types of imagery in equal measure (Overby et al. 335). The researchers also discovered dance teachers used indirect metaphorical imagery in the teaching of dance technique and choreography—a form of imagery also used by the figure skating coaches, but not to as great an extent; indirect metaphorical imagery was used very little by the soccer coaches (Overby et al. 335).

Modality-Specific Imagery Studies in Dance

Another way the effectiveness of imagery has been investigated in dance has been through modality-specific studies, including those based on visual, kinesthetic, or auditory imagery (Overby and Dunn 10). In one such study, the author was interested in learning whether dance teachers preferred using visual, kinesthetic, or other forms of imagery when teaching dance technique classes. The assessment instrument used in this study was the Systematic Observation Instrument (SOI) developed and tested by Overby; the four forms of imagery which can be recorded using the SOI are kinesthetic, visual, direct, and indirect imagery (Minton "Assessment" 280). Seven modern and jazz dance teachers volunteered for inclusion in the study (Minton "Assessment" 281). Overall, the teachers preferred using direct imagery, which was described in the SOI as mental rehearsal, with visual imagery as their second most preferred choice (Minton "Assessment" 280 & 287). The preference for visual imagery over kinesthetic imagery is ironic, considering dance is a kinesthetic endeavor.

An answer to the previous outcome might be that the visual system is the dominant sensory system in humans (Brodie and Lobel 24). In their article, Brodie and Lobel suggested ways to help students tune into their kinesthetic body feelings. In one of their exercises, these authors suggested standing with the eyes closed to become aware of the tiny shifting motions which the body produces to maintain an upright position—movements which are not noticed when the eyes are open. This exercise is followed by consciously shifting the weight from foot to foot while the eyes are closed to help understand how difficult it is to balance when vision is removed (25). The authors also suggested becoming more aware of kinesthetic body feelings by working with a partner. In one such exploration, the partners stand facing each other with the palms of both hands touching, and while one partner leads, the partners move the hands slowly in a horizontal circle (Brodie and Lobel 25).

In a second imagery modality-based study, the researchers were interested in studying the effect of visual and kinesthetic imagery on hip and pelvic kinematics during the performance of the plié and sauté. The twenty-four subjects were randomly assigned to one of three groups: visual imagery, kinesthetic imagery, or a control who performed a mental arithmetic task (Coker et al. 63) The result was that neither imagery practice increased external hip rotation, decreased sagittal pelvic excursion, or affected the dancers' ratio for hip to pelvic movements; it was proposed that the lack of imagery effect could have been due to the fact that elite dancers already use more imagery in class situations than novice dancers (Coker et al. 68).

In a third study in this category, four advanced high school ballet students suggested visual/kinesthetic images, such as thinking about the leg as an elastic band when performing a dégagé combination or visualizing a flowing piece of fabric when performing a pas de cheval; however, the teacher discovered that this imagery was most useful when the combinations were performed more slowly (Spagnuolo and Colket 92). Based on her students' responses, the teacher discovered that bringing the students' attention to aspects of anatomy through use of imagery was an excellent way to create anatomical awareness (Spagnuolo and Colket 93).

Imagery Studies Dealing with Specific Dance Movements

Another category of imagery research was based on learning the effect of imagery on the ability to perform specific dance movements. In one example of this type of research, Christine Hanrahan and a colleague used lines of movement imagery related to the desired direction of the movement and global images to study their effect on performance of the développé; more specifically, in terms of global imagery, the subjects were instructed to imagine their bodies as thin and luminous—a tactic which enhanced the performance of the targeted movement (Overby and Dunn 11).

In another study in this category, the researchers were interested in investigating the effect of mental imagery on movement intention in the performance of the demi-plié in preparation for jumping to optimize performance (Couillandre 91). The subjects, who included seven professional ballet dancers, experienced the following interventions in this study: a description of the articulations of the ankle, knee, and hip as they are influenced by kinetic muscle chains, rhythm, and dynamic alignment, and imagery, which involved giving a more dynamic reaction to the foot and a direct kinetic chain to the upper body (Couillandre 93). In the outcome of this study, no change was found in the depth of the demi-plié or jump height, although the dynamic alignment improved during both the demi-plié and jump due to changes in muscular activity (Couillandre 94–95).

In a third study investigating specific dance movements, the researchers, Teresa Heiland and Robert Rovetti, used a quasi-experimental design to assess the effectiveness of Franklin Method images on the subjects' jump height; eleven subjects, nine females and two male college dance majors whose jump height needed improvement, were recommended for participation in the study (144). The Franklin images selected for inclusion in the study were those that were kinetically charged and which could be described verbally and visually (Heiland and Rovetti 144). The four images used were visualizing the whole body as a spring, imagining the central axis as a rocket booster, feeling the feet as though they were stretching into sand, and picturing a lengthening and deepening of the spinal curves (Heiland and Rovetti 147). Although a wide range of consistency in jump height was observed, the mean jump height improved most with the use of the rocket image and least when the students focused on the spinal image (Heiland and Rovetti 150 & 152).

Imagery Studies Dealing with Posture and Turnout in Dance

While not a study of the effect of imagery on specific dance movements, the author of this book was interested in learning the effect imagery had on postural alignment of beginning modern dance students. During the six-week study, postural alignment was filmed and then measured pre and post from a profile view while the subjects were both in a still standing position and walking (Minton *The Effects* 127). Twenty students from each of three dance classes volunteered to be in the study (Minton *The Effects* 65) with a different type of imagery used as a teaching strategy in two of the classes. The images were anatomically based images using imagined lines of movement for postural correction (group 1), pictorial images devised by Sweigard for improving posture (group 2), and consciously suggesting that the students attempt to move their body segments in the desired direction to attain correct alignment (group 3) (Minton *The Effects* 128). While alignment improved in the classes overall, differences in alignment between treatments were minimal (Minton *The Effects* 134–35).

A study by Gayanne Grossman et al. was a second investigation which did not deal with specific dance movements but with improving turnout. In this study, imagery was used to help dancers find and maintain a neutral pelvis in which the hip is stable and the pelvis is not tilted in an anterior direction (17). One image described was to lie on the back and imagine a narrowing at the waist and sinking or hollowing at the front of the pelvis to activate the transverse abdominus muscle; another image described rolling over to a prone position, engaging the pelvic floor, and visualizing a flow of energy which is drawn up to the body's center from the pelvic floor, accompanied by a magnet which draws the waist in, the front of the pelvis toward the spine, and the pelvic floor in and upward (Grossman et al. 19). The second image was to be performed after the first image. In addition to the imagery work described in this article, the authors suggested that learning proper turnout may require periodic adjustment for optimal performance (Grossman et al. 26).

Anatomically Based Imagery Articles and Studies in Dance

Johanna Kirk was interested in introducing human biology into dance technique classes by beginning with an exploration of the respiratory system (61). One image used by Kirk was to trace the pathway of the breath in the body beginning with the nostrils and ending with tubules in the lungs, which become gradually smaller and more porous, allowing oxygen from the air to merge with the blood (63). Other images were to visually map parts of the lungs and kinesthetically feel how the chest moves during the process of breathing (Kirk 63–64). In her concluding statement, Kirk commented her imagery and somatics-based teaching techniques are created to enrich her students both as dancers and human beings, to help them feel whole and enjoy their individuality (Kirk 66).

In another anatomically based study, the teachers were interested in learning how they might help first-year modern dance students more fully understand anatomical/kinesthetic connections when they did not have this type of training prior to attending college (Moore and Moore 200). One technique used was to present the students with common, concrete three-dimensional objects which served as a type of image and could elicit the desired body movement involved in a technical skill; thus, as a first step, the physical object was presented along with the corresponding anatomical concept. Some examples were to use a yo-yo to represent feeling weighted and then rebounding from gravity or to have a slinky stand for articulations between the vertebrae (Moore and Moore 200). The initial presentations were followed with improvisation and partner work based on the movement concepts in which the students could learn about movement possibilities without having to perform a specific phrase; if a student was not satisfied with their movement responses, they had agency and could try again. The outcome was that the students made new connections and understandings which could lead to further inquiry (Moore and Moore 202).

Somatics-Based Imagery Studies in Dance

Work with mental imagery in dance has also been pursued using a somatics-based approach. Two researchers, Ashleigh Ritchie and Fiona Brooker, adopted this method because it supported a more collaborative experience for the teachers and students alike in higher education ("Imaging" 168). The imagery interventions used in a contemporary dance class study included guided imagery, which can calm students and provide a clear headspace, and cognitive-specific imagery, which allows for a mental rehearsal of the targeted movements; the two imagery approaches were blended to allow students to relax with using familiar imagery before the more complex mental rehearsal task (Ritchie and Brooker "Imaging" 171). Eight undergraduate ballet students participated in this study (Ritchie and Brooker "Imaging" 174). In response to this imagery approach, one of the students commented that learning in this class led to an embodied understanding of the movements, while another student stated she was able to feel rather than think about recalling class content (Ritchie and Brooker "Imaging" 175–76).

The two aforementioned researchers also used somatics-based imagery in another study. The twenty-four ballet students in this study experienced a research protocol in which they performed a targeted movement sequence, followed by assuming a resting position and imagining themselves dancing the material they had just performed while focusing on feedback they had received (Ritchie and Brooker "Democratic" 199–200). The images were multisensory in nature, although the students had some choice as to the image they could use; the outcome was that the students were able to approach the movement material with greater concentration, which resulted in being able to move with more clarity (Ritchie and Brooker

"Democratic" 199–200). The researchers also specified that use of imagery altered the way students approached and performed movements, but those who had the most prior experience with somatic imagery made the earliest progress ("Democratic" 201).

The Effect of Imagery on Psychological Skills in Dance

Some of those researching the use of imagery in dance have been interested in the effect of imagery use on various psychological skills and variables. In an investigation in this category, the researchers looked at the relationships between imagery ability, its use, and its learning style in thirty-four intermediate-level ballet and modern dance college students; the research instruments used in this study were the Movement Imagery Questionnaire-Revised (MIQ-R) and David Kolb's Learning Style Inventory-3 (LSI-3), which is based on how one gathers and processes information (Bolles and Chatfield 6–7). Thirty of thirty-four of the subjects displayed relative ease when using imagery based on their averaged MIQ-R scores (6). Another outcome of this study showed that the highest imagers preferred concrete or "feeling oriented" experiences during the information gathering learning stage (14). Eight students (four highest imagers and four lowest imagers) based on their MIQ-R scores were selected to participate in interviews to further assess their imagery use. While there appeared to be no difference in imagery use based on learning style, the high imagers came from a dance background, where they were exposed to much imagery, while the low imagers were not (9 & 11). One of the major themes that emerged from the interviews was that the subjects indicated imagery was important in their learning experiences (9).

A second study in this category included 216 subjects who performed in eight different dance styles with the goal of learning the relationship between the dancers' help-seeking behaviors, imagery use, and self-esteem in relationship to their injury status (Nordin-Bates et al. 76). Outcomes of this study showed a small, positive correlation between hours dancing per week and use of facilitative or helpful imagery, that those dancers who engaged in more imagery daily reported doing so even when injured, and those studying dance at vocational schools used more facilitative imagery than academic dance students (Nordin-Bates et al. 81–82).

Ellinor Klockare et al. also conducted a study investigating how dance teachers worked with psychological skills; interviews were conducted with six females who teach ballet, jazz, and contemporary dance to discover how they addressed their students' goal setting, imagery, performance preparation and evaluation, confidence, anxiety management, and how they supplied feedback (279–80). A qualitative analysis of the interviews revealed emergent themes, with the outcome that imagery was included under the theme of techniques used by the teachers (281). The researchers found the images used were of several types and included character or role-based images to help students' expressivity and emotional images connected to understanding how to perform a movement correctly; the teachers also encouraged students to experiment with imagery (285–86).

In another study, the researchers analyzed the relationship between perfectionism and creative expression and whether the two traits are compatible, with the premise that ballet training does not develop the latter quality (Karin and Nordin-Bates 1). Thirteen dance students (eight females and five males) were included in this study; the research instruments used included the Multidimensional Inventory of Perfectionism in Sport (MIPS), as a baseline assessment of perfectionism; the Perfectionistic Cognitive Inventory (PCI), used pre and post to assess the frequency of dancers' in-class perfectionistic thoughts; and a study-specific questionnaire which included an in-class creativity scale (3–4). During the course of the study, the students were exposed to an intervention focused on implicit learning and sensorikinetic images, with the outcome that perfectionistic comments were lower, and the dancers felt more creative after the intervention (7).

A second study conducted by Nordin-Bates was also based on the relationship between perfectionism and creativity; seventy-seven dance students from a national ballet school participated in this study (25). Perfectionism was evaluated using the Multidimensional Inventory of Perfectionism (MIPS), the Basic Needs Satisfaction in Sport Scale (BNSSS) was used to evaluate whether the students' need for autonomy and relatedness were met, and the Dancers Perceptions of the Creative Process Questionnaire (DPCPQ) captured the participants' self-rated creativity in dance, along with qualitative interviews (Nordin-Bates 26). Nordin-Bates indicated that the students demonstrated high scores for creativity and moderate to somewhat-high scores for perfectionism, although no significant relationships resulted between creativity and perfectionism (26–27). Of particular interest here, based on the interviews, was that the inspiration and imagery were reported to promote creativity, an outcome that agrees with earlier studies (Nordin-Bates 31).

Body Image Studies in Dance

The body image was the last form of imagery discussed in the section prior describing imagery types. In her article on body image and dance class, Wendy Oliver noted the following about dance and a dancer's body. She wrote, "Body image is not just about maintaining a certain weight; in dance it can refer to specific 'body flaws,' such as bowlegs, elevated shoulders, or a hyperextended back" (18).

It was decided to limit summaries of research on dance and body image to those published in the last ten years due to the proliferation of studies dealing with this topic. In one study, the researchers were interested in learning about the relationship between dance studio mirrors and the body image of high- and low-performing beginning ballet students. In this study, twenty-three students were taught using mirrors, and twenty-three were taught in the absence of mirrors; all were female ballet dancers (Radell et al. "Impact"108). All students in the study completed the Cash 69-Item Body Self-Relations Questionnaire pre and post and were videotaped in the fifth and fourteenth weeks of the semester (Radell et al. "Impact" 108). The videotapes were scored independently on a one-to-five scale by two ballet teachers; those receiving a score of 3 or higher were classified as high performers, while those with a score below 3 were designated as low performers (Radell et al. "Impact" 108). The result of this study showed that while the mirror can afford feedback, higher-performing dancers had a more positive body image when a mirror was not present, but lower-performing dancers who used a mirror seemed less worried about their weight than low-performing dancers who did not use a mirror (Radell et al. "Impact" 108).

The Cash 69-Item Body Self-Relations Questionnaire was used in a second study along with semistructured interviews of five randomly selected students; a mirror was used to teach thirty-six beginning-level ballet students and sixteen advanced-level ballet students (Radell et al. "Comparison" 135). By the end of the semester, there was a decrease in the body image satisfaction for both groups, although the interviews revealed the beginning dancers experienced an increase in self-consciousness, but the advanced dancers developed ways to avoid focusing on the mirror, such as feeling the movements muscularly (Radell et al. "Comparison" 135).

A third study by Sally Radell et al. seemed to confirm the findings, in part, of the two previous studies. In this study, the researcher investigated the effect of using a mirror on body image throughout the classes in comparison to using the mirror during only part of the class when both classes included beginning-level ballet students (Radell et al. "Body Image" 1). Those students who learned in the partial mirror environment seemed to become more aware of their overall bodily feelings, whereas the full mirror group learned to focus more on how specific aspects of their ballet movements such as turning out or flexibility improved (Radell et al. "Body Image" 5).

Kelly Culver also did a research study in which she attempted to improve her dance students' body image. In this study, the researcher used a choreography curriculum which included meditation, improvisation, and creation to help the students develop a more positive body image and an improved appreciation for their bodies (iii). Twenty-two high school dance students participated in this study, in which they completed a pre- and post-survey, weekly journal entries, and an exit questionnaire (Culver iii). Based on the outcome of earlier studies, the researcher covered the dance studio mirrors for the eight-week duration of the study (Culver 45). Culver used the theme and variations dance form during the creative portions of the study to encourage the students to focus on a body part about which they felt insecure (50). The outcome of the study was that some students became more confident about their bodies, worried less about how others perceived their bodies, no longer felt pressure to look a certain way, and found ways to rid themselves of negative thoughts about their bodies (Culver 55–59).

In a fifth study, college dancers' body image was evaluated based on their conversations about weight and body dissatisfaction. During the study, 116 students responded to hypothetical fat talk scenarios and completed the Body Esteem Scale (BES) (Kartawidjaja and Codero 122). The outcome of this study showed the least-severe levels of fat talk were among dance majors, in comparison to those students who danced but were not dance majors, and also when compared to the nondance college students; there was no significant difference between the students' BES scores among the three groups (Kartawidjaja and Codero 126).

Other studies about dance and body image explored the connection between body image and eating disorders. In one piece of research conducted in Israel, the Collins Body Image Silhouettes Questionnaire and the Eating Attitudes Test (EAT-26) were completed by forty-seven dancers or former dancers and forty-three nondancers aged 15 to 30 years; the first of these instruments was used to examine subjects' opinions about their body image based on seven silhouettes, which range from thin to full bodied, and the second instrument, which screens for symptoms indicative of eating disorders (Walter and Yanko 244). The hypothesis that differences would be found between dancers, former dancers, and nondancers for eating disorders and body image was not confirmed, nor was the premise that there is a correlation between body image and eating disorders; these findings contrast with the outcome of earlier studies (Walter and Yanko 246–47).

The EAT-26 test was also used in another study conducted in Greece, along with using the Social Physique Anxiety Scale (SPAS) and a questionnaire to assess parental and peer pressure from significant others; the subjects were 108 professionals who performed the genres of ballet (thirty-seven), Latin (thirty-one), and traditional dance (forty) (Kalyva et al. 1 & 4). No statistically significant differences were found between the three groups of subjects on any of the research instruments, although seven of the dancers' scores indicated they had abnormal eating habits (Kalyva et al. 5).

Finally, in another recent study, 320 Brazilian professional ballroom dancers completed a body image satisfaction scale which included nine body silhouettes, varying from thin to severely obese; 187 of the subjects were male, and the mean age for both sexes was 31.48 years (Cardoso et al. 19). The majority of the dancers in this study were dissatisfied with their body image, especially the women, but displayed a low risk for developing eating disorders, although another instrument, the Bulimic Investigatory Test Edinburgh (BITE), did provide evidence of compulsive eating and purging among the dancers (Cardoso et al. 20).

The outcome of some of the body image/eating disorder studies described previously seemed to display a need for an alternative research approach. It could be that a qualitative assessment might produce more definitive data of the relationship between dance and body image issues. Sherrie Barr and Wendy Oliver suggested broadening the teaching strategies used in dance technique classes as they relate to body image by incorporating feminist pedagogical approaches (97). In contrast to authoritarian teaching approaches, "feminist pedagogy gives attention to teaching approaches... honoring individual voices, collaborative learning, de-centering the teacher-student relationship, inclusivity, and critical reflection" (Barr and Oliver 98). Thus, dance technique teachers who strive to nurture their students' artistic identity and its development should foster a classroom environment of community and one in which diverse viewpoints are respected (Barr and Oliver 107).

Imagery Applications in the Choreographic Process

Jacqueline Smith-Autard remarked that the choreographer can imagine his or her use of the elements of the craft of choreography, such as the climax for a work; imaginative or original thoughts could produce even richer forms than the choreographer imagined in the early stages of dance making. Smith-Autard challenged readers to let their imaginations run away with the process because the outcome can be surprising (214).

While dancers frequently use their imagination as a motivation for creating movement and dances, the most vivid images will produce the best results. Choreographers can use images based on multiple sensory modalities, but the best advice is to use inspirational images that fit one's learning style. Success in working with imagery as an inspiration also means being able to focus on one's inner realm, and it may help to close one's eyes when beginning to create movement based on imagery (Minton *Choreography* 8). It is during the feeling and forming phase of the choreographic process that mental imagery is transformed into actions.

In a review of imagery used in dance, Pavlik and Nordin-Bates indicated that choreographers use varied images to inspire movement creation and for problem-solving when working on a piece; some of the images used, as reported by dancers to make movement choices, included abstract ideas, the surrounding space, and their own bodies (56). During improvisation, a dancer can stumble on an image which provides a new avenue for movement exploration, although some choreographers supply their dancers with imagery during their creative process (Pavlik and Nordin-Bates 58).

Vicky Fisher pointed out that a single mental image can have multiple impacts depending on the context, one of which is to use imagery to inspire and guide movement creation (259–60). Fisher continued that almost any image can stimulate improvisation, whether the focus is on exploring the physical aspects of movement or creating movements, with the purpose of meaning making; image use in choreography is similar to its use in improvisation, but with the goal of setting movement to form a dance (261). Furthermore, Fisher indicated that imagery use in developing and structuring a choreography creates meaning through internal logic in association with external entities; the meaning domain of imagery is related to its cognitive use and involves an exploration of the ideas embedded in the image (263–64).

In their exploration of imagery, Jonathan Clark and Taku Ando sought to discover the types of imagery used by choreographers. These authors indicated movement creation is often initiated in response to mental imagery based on both verbal and nonverbal instructions which relate to various sensory modalities, but kinesthetic images, in particular, have intrinsic spatial properties (180).

The previous authors mentioned specific choreographers and how they relied on their image of space to create movement. For example, Balanchine's use of space was defined by the dancers, Cunningham created movements which are scattered and spread in the performance space, and Forsythe's improvisations are related to a series of markers on a body, enabling the dancers to coordinate their movements in relation to bodily points (181–82). The authors also discussed the kinesthetic nature of imagery in its many iterations, stating that "movement may be simultaneously carried out, anticipated or imagined whilst generating certain types of images, called kinaesthetic images" (184). Finally, the types of imagery used by Ando in his choreographic instructions to dancers involved asking them to conceive of an image based on their own movements instead of using imagery derived from forms and external structures; then Ando changed these images by twisting or stretching them to create new movements (189).

In her effort to understand and describe the best strategies for teaching choreography and enhance creativity, Na-ye Kim interviewed ten professional choreographers—five who were Korean, and five who were American (5). Based on the interviews, Kim was able to discover choreographic teaching styles which she found could be coalesced into three categories (7). Under one of these categories, unfold thematizing, she discussed how student choreographers can be taught to tap into themes from their own lives and translate the perceived information into images (13). In Kim's words, "[t]he scenes that choreographers construct are images in their minds that have been translated into something tangible and visible" (14).

Other content related to the use of imagery as part of the choreographic process was based on research to determine its effectiveness on creativity. In one study, 240 undergraduate dance students were subjects in a study to assess the effectiveness of workshops designed to develop metacognitive skills with imagery which could support creativity during the choreographic process; there were 111 students in the control group, while 129 students received the imagery training (May et al. "Enhancing" 1 & 4). The metacognitive imagery-based creativity training used in the workshops applied mental representations known as Interacting Cognitive Subsystems (ICS), which is based on imagery about space and movement, sound and speech, and intuitive emotional schemas (May et al. "Enchancing" 3). The Abbreviated Torrance Test for Adults (ATTA) was administered at the beginning of the study prior to the creativity training, and the students completed the Flexible Thinking Test (FTT) before and after the workshops; during the study, the students also created and received feedback on dance pieces they created as a measure of their creativity (May et al. "Enhancing" 1 & 4). At the conclusion of the research, the groups did not differ in creativity and the control group had higher scores for use of imagery, although three months later, the imagery group had better scores for creativity and their use of imagery ideas (May et al. "Enhancing" 7–8).

In another study led by Jon May, the researchers wanted to learn how forms of mental imagery activated various brain structures, and supported the creative work of choreographer Wayne McGregor, in which he asked dancers to create movement in response to tasks (May et al. "Points" 404). The task instructions McGregor used require mental imagery along with decision-making; he then selected and amplified sections of the dancers' movements (May et al. "Points" 406). An example of one of McGregor's tasks was:

> Imagine an object. Reduce it to a line drawing. Visualise an element of it. Describe what is visible. The other condition was based upon emotional

instructions: one example from this experiment being "Think of a familiar song. . . . Focus on the memories, feelings or sensations it evokes, in you or someone else. Translate it into 3d and draw the meaning."

(May et al. "Points" 409)

In a pilot investigation which was part of the previous study, the investigators found different neural networks were active in response to different imagery tasks; fMRI data showed spatial practice, and emotional imagery tasks activated the orbitofrontal cortex, middle temporal regions, and occipital cortex, although spatial imagery activated the premotor and parietal cortices (May et al. "Points" 426–27). While the outcome of this study demonstrated that varying imagery use could contribute to creating different movements, the researchers offered their fMRI results with caution because the dancer was stationary during this part of the study, a condition which may have changed her ability to focus on the targeted imagery (May et al. "Points" 429).

Exploration Experiences

These explorations are based on the content of Chapter 3: body awareness, the role of attention and mental imagery, including exercises which deal with information in the subsections under the previous main headings.

Basic Body Awareness Explorations

1. It is understood that body awareness is a subjective experiencing of one's own body. However, the type and level of one's body awareness can be altered by other sensory input. Lie down on a mat or soft carpet and close your eyes. After taking several deep breaths, scan your entire body for any bodily feelings you are experiencing, including any interoceptive sensations from inside your body. Next, shift your attention to another of your sensory modalities, such as vision or hearing, and focus on the input you see or hear. How did your experiences during the first part of this exercise compare with those you experienced during the second part?
2. Stand in a room in your house and again bring your focus to your body and the sensations you are experiencing. Continue to focus on your bodily sensations but simultaneously extend your awareness to surroundings in the room. Did you experience any difference in your bodily sensations when you began to be more aware of your surroundings? Repeat the same exploration in an outdoor location and describe any differences you noticed between the two experiences.
3. Perform a simple movement skill, such as bending over toward the floor to retrieve an object, but focus outwardly by being aware of the spatial pathway of your action and the fact that you are changing levels. Then, perform the same action, but this time focus on the changing body shapes through which you

moved while performing the action. Describe the differences you experienced in your bodily sensations when performing this action in two ways.

4. Perform another simple action while focusing on the process of performing the action. This means you are going to experience and then be able to describe how each part of the action felt in your body. Follow this by performing the same action, by focusing on the end goal of the action. Did you notice any differences in body awareness when performing these two iterations of the same action?

5. There are many techniques used in somatics to help one be more aware of one's body. One of these is to breathe with your movements. Create a short movement pattern with one body part that moves up and then down or away from and then toward the floor. Perform this action as you would normally, followed by performing the same pattern while breathing in as you move the body part up and out as you move in down. Did your awareness of the body part change when you accompanied it with breathing?

6. Some somatic practices are concerned with body alignment or posture. Walk across a room using your normal posture. Then, attempt to lift and engage your core and make sure your shoulders are above your hips as you walk along the same pathway in the room. How would you describe your bodily sensations during each walking experience? Did one walking experience feel different from the other one? Was one easier to perform?

7. Having a clear movement intention is also a concern in many somatic systems. Walk across the room again using your usual approach, followed by covering the same pathway in space, with the intent of reaching the other side of the room. How would you compare your bodily feelings in each experience?

8. Balance on one foot with your visual focus straight ahead and your arms hanging at your sides. You should notice subtle changes and adjustments your body makes to maintain balance. Describe each of the bodily sensations you experienced in this exploration.

9. The influence of African dance on Western dance forms was mentioned in this chapter. One of the characteristics of African dance is that it is connected or grounded to the earth by using a bent knee stance. Practice walking in your normal manner. Then try walking with bent knees and by focusing on connecting the center of your body with the ground. Did your body feel different during each mode of walking?

10. Sit in a chair and slump forward. Next, remain seated while you arch your back. Finally, assume a seated position which is a neutral position located between the two previous positions and in which your shoulders are aligned above your hips. Which position felt more comfortable based on your bodily feelings?

11. The spine can be moved in multiple ways. These include rotation or twisting from side to side, curving forwards, arching backwards, and bending laterally to the right and left sides. Sit in a chair and practice moving your spine in the four different ways described in the preceding sentence. Then, perform each

of the spinal movements again, but this time be particularly aware of your bodily feelings as you perform each of these movements. Did you notice any differences in how your body felt as you performed each action? Did some of these actions feel relaxed while others felt tense?
12. Review the muscular anatomy of your leg. Then, hold onto a chair with one hand and swing the opposite leg to the front and back from the hip. Follow this by performing the same action while focusing on how specific muscles contract and relax as you perform the leg swing. Did your leg feel any different when you performed the leg swing under the two conditions?
13. Perform the same leg swing as the one described in the preceding exploration, but this time place your forefinger at the front of your hip joint as you perform the action, followed by placing your finger on the side of your hip while you perform the same action. Did touching the active part of your body as you performed the leg swing change your body awareness?
14. Did you experience any difficulty when performing the previous explorations. In particular, did any of the positions or movements feel more comfortable when you performed them in your usual manner in comparison to performing them in the altered manner?

More Complex Body Awareness Explorations

1. Watch an instructional ballet video and select a short movement sequence you wish to perform from the video. Perform the movement sequence once for practice. Then, perform it again, paying attention to how one part of your body feels as you perform the movements. Next, perform the same movement sequence again, but this time focus on the sounds you hear as you perform the movements. Did you have a different sense of your bodily feelings when you focused on the sounds?
2. Perform the preceding movement sequence again, but this time focus on visual aspects of your surroundings. Did this change in focus make it easier or more difficult for you to perform the movements?
3. Try performing the same ballet movement sequence in two different ways. First, perform it while focusing internally on how the movements feel in your body. Second, perform the movement sequence using an outward focus by emphasizing the direction, size, timing, or quality of the movements. Which method of performing the movement sequence did you prefer? Explain why you preferred performing the movements in one manner over the others.
4. Watch a video of a solo modern dancer who is traveling across the dance space while also moving at different levels. Then, select a short movement sequence from the video and practice it. Next, perform the movements, taking care to pay attention to the process of performing the actions by noting changes in your bodily feelings. Finally, perform the same movement sequence by focusing on the end goal of your movements. Which approach to performing these movements was most fulfilling for you, and why?

Connections between Body, Brain, Mind, and Thinking   **101**

5. Perform the preceding modern dance movement sequence as you normally would. Then, perform it again while breathing in during the upward movements and out on the downward parts of the movement sequence. How would you describe your body feelings as they are related to your breath during each part of the movement sequence?
6. Perform the same modern dance movement sequence. Then, describe the changes you experienced in your alignment or posture and how these changes felt in your body.
7. Analyze the preceding modern dance movement sequence based on your intent at three points in the sequence, followed by performing the movements as you focus on your selected intents. Do you think focusing on the intents improved your performance of the movement sequence?
8. Position your body in an arabesque and analyze the adjustments you need to make in different parts of your body to maintain balance.
9. Watch a video of African dance and then select a short sequence of movement from the video. Practice performing the movement sequence, and then analyze the bodily feelings you experienced in the lower half of your body.
10. Perform two of the movement sequences you experienced previously in earlier explorations. Then, perform them again and describe the movements of your spine during each sequence. Was there a variation in the way you moved your spine during each sequence?
11. Choose one of the movement sequences you already performed and analyze how the muscles of your legs worked together to enable you to perform the movements.
12. Heighten your awareness of how your muscles worked in the previous exploration by placing your forefinger at different points on your body when you perform it again. Did the use of your tactile sense help you understand how your muscles worked to perform the movement sequence? Were you more aware of your bodily feelings when using your tactile sense?

Basic Attention Explorations

1. The point of the following exploration is to tune into changes in your stream of attention. Begin by performing a simple task, such as pushing a moderately heavy object forward. Then perform this action again while paying attention to the feelings you experience in your hands, followed by changing your attentional focus to feelings you experience in your arms or in another body part. How would you compare these two body awareness experiences?
2. Select one of the preceding explorations. Then, based on the content in the chapter section on attention, decide whether you were using controlled or automatic attention while performing the movements.
3. Eastern movement practices distinguish between foundations which are outwardly and inwardly directed. Outwardly directed foundations include body alignment and posture, while inwardly directed foundations are based on the

use of energy, breath, attention, and focus. Practice sitting down and standing while paying attention to your posture. Then, shift your attention to focusing on your breath while sitting down and standing. Describe the differences you experienced in each exploration.

4. The practice of tai chi chuan is based on flowing between prescribed postures. Create four different body shapes. Then, perform these body shapes while transitioning or moving between them, stopping momentarily in each one. Next, perform the body shapes without stopping in each one but while flowing through them. How would you describe your attention in each experience?

5. Perform the preceding shape-based movement sequence again, but this time pay attention to the movement connections between the body shapes and the effort or energy required to move from shape to body shape. How would you describe the effort you needed to expend to move from one body shape to the next one? Did your use of energy or movement quality change as you moved from shape to shape?

6. Perform the shape-based movement sequence a third time, but this time focus your attention on different body systems. First, focus on the movements of your bones. Then, focus your attention more deeply on the inside of your body. Did changing your attentional focus change the way you experienced these movements?

7. Create a short, simple movement sequence. For example, sitting down, standing up, and then walking in different directions constitute a short, simple movement sequence. However, as you create the movement sequence, try to remember which aspects of creating the movement attracted your attention. Then, explain why certain aspects of movement sequence stood out for you.

More Complex Attention Explorations

1. Watch a video of a solo modern dancer performing a simple movement sequence. Then, select a short phrase from this sequence and perform it by using an internal focus. Finally, perform the same movement sequence while using an external focus. You should have been aware of different aspects of this movement experience when using the two different types of foci. Compare and describe these differences.

2. If you were teaching the preceding movement phrase, describe some verbal cues you might use to encourage the students to use an external focus. What about the use of cues which could be used to encourage an internal focus when performing the same phrase?

3. If you were teaching the same phrase, how might you use movement exploration or improvisation to help beginning students pay attention to changes in their bodily feelings or an internal focus while performing it?

4. Look at the feather pictured in Figure 3.5. This feather is bright pink, very soft to the touch, about a foot and one-half in length, and curved to the left. Each

FIGURE 3.5 Image of bright-pink feather.

Source: Photo by author.

part of the feather is attached at its center to the shaft, which is the same color but hard to the touch. Focus your attention on one aspect of this feather and use it as your inspiration to create a movement. Then, shift your attention to another part of the feather and create another movement. Describe how shifting your attention to a different part of the inspiration altered the movements you created.
5. Shift your attention to the kinesthetic body feelings you experienced when you created the two previous movements inspired by the feather. How might you use these body feelings to help you create more movements based on the same inspiration? In other words, where do these body feelings seem to lead you next in your creative process?
6. When you created the preceding movements, did you pay attention to or recall any memories? If so, how would you describe these memories and their relationship to your creative process?

Basic Imagery Explorations

1. This first exploration is based on mental practice or rehearsing a movement or sequence in your mind without performing it physically. Think of an action or a task you do regularly and then see yourself doing it in your mind. Following this rehearsal, describe some of the aspects or parts of the task and whether you experienced any bodily feelings.
2. Focus on the same task you used in the preceding exploration, but this time imagine you are watching someone else perform this task. This is an example of using an external image. How did this use of imagery differ from the use

you experienced in the preceding exploration, which was an internal imagery experience?
3. Focus again on the same task, but this time see a visual picture in your mind of your body at the beginning and at the end of the task. How was your body or its parts shaped at these two points in the task?
4. Rehearse the same task once more while focusing on your bodily feelings. These would be the kinesthetic images that accompany performance of the task. Now, describe one or two of these kinesthetic bodily feelings.
5. Direct imagery is based on imagining your body or its parts as an outside moving object. To walk forward with an energetic and determined feeling, imagine you are a runner in a race moving along a straight track. Next, imagine you want to walk forward in a relaxed and indeterminate way by pretending you are a child who is dawdling and procrastinating on their way to school. Then, compare your experience of the two ways of imagined walking.
6. Indirect or metaphorical imagery is not literal, because it serves as a way you could move in relation to the movements of an outside object. Select one part of your body which you want to move in a specific way. Then, create a metaphorical image which could help you move in the desired way.
7. This exploration is based on a line-of-movement image. You are going to slowly unfold or reach one arm out to the side of your body, but as you do this, imagine that there is a string that connects your shoulder and the tip of your forefinger. Then, perform the same movement without using the image. Did your arm feel different when performing the action under the two conditions?
8. Decide on a movement quality you would like to use as you walk forward. Then, imagine a global image which could help you move in this way. For example, you could imagine you are in a hot tropical climate to be able to walk slowly and in a relaxed way.
9. Anatomical imagery is involved with focusing on parts of the body to assist in the performance of a movement. This time you are going to reach your arm to the side of your body as you simultaneously turn your palm to face upward. As you perform this action, focus on the head of your upper arm bone or humerus as it rotates inside your shoulder joint while turning your palm upward.
10. The final exploration in this section is based on your body image. To explore your body image, lie down on a mat or carpet with your legs straight and your arms at your sides. Then, close your eyes and take a few deep breaths. Next, mentally scan your entire body. How would you describe the picture you have in your mind of your body? Are there parts of your body you really like and parts of which you are less fond? Your feelings about different parts of your body factor into your overall body image.

More Complex Imagery Explorations

1. Create a short dance movement sequence in the genre of your choice. Then, mentally rehearse this sequence in your mind. Which details in the movement sequence stood out?

Connections between Body, Brain, Mind, and Thinking   105

2. Imagine you are watching someone else perform the preceding movement sequence. Were different movement details apparent this time?
3. Mentally review the same movement sequence again, but this time focus on the visual aspects of the movements. Visual movement aspects include direction, level, relative size, shape, pathway, or position of body parts. Which visual aspects of the movement sequence were most prominent?
4. Perform the same movement sequence again while focusing on your kinesthetic bodily feelings which make up the kinesthetic imagery connected to the movements. Then, write a description of the two most prominent body feelings you experienced.
5. Think of an outside moving object that could help you perform the same movement sequence. Then, focus on this object as if it were a part of your body as you perform the movements. Did focusing on the image of the outside object help you perform the movements?
6. Imagine another outside moving object which could serve as a metaphor for your movements. How would you describe the quality of this imagined moving object? Describe that quality and then perform the same movement sequence again. Explain why the use of the indirect, metaphoric image was helpful or was not helpful in your performance of the movement sequence.
7. How might you use the image of a line-of-movement to aid in the performance of the same movement sequence?
8. Describe an overall global image you could use to capture the essence of the same dance movement sequence.
9. Review the same dance movement sequence to describe how specific parts of your anatomy function. Then, focus on one of these anatomical images as you perform the dance movement sequence again. Was focusing on the anatomical image helpful or not?
10. Review the analysis of your body image which you described in exploration 10 from the first set of previous exercises. Now, focus on your description of your body image as you perform the same dance movement sequence. Did focusing on your body image contribute to or detract from your performance?
11. Do you think you are a visual, auditory, or tactile/kinesthetic learner? Select one from the three learning styles and create an image that is based on that style. If you are primarily a visual learner, your image will be a mental picture. If you are an auditory learner, your image will be a targeted sound. If you are a tactile/kinesthetic learner, your image will be a body feeling. Now, focus on the image you created and devise one or two movements based on it. In what way do you think the movements you created capture the essence of your image?
12. In the previous text, there are some examples of spatial imagery. Create an image of a space in your mind. Continue to focus on this space and create movements in which you explore this imaginary space.
13. Think of a scene from your own life and create a mental image based on that scene. Continue to focus on the image of this scene as you create movements based on it.

14. What emotion do you associate with the preceding imagined scene? Focus on the emotion along with focusing on the same scene you used in the previous exploration as you create movements inspired by the emotion. Were the movements you created this time similar or different?

References

Alix, Sébastien-Akira. "The Hand As Agent of the Mind? The Irony of Manual Training Reform in Menomonie, Wisconsin (1890–1920)." *History of Education*, vol. 48, no. 4, 2019, pp. 479–95.

Andersen, Hannah. "Somatics, Transfer Theory, and Learning." *Journal of Dance Education*, vol. 18, no. 4, 2018, pp. 164–75.

Bailey, Richard. "Educating with Brain, Body and World Together." *Interchange*, vol. 51, 2020, pp. 277–91.

Bales, Melanie. "Body, Effort, and Space: A Framework for Use in Teaching." *Journal of Dance Education*, vol. 6, no. 3, 2006, pp. 72–77.

Banks, Ojeya Cruz. "Stories of West African and House Dance Pedagogies: 4E Cognition Meet Rhythmic Virtuosity." *Journal of Dance Education*, vol. 21, no. 3, 2021, pp. 176–82.

Bannon, Fiona, and Carole Kirk. "Deepening Discipline: Digital Reflection and Choreography." *Research in Dance Education*, vol. 15, no. 3, 2014, pp. 289–302.

Barr, Sherrie, and Wendy Oliver. "Feminist Pedagogy, Body Image, and the Dance Technique Class." *Research in Dance Education*, vol. 17, no. 2, 2016, pp. 97–112.

Batson, Glenna, and Ray Schwartz. "Revisiting the Value of Somatic Education in Dance Training Through an Inquiry into Practice Schedules." *Journal of Dance Education*, vol. 7, no. 2, 2007, pp. 47–56.

———. "Improving Postural Control in Battement Tendu: One Teacher's Reflections and Somatic Exercises." *Journal of Dance Education*, vol. 10, no. 1, 2010, pp. 6–13.

Batson, Glenna, and Margaret Wilson. *Body and Mind in Motion: Dance and Neuroscience in Conversation*. Intellect, 2014.

Berg, Tanya. "Ballet As Somatic Practice: A Case Study Exploring the Integration of Somatic Practices in Ballet Pedagogy." *Journal of Dance Education*, vol. 17, no. 4, 2017, pp. 147–57.

Bergentoft, Heléne. "Running: A Way to Increase Body Awareness in Secondary School Physical Education." *European Physical Education Review*, vol. 26, no. 1, 2020, pp. 3–21.

Bolles, Gina, and Steven Chatfield. "The Intersection of Imagery Ability, Imagery Use, and Learning Style: A Exploratory Study." *Journal of Dance Education*, vol. 9, no. 1, 2009, pp. 6–16.

Bradshaw-Yerby, Alexandra. "Dance Lessons for Writers: Embodied Language Applications for Movement Classrooms." *Journal of Dance Education*, vol. 21, no. 3, 2021, pp. 192–97.

Brodie, Julie, and Elin Lobel. "More Than Just a Mirror Image: The Visual System and Other Modes of Learning and Performing Dance." *Journal of Dance Education*, vol. 8, no. 1, 2008, pp. 23–31.

Busch, Lena, et al. "The Influence of Fitness-App Usage on Psychological Well-Being and Body Awareness—A Daily Randomized Trial." *Journal of Sport and Exercise Psychology*, vol. 42, 2020, pp. 249–60.

Carbone, Elena, et al. "Supporting Learning in Older Adults: The Role of Imagery Strategy." *Aging and Mental Health*, vol. 25, no. 8, 2021, pp. 1564–71.

Cardoso, Allana, et al. "Body Image Dissatisfaction, Eating Disorders, and Associated Factors in Brazilian Professional Ballroom Dancers." *Journal of Dance Medicine & Science*, vol. 25, no. 1, 2021, pp. 18–23.

Carey, Katy, et al. "Learning Choreography: An Investigation of Motor Imagery, Attentional Effort, and Expertise in Modern Dance." *Frontiers in Psychology*, 2019, pp. 1–11.

Cash, Thomas, and Linda Smolak. "Understanding Body Images: Historical and Contemporary Perspectives." *Body Image: A Handbook of Science, Practice and Prevention*. 2nd ed. edited by Thomas Cash and Linda Smolak, The Guilford Press, 2012, pp. 3–11.

Cheville, Julie. "Confronting the Problem of Embodiment." *International Journal of Qualitative Studies in Education*, vol. 18, no. 1, 2005, pp. 85–107.

Clark, Jonathan, and Taku Ando. "Geometry, Embodied Cognition and Choreographic Praxis." *International Journal of Performance Arts and Digital Media*, vol. 10, no. 2, 2014, pp. 179–92.

Coker, Elizabeth, et al. "Motor Imagery Modality in Expert Dancers: An Investigation of Hip and Pelvis Kinematics in Demi-Plié and Sauté." *Journal of Dance Medicine & Science*, vol. 19, no. 2, 2015, pp. 63–69.

Cornell, Ann Weiser, and Barbara Mc Gavin. "The Concept of 'Felt Sense' in Embodied Knowing and Action." *The Art and Science of Embodied Research Design: Concepts, Methods and Cases*, edited by Jennifer Frank Tantia, Routledge, 2021, pp. 29–39.

Costa, Ana, and Thorsten Barnhofer. "Turning Towards or Turning Away: A Comparison of Mindfulness Meditation and Guided Imagery Relaxation in Patients with Acute Depression." *Behavioral and Cognitive Psychotherapy*, vol. 44, 2016, pp. 410–19.

Couillandre, Annabelle, et al. "Exploring the Effects of Kinesiological Awareness and Mental Imagery on Movement Intention in the Performance of Demi-Plié." *Journal of Dance Medicine & Science*, vol. 12. No. 3, 2008, pp. 91–98.

Courtney, Rosalba. "Breath, Mind Body." Breath, Mind and Body—Dr Rosalba Courtney, accessed 9 Dec. 2021.

Culver, Kelly. *Reflection, Creation, Transformation: Fostering a Positive Body Image in Female High School Dancers Through a Creative Choreography Curriculum*. MA Thesis, University of Northern Colorado, 2021.

Damasio, Antonio. *Descartes' Error: Emotion, Reason, and the Human Brain*. Grosset/Putnam, 1994.

Damasio, Antonio, and Hanna Damasio. "Minding the Body." *Daedalus*, vol. 135, no. 3, 2006, pp. 15–22.

Delinsky, Sherrie Selwyn. "Body Image and Anorexia Nervosa." *Body Image: A Handbook of Science, Practice and Prevention*. 2nd ed. edited by Thomas Cash and Linda Smolak, The Guilford Press, 2012, pp. 279–87.

Dragon, Donna. "Creating Cultures of Teaching and Learning: Conveying Dance and Somatic Education Pedagogy." *Journal of Dance Education*, vol. 15, no. 1, 2015, pp. 25–32.

Eddy, Martha. "The Practical Application of Mind-Body Centering (BMC) in Dance Pedagogy." *Journal of Dance Education*, vol. 6, no. 3, 2006, pp. 86–91.

———. *Mindful Movement: The Evolution of the Somatic Arts and Conscious Action*. Intellect, 2017.

Ferrari, Michel, et al. "Piaget's Framework for a Scientific Study of Consciousness." *Human Development*, vol. 44, no. 4, 2001, pp. 195–213.

Fish, Lee, et al. "Investigating the Use of Imagery by Elite Ballet Dancers." Hall, Craig. Personal Email Communication. 5 Sept. 2021.

Fisher, Vicky. "Unfurling the Wings of Flight: Clarifying 'the What' and 'the Why' of Mental Imagery Use in Dance." *Research in Dance Education*, vol. 18, no. 3, 2017, pp. 252–72.

Fonow, Margaret, et al. "Using the Feldenkrais Method of Somatic Education to Enhance Mindfulness, Body Awareness, and Empathetic Leadership Perceptions among College Students." *Journal of Leadership Education*, vol. 15, no. 3, 2016, pp. 116–29.

Fortin, Sylvie, and Fernande Girard. "Dancers' Application of the Alexander Technique." *Journal of Dance Education*, vol. 5, no. 4, 2005, pp. 125–31.

Franklin, Eric. *Dance Imagery for Technique and Performance*. 2nd ed. Human Kinetics, 2014.

Frith, Emily, et al. "Keeping Creativity Under Control: Contributions of Attention Control and Fluid Intelligence to Divergent Thinking." *Creativity Research Journal*, vol. 33, no. 2, 2021, pp. 138–57.

George, Doran. *The Natural Body in Somatics Dance Training*. Oxford UP, 2020.

Gibbs, Raymond. *Embodiment and Cognitive Science*. Cambridge UP, 2005.

Giguere, Miriam. "The Social Nature of Cognition in Dance: The Impact of Group Interactions on Dance Education Practices." *Journal of Dance Education*, vol. 21, no. 3, 2021, pp. 132–39.

Gose, Rebecca. "Extraordinary Dancing Requires Extraordinary (Motor) Learning." *Journal of Dance Education*, vol. 19, no. 1, 2019, pp. 34–40.

Green, Diana. *Choreographing from Within: Developing the Habit of Inquiry as an Artist*. Human Kinetics, 2010.

Green, Jill. "Foucault and the Training of Docile Bodies in Dance Education." *The Journal of the Arts and Learning Special Interest Group of the American Education Research Association*, vol. 191, no. 1, 2003, pp. 99–125.

Grossman, Gayanne, et al. "Effective Use of Turnout: Biomechanical, Neuromuscular, and Behavioral Considerations." *Journal of Dance Education*, vol. 5, no. 1, 2005, pp. 15–27.

Grossman, Susan. "Empirical Evidence of the Embodiment Awareness Changes in Somatic Focused Gestalt Psychotherapy." *The Art and Science of Embodied Research Design: Concepts, Methods and Cases*, edited by Jennifer Frank Tantia, Routledge, 2021, pp. 76–85.

Guilbert, Jessica, et al. "Motor Imagery Development and Proprioceptive Integration: Which Sensory Reweighting During Childhood?" *Journal of Experimental Child Psychology*, vol. 166, 2018, pp. 621–34.

Guss-West, Clare. *Attention and Focus in Dance: Enhancing Power, Precision, and Artistry*. Human Kinetics, 2021.

Hartelius, Glenn. "Somatic Phenomenology: Maps of Body-Felt Experience." *The Art and Science of Embodied Research Design: Concepts, Methods and Cases*, edited by Jennifer Frank Tantia, Routledge, 2021, pp. 87–99.

Heiland, Teresa, and Robert Rovetti. "Examining Effects of Franklin Method Metaphorical and Anatomical Mental Images on College Dances' Jumping Height." *Research in Dance Education*, vol. 14, no. 2, 2013, pp. 141–61.

Henley, Matthew. "Thinking About Thinking: Dance Education and 4E Cognition." *Journal of Dance Education*, vol. 21, no. 3, 2021, pp. 129–31.

Herman, Frederik, and Michèle Hofmann. "Bodies and Minds in Education." *Journal of the History of Education Society*, vol. 48, no. 4, 2019, pp. 443–51.

Honig, Alice Sterling. "Teachers Can Help Promote Children's Body Awareness and Imagination." *Early Child Development and Care*, vol. 190, no. 14, 2020, pp. 2291–96.

Hutt, Ethan. "Afterword [Part 1]: The Practice of Attending to Bodies and Minds in Education." *History of Education*, vol. 48, no. 4, 2019, pp. 546–52.

Johnson, Jessica. "Finding Center: Strategies for Awakening Proprioceptive Awareness for More Embodied Performance." *Wellness*, June–July, 2020, pp. 18–21.

Kalyva, Stavroula, et al. "Disturbed Eating Attitudes, Social Physique, Anxiety, and Perceived Pressure for Thin Body in Professional Dancers." *Research in Dance Education*, 2021, pp. 1–12.

Kandel, Eric. *In Search of Memory: The Emergence of a New Science of Mind*. Norton, 2006.

———. "The New Science of Mind." *New York Times*. 8 Sept. 2013.

Karin, Janet, and Sanna Nortin-Bates. "Enhancing Creativity and Managing Perfectionism in Dancers Through Implicit Learning and Sensori-Kinetic Imagery." *Journal of Dance Education*, vol. 20, 2020, pp. 1–11.

Kartawidjaja, Jenae, and Elizabeth Cordero. "Fat Talk and Body Dissatisfaction Among College Dancers." *Journal of Dance Education*, vol. 13, no. 4, 2013, pp. 122–29.

Kearns, Lauren. "Somatics in Action: How 'I Feel Three-Dimensional and Real' Improves Dance Education and Training." *Journal of Dance Education*, vol. 10, no. 2, 2010, pp. 35–40.

Kim, Na-ye. "Identifying Choreographic Phronesis Teaching Styles for Creativity." *Research in Dance Education*, 2020, pp. 1–23.

Kirk, Johanna. "Experiencing Our Anatomy: Incorporating Human Biology into Dance Class vis Imagery, Imagination, and Somatics." *Journal of Dance Education*, vol. 14, no. 2, 2014, pp. 59–66.

Klockare, Ellinor, et al. "An Interpretative Phenomenological Analysis of How Professional Dance Teachers Implement Psychological Skills Training in Practice." *Research in Dance Education*, vol. 12, no. 3, 2011, pp. 277–93.

Knaster, Mirka. *Discovering the Body's Wisdom*. Bantam Books, 1996.

Kosslyn, Stephen, et al. "Neural Foundations of Imagery." *Nature Reviews: Neuroscience*, vol. 2, 2001, pp. 635–42.

———. *The Case for Mental Imagery*. Oxford UP, 2006.

Krasnow, Donna, and Virginia Wilmerding. *Motor Learning and Control for Dance: Principles and Practices for Performers and Teachers*. Human Kinetics, 2015.

Kronsted, Christian. "Using Affordances to Teach Improvisational Dance." *Journal of Dance Education*, vol. 21, no. 3, 2021, pp. 168–75.

Lachance, Josée, et al. "Learning to Be a Sensitive Professional: A Life-Enhancing Process Grounded in the Experience of the Body." *Adult Education Quarterly*, vol. 69, no. 1, 2019, pp. 24–41.

Leitch, Laurie, et al. "Somatic Experiencing Treatment with Social Services Workers Following Hurricanes Katrina and Rita." *Social Work*, vol. 54, no. 1, 2009, pp. 9–18.

Lester, Kelly Ferris. "Somatics: A Buzzword Defined." *Journal of Dance Education*, vol. 17, 2017, pp. 31–33.

Lindberg, Lindsay, et al. "Improvisational Dance as Enactive Cognition: What Do Novice Dancers Teach Us About Embodied Cognition in Dance?" *Journal of Dance Education*, vol. 21, no. 3, 2021, pp. 1–12.

Lowry, Natalie, et al. "Acute Impact of Self-Guided Mental Imagery on Craving in Cocaine Use Disorder: A Mixed-Methods Analysis of a Randomized Controlled Trial." *Addiction*, vol. 116, no. 9, 2021, pp. 2418–30.

Lunke, Katrin, and Beat Meier. "Disentangling the Impact of Artistic Creativity on Creative Thinking, Working Memory, Attention, and Intelligence: Evidence for Domain-Specific Relationships with a New Self-Report Questionnaire." *Frontiers in Psychology*, vol. 7, 2016, pp. 1–11.

Mattes, Josef. "Attentional Focus in Motor Learning, the Feldenkrais Method and Mindful Movement." *Perceptual and Motor Skills*, vol. 123, no. 1, 2016, pp. 258–76.

May, Jon, et al. "Points in Space: An Interdisciplinary Study of Imagery in Movement Creation." *Dance Research: The Journal of the Society for Dance Research*, vol. 29, no. 2, 2011, pp. 404–32.

———. "Enhancing Creativity by Training Metacognitive Skills in Mental Imagery." *Thinking Skills and Creativity*, vol. 38, 2020, pp. 1–10.

McCreary, Donald. "Body Image and Muscularity." *Body Image: A Handbook of Science, Practice and Prevention*, edited by Thomas Cash and Linda Smolak, The Guilford Press, 2012, pp. 198–205.

Minton, Sandra, and Karen McGill. "The Effects of Participation in Dance Technique Classes on Student Performance on a Spatial Kinesthetic Awareness Test." *Journal of Dance Medicine & Science*, vol. 2, no. 2, 1998, pp. 68–72.

———. "Assessment of High School Students' Creative Thinking Skills: A Comparison of Dance and Non-Dance Classes." *Research in Dance Education*, vol. 4, no. 1, 2003, pp. 31–49.

———. *Choreography: A Basic Approach Using Improvisation*. 4th ed. Human Kinetics, 2018.

Mokienko, Olesya, et al. "Motor Imagery and Its Practical Application." *Neuroscience and Behavioral Physiology*, vol. 44, no. 5, 2014, pp. 483–89.

Moore, Christi Camper, and David Moore. "The Extended Mind: Physical Tools to Expand Cognition in the Collegiate Modern Dance Class." *Journal of Dance Education*, vol. 21, no. 3, 2021, pp. 198–202.

Moran, A., et al. "Re-Imaging Motor Imagery: Building Bridges Between Cognitive Neuroscience and Sport Psychology." *British Journal of Psychology*, vol. 103, 2012, pp. 224–47.

Nabors, Laura, et al. "Implementing the Coping Positively with My Worries Manual: A Pilot Study." *Journal of Child and Family Studies*, vol. 28, 2019, pp. 2708–17.

Neal, Allyson Matney. "Somatic Interventions to Improve Self-Regulation in Children and Adolescents." *Journal of Child and Adolescent Psychiatric Nursing*, vol. 34, 2021, pp. 171–80.

Newen, Albert, et al. *The Oxford Handbook of 4E Cognition*. Oxford UP, 2018.

Nordin, Sanna, and Jennifer Cumming. "Measuring the Content of Dancers' Images: Development of the Dance Imagery Questionnaire (DIQ)." *Journal of Dance Medicine & Science*, vol. 10, nos. 3&4, 2006, pp. 85–98.

Nordin-Bates, Sanna, et al. "Injury, Imagery, and Self-Esteem in Dance: Healthy Minds in Injured Bodies." *Journal of Dance Medicine & Science*, vol. 15, no. 2, 2011, pp. 76–85.

———. "Striving for Perfection or for Creativity?" *Journal of Dance Education*, vol. 20, 2020, pp. 23–34.

Oliver, Wendy. "Body Image in Dance Class: Dance Educators Can and Should Help Their Dancers Develop and Maintain a Positive Body Image." *Journal of Physical Education, Recreation & Dance*, vol. 79, no. 5, 2008, pp. 18–41.

Overby, Lynnette Young, et al. "A Comparison of Imagery Used by Dance Teachers, Figure Skating Coaches, and Soccer Players." *Imagination, Cognition and Personality*, vol. 17, no. 4, 1997–98, pp. 323–37.

Overby, Lynnette Young, and Jan Dunn. "The History and Research of Dance Imagery: Implications for Teachers." *The IADMS Bulletin for Teachers*, vol. 3, no 2, 2011, pp. 9–11.

Pavlik, Katherine, and Sanna Nordin-Bates. "Imagery in Dance: A Literature Review." *Journal of Dance Medicine & Science*, vol. 20, no. 2, 2016, pp. 51–63.

Radell, Sally, et al. "The Impact of Mirrors on Body Image and Performance in High and Low Performing Female Ballet Students." *Journal of Dance Medicine & Science*, vol. 15, no. 3, 2011, pp. 108–15.

———. "Comparison Study of Body Image Satisfaction Between Beginning- and Advanced-Level Female Ballet Students." *Journal of Dance Medicine & Science*, vol. 21, no. 4, 2017, pp. 135–43.

———. "Body Image and Mirror Exposure: The Impact of Partial Versus Full Mirror Use on Beginner-Level Ballet Students." *Journal of Dance Education*, 2021, pp. 1–8.

Ramachandran, V. S. *The Tell-Tale Brain: A Neuroscientist's Quest for What Makes Us Human*. Norton, 2011.

Rimmer, Rachel. "Improvising with Material in the Higher Education Dance Technique Class: Exploration and Ownership." *Journal of Dance Education*, vol. 13, no. 4, 2013, pp. 143–46.

Ritchie, Ashleigh, and Fiona Brooker. "Imaging the Future: An Autoethnographic Journey of Using a Guided and Cognitive-Specific Imagery Intervention in Undergraduate Release-Based Contemporary Dance Technique." *Research in Dance Education*, vol. 19, no. 2, 2018, pp. 167–82.

———. "Democratic and Feminist Pedagogy in the Ballet Technique Class: Using a Somatic Imagery Tool to Support Learning and Teaching of Ballet in Higher Education." *Journal of Dance Education*, vol. 20, 2020, pp. 197–204.

Schack, Thomas. "Building Blocks and Architecture of Dance." *The Neurocognition of Dance: Mind, Movement and Motor Skills*. 2nd ed., edited by B. Blassing et al., Routledge, 2019, pp. 117–38.

Schilder, Paul. *The Image and Appearance of the Human Body*. International UP, 1950.

Seago, Catherine. "A Study of the Perception and Use of Attention in Undergraduate Dance Training Classes." *Research in Dance Education*, vol. 21, no. 3, 2020, pp. 245–61.

Seiler, Brian, et al. "Biological Evidence of Imagery Abilities: Intraindividual Differences." *Journal of Sport & Exercise Psychology*, vol. 37, 2015, pp. 421–35.

Sheets-Johnstone, Maxine. "The Lived Body." *The Humanistic Psychologist*, vol. 48, no. 1, 2020, pp. 28–53.

Smith-Autard, Jacqueline. *Dance Composition: A Practical Guide to Creative Success in Dance Making*. 6th ed. Bloomsbury, 2010.

Solomon, Ruth. "An Efficient Warm-Up Based on Anatomical Principles." *Preventing Dance Injuries*. 2nd ed., edited by Ruth Solomon, John Solomon, and Sandra Cerny Minton, Human Kinetics, 2005, pp. 111–28.

Sorri, Mari. "The Body Has Reasons: Tacit Knowing in Thinking and Making." *The Journal of Aesthetic Education*, vol. 28, no. 2, 1994, pp. 15–26.

Spagnuolo, Lauren, and Laura Colket. "Slightly Off-Balance: Learning How to Teach Anatomical Awareness in the Dance Classroom." *Research in Dance Education*, vol. 17, no. 2, 2016, pp. 86–96.

Stuart, Susan. "The Union of Two Nervous Systems: Neurophenomenology, Enkinaesthesia, and the Alexander Technique." *Constructivist Foundations*, vol. 8, no. 3, 2013, pp. 314–23.

Sullivan, Jaclynn. "Learning and Embodied Cognition: A Review and Proposal." *Psychology Learning & Teaching*, vol. 17, no. 2, 2018, pp. 128–43.

Sweigard, Lulu. *Human Movement Potential: Its Ideokinetic Facilitation*. Dodd Mead, 1974.

Todd, Mabel Ellsworth. *The Thinking Body*. Dance Horizons, 1975.

Toner, John, et al. "Reflective and Pre-Reflective Awareness in Skilled Actions." *Psychology of Consciousness: Theory, Research and Practice*, vol. 3, no. 4, 2016, pp. 303–15.

Torres-Unda, Jon, et al. "The Feldendrais Method Improves Functioning and Body Balance in People with Intellectual Disability in Supported Employment: A Randomized Clinical Trial." *Research in Developmental Disabilities*, vol. 70, 2017, pp. 104–12.

Vroegh, Thijs. "Visual Imagery in the Listener's Mind: A Network Analysis of Absorbed Consciousness." *Psychology of Consciousness: Theory, Research and Practice*, 2021, pp. 1–24.

Walter, Ofra, and Sivan Yanko. "New Observations on the Influence of Dance on Body Image and Development of Eating Disorders." *Research in Dance Education*, vol. 19, no. 3, 2018, pp. 240–51.

Watson, Debbie, et al. "Facilitating and Nurturing Creativity in Pre-Vocational Dancers: Findings from the UK Centres for Advanced Training." *Research in Dance Education*, vol. 13, no. 2, 2012, pp. 153–73.

Whittier, Cadence. "Laban Movement Analysis Approach to Classical Ballet Pedagogy." *Journal of Dance Education*, vol. 6, no. 4, 2006, pp. 124–32.

Yagci, Gozde, et al. "Body Awareness and Its Relations to Quality of Life in Individuals with Idiopathic Scoliosis." *Perceptual and Motor Skills*, vol. 127, no. 5, 2020, pp. 841–57.

Zull, James. *From Brain to Mind: Using Neuroscience to Guide Change in Education*. Stylus, 2011.

Zvyagintsev, Mikhail, et al. "Brain Networks Underlying Mental Imagery of Auditory and Visual Information." *European Journal of Neuroscience*, vol. 37, 2013, pp. 1421–34.

4
THE ROLE OF THE BODY IN INTERPERSONAL CONNECTIONS AND COMMUNICATIONS

Introduction

The fact that we are part of the larger human community is often forgotten in our quest for individuality and personal choice. This issue surfaced prominently amid the coronavirus pandemic and whether it was a personal choice to get vaccinated as a precaution against the spread of a deadly pathogen.

In her book *Culturally Responsive Teaching & the Brain*, Zaretta Hammond wrote that one way to understand individuality and personal choice is to view these traits from a cultural perspective. However, understanding a cultural group does not mean experiencing its more superficial aspects, such as typical foods or holidays, but focusing on its roots or worldview, core beliefs, and group values (24–25). Hammond calls these aspects of a culture universal patterns or cultural archetypes; "cultures might be different at the surface and shallow levels, [but] at the root of different cultures there are common values, worldviews, and practices that form these archetypes" (25). A common cultural archetype is a group's orientation toward viewing the cultural group as a collective or made up of many interconnected individuals (Hammond 25).

Originally, humans were more oriented toward collectivism, but with the move to cities, a more individualistic bent took over (Hammond 25). As has been noted in earlier chapters, there is a different orientation between Western and Eastern thinking concerning the mind-body dichotomy and practices involving body awareness and attention. This difference in thinking extends to the collectivism or community orientation versus individualism as well. Hammond wrote:

> Most European cultures were rooted in an individualistic mindset, while the collectivist worldview is common among Latin American, Asian, African, Middle Eastern, and many Slavic cultures. . . . Collectivistic societies

DOI: 10.4324/9781003258926-4

emphasize relationships, interdependence within a community, and cooperative learning. Individualistic societies emphasize individual achievement and independence.

(25)

Today, multiple cultures live on the same planet, and interconnections between them are increasing due to travel and migrations. Different cultures, religions, and worldviews have become neighbors in today's world, accompanied by a lack of understanding and creation of suspicion (de Souza 48). Sara Konrath et al. reported that a standardized test used to measure college students' level of empathy showed that the ability to stand in another person's shoes has declined by 34 points since 1980 (Shushok 2). The question is how to bridge this divide and create a more humanistic world and worldview. It seems one key to answering this question is developing a sense of understanding and empathy between individuals and cultures.

Empathy

So what, then, is *empathy*? In its original use in English at the beginning of the twentieth century, empathy meant a strong physical response to people and objects; however, this meaning, when interpreted by psychologists, became connected with an emotional experience instead of a physical experience (Foster 10). Empathy has been described elsewhere as having an openness to others (Bialystok and Kukar 24). Having empathy establishes connections and creates a sense of community since the person who is empathizing needs to, in many instances, overlook his or her own viewpoint to understand the other (Detrick 6).

In her efforts to understand empathy, Rebecca Detrick defined it as:

> [T]he visceral/emotional response to the shared and universal human experience. It requires recognition, validation, and possibly affirmation of a person's emotional reaction to his/her own life experiences. The event/experience itself may be foreign to the empathetic person, but the feeling—the reactionary response to an event—is universal and shared.
>
> *(6)*

Other authorities who have studied empathy, including its neural basis, distinguished between affective and cognitive empathy; *affective empathy* is the ability to experience what it feels like when another person experiences a particular emotion, while *cognitive empathy* is understanding what the thoughts and emotions of another person might be without becoming emotionally involved (van Zonneveld et al. 914).

In a study of 114 8- to 12-year-old children that appeared to be at a high risk for developing criminal behaviors, the researchers found that antisocial behaviors are based on an impairment of empathy, especially affective empathy (van Zonneveld et al. 913 & 918). Based on the cognitive aspects of empathy and the demands placed on them, a sense of empathy cannot be fully developed until around the age of 12, when children gain the ability to think abstractly (Walker and Weidenbenner 120).

Some believe empathy can be taught or at least encouraged through various approaches. In fact, a volume of educational literature promotes empathy along with authenticity as educational traits that transcend teaching curricular content (Bialystok and Kukar 23). Many believe developing a sense of empathy is based on listening well, making an attempt to validate the feelings of another person, understanding that those feelings are real and important, and often, letting one's own social/cultural stereotypes go (Detrick 6). Some writers indicated that being empathetic can be learned through experience and a gradual refinement of a child's ability to recognize the emotional signals of others (van Zonneveld et al. 3). Others described the connection between having a low level of empathy and displaying aggressive behaviors; the belief was that targeting the mindset of such individuals by convincing them that empathy is malleable could lead to their acceptance of techniques designed to enhance their empathy (Gandhi et al. 1).

Programs that promote children's awareness that they are connected to others can also promote empathy, especially in multicultural, multireligious societies, where differences between individuals and groups predominate (de Souza 52). Some techniques incorporated in such programs include sharing personal stories and mirroring experiences from these stories, emphasizing similarities instead of differences, offering creative activities based on thinking that extends beyond the usual framework, realizing the arts can enhance empathy and expression, and demonstrating empathetic responses when teaching (de Souza 52–53).

Developing a sense of empathy has also been connected to improving intercultural communication and competency. Aminu Amman described this trait as cultural empathy, pursued by fulfilling the role of a cultural intermediary between one's own culture and one that is foreign (Mai 564). An interview study included nineteen Vietnamese graduates and six international managers who were from the USA, Sweden, the Netherlands, and UK; all were working for international non-governmental organizations (INGOs) (Mai 566). The outcome of the interviews was that the graduates encountered misunderstandings due to cultural differences because they lacked intercultural knowledge and competencies (Mai 566). The researcher also learned that the managers needed to overcome cultural differences or become more culturally empathetic to communicate more effectively (Mai 568).

Connection to Social Emotional Learning

Social emotional learning (SEL) seeks to enhance the social and emotional abilities of children, including their self-awareness, self-management, social awareness, relationship skills, and responsible decision-making (Green et al. "Evaluation" 531). SEL is also the basis of theory of mind skills (Walker and Weidenbenner 116) or the ability to attribute mental states to oneself or others as a foundation for social interactions.

The components of SEL have been described by the Collaborative for Academic, Social, and Emotional Learning (CASEL) in the following way:

> [S]elf-awareness refers to the ability to recognize emotions and thoughts and their influence on behavior and assess personal strengths and limitations. Self-management refers to the ability to effectively regulate emotions, thoughts, and behaviors in different situations and to set and work toward goals. Social awareness refers to the ability to take the perspective of and empathize with others, to understand social and ethical norms for behavior, and to recognize available resources and supports. Relationship skills refer to the ability to establish and maintain healthy relationships, communicate well with others, negotiate conflict, and seek and offer help when needed . . . .. responsible decision-making refers to the ability to make constructive choices about personal behavior and social interactions, evaluate consequences of actions, and consider the well-being of self and others.
>
> *(qtd. in Green et al. "Evaluation" 532–33)*

Based on the information in the preceding section about empathy and the preceding content, it is possible to discern the connections between empathy and SEL skills. Developing social and emotional competencies is important in childhood for maintaining healthy relationships, creating the ability to cope with difficulties, and to one's overall well-being; proponents of SEL value its possible effect on the prevention of later problems and development of students' resiliency (Green "Evaluation" 532–33).

Developing SEL Abilities in Students

Various suggestions have been offered for improving students' SEL abilities. An article in an educational publication included information about how to improve such abilities in young people. The suggestions included (1) challenging students to become more self-aware, especially of their strengths, by using reflection to describe how they fit into the world; (2) creating exercises for students to mingle with their peers when discussing a topic; (3) practicing stress management through the use of mindfulness and breathing exercises and by journaling or becoming involved in the expressive arts; (4) providing opportunities to work with peers to achieve a common goal; and (5) teaching lessons to help students learn life skills, including responsible decision-making (Norris 17–18).

A high school English Language Arts (ELA) teacher also described how her curriculum can be used to develop students' SEL skills. Literature can evoke emotional responses and describe questions and uncertainties encountered in life (Coleman 2). The author noted that the SEL activities can be used to promote both self-awareness and social awareness. For example, students can freewrite based on emotions, or a text can be chosen in which the protagonist discusses his or her self-identity and grapples with it, accompanied by questions in which students make connections between themselves and the character; the students were also encouraged to interact with each other based on open-ended topics (Coleman 3).

The safe, positive, accountable, respectful, and kind program (SPARK) is an elementary-level SEL program designed to reduce risk factors, initiate resilience, and promote well-being by employing principles of mind, thought, and consciousness (Green et al. "Evaluation" 534). Green et al. conducted a study to determine the effectiveness of this program on ninety-four fourth and fifth graders from one elementary school. An outcome of the study was that the researchers found a significant difference between the students who received the SPARK intervention and those who did not based on their understanding of the program's principles of communication, decision-making, and problem-solving skills, along with their emotional regulation and resilience (Green et al. "Evaluation" 531).

Considering the amount of time youth spend online, other researchers were interested in learning how technology could be used to promote growth in SEL skills. One of the points made in this article was that skills learned in a virtual environment do not necessarily ensure success when transferring them to real life (Walker and Weidenbenner 125). What is needed for successful transfer from the virtual world is the human element. This means a human, such as a teacher, parent, or peer, must mediate the understanding of the processes experienced virtually (Walker and Weidenbenner 127). Thus, technology can be used for developing SEL skills, but only with human mediation, although advancements in technology have been increasingly able to mimic human interactions (Walker and Weidenbenner 123).

Studies on Movement and Dance and Social Emotional Learning

While the physical education curriculum is not the same as dance curricula in terms of the goals and the end product, it is focused on movement. Thus, planned and well-designed physical education programs have been proposed as a method to improve students' SEL abilities. In their article, the authors created and described a teaching personal social responsibility (TPSR) model as a method to use physical activity to teach at-risk youth social responsibility, indicating that such models were previously created by noted physical educators Don Hellison and Daryl Siedentop (Olive et al. 21). The authors explained that the following components were included in their physical activity model to help develop SEL skills: (1) relational time, (2) awareness talks, (3) physical activity, (4) group meetings, and (5) time for reflection (Olive et al. 21).

Olive et al. also explained that another important part of teaching SEL skills is helping students understand the SEL language; when students understand these competencies, they are more likely to ask for help, manage their emotions, and solve problems (22). In one physical activity program, the treatment group received SEL training while the control group did not; surveys measuring the students' SEL knowledge and self-perceptions were given pre and post. After four weeks, there was no change in the students' self-perceptions, although staff noticed the students changed the way they talked to each other (Olive et al. 23).

Other studies were concerned with using dance in relation to social-emotional intelligence. In an article, the researchers analyzed scientific literature on dance and emotional intelligence with the outcome that sixty-six documents were retrieved, with forty-nine selected for further analysis, since they presented dance in some way as having a relationship with emotional intelligence and emotions (San-Juan-Ferrer and Hipola 67). Ideas presented in four of the studies were to separate dance from physical education, that dance can serve as a form of social relationship, and the use of dance to develop nonverbal body language to express emotions (San-Juan-Ferrer and Hipola 67 & 74).

In one of the pieces of dance research analyzed in the preceding study, it was discovered children between the ages of 4 and 7 learned to control their emotions and impulses and became more considerate of the emotions of others and in relationships with teachers and friends (San-Juan-Ferrer and Hipola 74). Several studies completed on secondary, university, and professional dancers indicated there was improvement in emotional regulation (San-Juan-Ferrer and Hipola 74–75). Taken together, these studies demonstrated a relationship between involvement in dance and emotional intelligence, well-being, self-efficacy, and emotional control (San-Juan-Ferrer and Hipola 75).

Another review of past SEL studies revealed that a cognitive-based creative dance curriculum might support learning socioemotional and communication skills along with developing a sense of identity, increased self-confidence, self-awareness, relationship skills, empathy, creativity, and the ability to make decisions (Payne and Costas 282). In a study on this topic conducted by the researchers, Pereira and Marques-Pinto, it was learned that dance improved students' self-management and relationship skills, while a second study by Horwitz et al. showed dance seemed to be involved with interpersonal emotional interplay (Payne and Costas 282). The authors pointed out that relationships can be developed nonverbally when students collaborate to make dances, while such a curriculum can promote emotional literacy or the ability to communicate emotions and sense them in others through movement (Payne and Costas 282).

Other authors were interested in why creative dance could be used to help preschool children express their emotions and develop socioemotional skills. The argument of these researchers was based on the fact that emotional experiences are extremely important in humans beginning at very early ages and that young children need to learn appropriate and socially acceptable ways to regulate their emotions (Cetin and Cevikbas 329). Since preschoolers often resort to expressing themselves nonverbally, creative dance is an appropriate instrument of expression for them (Cetin and Cevikbas 330). In addition, the authors pointed out that there is a strong connection between physical movement and emotional expression, although Canadian physical education professor Sheryle Bergmann promoted creative dance as more effective in this respect than learning sports skills, because creative movement can be used to express one's thoughts (Cetin and Cevikbas 332–33).

In 2019–2020, two New York schools provided a dance-based approach for third and fourth grade students to help them learn about SEL. The classes in this program combined five basic dance concepts with four aspects of SEL through a scaffolded use of inquiry, brainstorming, games, and debriefing; the students explored how language and movement choices connect with their senses, emotional expression, relationships, and the environment (Eddy et al. 196). The outcome of this program affected how the students experienced their environment, communicated, and dealt with conflicts; they also learned that body language affected their perceptions, increased meaning in verbal expressions, and improved how they approached conflict (Eddy et al. 196).

Another initiative was conducted through the educational programs' residency of the Hubbard Street Dance Chicago, with the purpose of focusing on how SEL competencies evolve during a dance residency through examination of the choreographic process and with the purpose to develop an academic mindset, social skills, and learning strategies; the most recent program included 2,100 students and seventy teachers across nine schools (Eddy et al. 198). After examining the residency videos, the researchers found the curriculum facilitated many SEL characteristics; in terms of self-awareness, the students demonstrated improved participation and performance, social skills became evident in the students' ability to collaborate, while they used self-management techniques to accomplish their goals (Eddy et al. 199).

Considering the preceding content, it should be recognized there are many points during which teaching dance and developing empathy and SEL skills intersect, leading to suggestions for the use of dance to develop these abilities.

Empathy and the Arts

Many advantages have been attributed to participation in the arts, including academic achievement and personal development in the form of inter- and intrapersonal traits. Some authorities believe that the most effective approach to school safety amid bullying incidents and violence is to address the students' emotional and psychological safety. "Creating school environments where students feel emotionally safe and valued as individuals not only helps with mental health issues . . . but also supports better student achievement" (Goodwin 83). Such goals can and should be nourished through participation in the arts, which provide opportunities for emotional expression and the satisfaction of personal achievement. At the end of the twentieth century, the Arts Education Partnership (AEP) published a collection of reports which showed low-income students who were high arts participants were more successful in school and life than their peers who were not as involved in the arts (Rabkin 7).

Recently, AEP indicated further research was needed to investigate the intersections between participation in the arts and the development of students' social skills (Omasta et al. 158–59). In their study, a research team used a technique called interpretive content analysis to determine the degree of alignment between the

National Core Arts Standards (NCAS) and SEL goals. The intersections of the arts and SEL standards were classified as either directly aligned (complete fulfillment of the arts standard and paired SEL goal), indirectly aligned (complete fulfillment of the arts standard and part of the paired SEL goal), or not aligned (no clear relationship between the arts standard and SEL goal (Omasta et al. 162).

When considering overall alignment among all arts disciplines and SEL goals, the researchers found the percentage of alignment ranged from 50% to 82%, although a much more modest outcome was achieved when comparing NCAS individually to ten meso-level SEL goals (Omasta et al. 164). In this study, the majority of dance standards did align with the SEL goals in terms of intrapersonal skills, but only a few aligned with the SEL goal of decision-making and responsible behavior (Omasta et al. 164). The recommendation of the researchers was that greater alignment between NCAS and the SEL goals might be achieved through deliberate lesson planning to make sure both types of learning goals are achieved (Omasta et al. 158).

Such deliberate lesson planning was adopted in New Jersey to intentionally connect SEL goals to work done in arts classrooms through the development of a matrix to provide arts educators with information needed to embed SEL components in their revised curricula. To do this, the revisions team explored all the intersections between the arts standards and SEL goals that would inform their revised teaching approach (Edgar and Morrison 146). Other points raised in this article were promoting the connection between the arts and SEL skills by emphasizing the relationship built between arts teachers and their students, focusing on the perseverance needed to achieve artistic excellence, understanding the autonomy developed by doing creative work, and creating the opportunity for discussions, acceptance, and appreciation of diversity (Edgar and Morrison 149).

In a study done in China, the researchers wanted to learn about the connection between arts participation and the social-emotional development of preschool students. Three hundred preschoolers were involved in this study, in which an experimental group was offered art appreciation and art creation activities on an alternative basis (Qiao et al. 2). Some of the art appreciation activities were observing paintings or ballet videos, while creative activities included drawing simple objects, making simple musical sequences, or role-playing in the form of simple scenes (Qiao et al. 2–3). The outcome of this study revealed improvement in emotional knowledge in both the experimental and control groups, although improvement was more significant in the experimental group (Qiao et al. 4).

Empathy and Dance

Susan Leigh Foster emphasized the importance of empathy in today's world, especially in relation to choreography. She wrote:

> As the degree of suffering among the world's impoverished peoples escalates along with the violence wrought by humans upon one another, the capacity

for empathy is being debated and reexamined. What has seldom been questioned in these debates . . . is the nature of the body itself that is claiming to feel what another body is feeling. . . . Choreography, whatever its meaning, can provide clues to this specific experience of the physical in the ways that records or documents movement, and also in the ways that it sets forth principles upon which movement is to be learned and crafted.

(174–75)

Studies on Developing Empathy through Dance

It is the belief of this author that what can be learned from and through movement and dance and what can be communicated is just being discovered and revealed. The following studies are some examples of research that has been completed with the goal of exploring the capacity of movement and dance to develop empathy among students.

In a study about creating empathy between students, the researcher Rebecca Epstein wanted to discover how movement and dance could be used to help fifth grade students be more empathetic toward each other even though they were from different cultural backgrounds. In this study, the students worked with a partner or partners with a different ethnic background to learn more about their culture (Epstein 29). To further her goals, the researcher, who was also the dance teacher, used teacher-to-student interviews and student-to-student interviews with the purpose of helping the students learn more about the cultural backgrounds of the other students in her classes (Epstein 30–32). Creative work was incorporated in the study by having the students write "I am" poems, create a visual artwork motif, and choreograph dances which were performed later; all creative work was based on the students' cultural backgrounds (Epstein 55–58). Overall, the researcher concluded participation in dance did seem to influence how empathetic the students became toward each other, an outcome that was especially evident in the final dance performance (Epstein 68).

Another dance teacher, Arianne MacBean, used inductive movement explorations and dance making to promote self-discovery and empathy among students. In one exercise, the teacher had her seventh graders bend down to the ground as if they were picking cotton from low bushes so they would experience the bodily feelings of African Americans who worked on the plantations in the past (MacBean 118). In another exercise, the students wrote "When you look at me, you see" on one side of a paper, and "When you look at me, you don't see" on the other side of the paper, followed by filling the paper with freewriting based on their responses to these statements. After circling five words that stood out, the students created movement phrases based on the words and later taught their phrases to their group, followed by a discussion to expose assumptions the students may have had about each other (MacBean 119).

In a third effort, a dance-for-camera project, the professors Rosely Conz and Stephany Slaughter used kinesthetic empathy to help college students understand

and connect with the instability experienced by immigrants; initial strategies used to create the film were to cast college students of different ethnicities in the film and include personal stories as told by community immigrants (3 & 5–6). Improvisation exercises based on the students' own immigrant experiences, creating a gesture expressing their personal identity and words related to the immigrant experience suggested by the professors, were used as inspirations to create movements for filmed dances (Conz and Slaughter 7). Later, the dance films were used as a catalyst in community workshops for younger dancers aged 11 to 17 to help them explore and understand immigration and its ramifications (Conz and Slaughter 9).

Finally, a study by Rachel Wade was based on the goal of creating more empathy for an individual who participated in the civil rights movement using a choreographic process designed for high school students (23). All the students had a chance to interview the individual on whose personal experiences their choreography was based, and later were divided into groups by choosing aspects of the interviewee's experiences in which they were most interested; pre- and post-surveys and journal reflections were used to assess the students' developing empathy for and understanding of the civil rights movement and for the person who participated in it as choreographic source material (Wade 25–27). The outcome of this project was that the students learned much about the brutality of the civil rights movement, how to collaborate with their peers, that they were more creative than they thought, and that choreography can be used as a mode of communication (Wade 52–55).

Neuroscience and Empathy

There is ample evidence that human empathy has a physical, bodily origin. One of the probing questions neuroscientist V. S. Ramachandran asked is whether human brains are hardwired for empathy and compassion. He asked this question because it appeared certain neurons in the brain fired when a patient's hand was poked and when someone watched the hand of this person being poked (6).

There are three areas in the brain which seem to have the ability to respond, as described in the preceding paragraph. These areas are Wernicke's area in the left temporal lobe, the prefrontal cortex, and the IPL, or inferior parietal lobule, in each parietal lobe; within these areas, there are a special class of nerve cells known as mirror neurons which fire when you perform an action and when you watch another person perform the same action (Ramachandran 22). Thus, mirror neurons empathize with the other person by reading their intentions and are usually accurate in guessing the intentions of another (Ramachandran 22). However, according to Ramachandran, there may be frontal inhibitory circuits that suppress automatic mimicry when it is not appropriate (124).

Mirror neurons also play a role in what can be termed mastery because the combination of sensory perception and responding motor actions of seeing a movement and mimicking it means, in many instances, the movement becomes automatic and a part of daily life and no longer requires conscious thought (Zull

36). In addition, the basis of learning to write involves mimicry in the form of copying letters (Zull 163).

In humans, the mirror neuron system may have turned inward, providing a person with a representation of one's own mind, leading to the human capacity for self-awareness. Disturbances in the human mirror neuron system can lead to a wide range of symptoms—dissolution of internal boundaries and personal identity and body image issues (Ramachandran 260–61).

The preceding information about empathy and the human mirror neuron system can also be related to the increasingly multicultural world in which one lives today. If the brain is presented with stimuli that are unfamiliar or uninteresting, the mirror neuron system might ignore it, although there could be an attempt to interpret such stimuli in a meaningful way—a response which could lead to a negative or embarrassing outcome. Such an outcome might be experienced by someone attempting to become assimilated in a new culture (Westbrook 327).

Studies on Movement and Mirror Neurons

As explained in Chapter 3, gestures have been successfully used to complement and communicate lesson content—a technique which could be helpful to learners with low visuospatial abilities (Brucker et al. 27–28). In their study, a group of researchers wanted to learn whether gestures performed by others are helpful in learning about nonhuman movements and if activation of the learner's mirror neuron system was involved. The results of this research showed that performing gestures related to the to-be-learned movements activated the mirror neuron system of low-visuospatial learners, enabling them to achieve the same learning outcomes as the high-visuospatial learners (Brucker et al. 35). However, the results were different when noncorresponding gestures were used in the lessons, since learning in the low-visuospatial learners depended on activation of their inferior parietal cortex; when this area of the brain was not activated, this group achieved poor results (Brucker et al. 35). The two conditions used in this study were movement patterns performed in animations of a swimming fish accompanied by corresponding human hand gestures, and the same fish animations accompanied by noncorresponding human hand gestures. (Brucker et al. 29).

Many mirror neuron studies have been done on monkeys, and this was originally how the operation of mirror neurons was discovered. In one such study, the researchers were interested in studying the relationship between gaze direction and actions performed by others. In this study, a monkey watched while the experimenter performed a grasping action while orienting his gaze either toward or away from the targeted object (Coudé et al. 3145). As a result, the researchers found mirror neuron properties are not limited to actual physical cues but extend to social signals, such as the direction of the experimenter's gaze as a representation of intention (Coudé et al. 3152). Counterintuitively, one-half of the targeted neurons responded to the use of a congruent gaze directed toward the object, while the other one-half were activated in response to a noncongruent gaze away from the object—an outcome that may have demonstrated plasticity of the mirror neuron system (Coudé et al. 3152).

Neuroscience, Empathy, and Dance

Some neuroscience studies have involved dance. Emily Cross and her colleagues have been interested in studying the responses of the mirror neuron system or, more broadly, the action observation network (AON) of novice and expert dancers. These researchers prefer to study responses in the AON because it encompasses all brain regions involved with observing actions (Cross 215–17). When the brains of expert dancers were scanned, Cross and her associates learned there were precise and rapid changes in the AON when the dancers were learning new dance movements, particularly in the left premotor cortex and left inferior parietal lobule—areas which contain the major mirror neuron systems in humans (219).

In another study, Cross was interested in studying novice dancers using fMRI sessions, with the result that physical practice engaged targeted components of the AON above passively observing movements (223–25). This outcome might suggest that previous physical practice is an important component of learning in dance through mimicry.

Some of the neuroscience studies of dance have been concerned with what goes on in the mind of one observing dance. During a dance performance, two processes are occurring simultaneously; one is the dancer performing on the stage, and the other is the audience member who views the onstage actions with both entities focusing on the movements (Calvo-Merino 195). One point made by Beatriz Calvo-Merino is that many academics and philosophers like Lotze, James, or Munsterberg have supported the idea that there is a common, shared mental mechanism for both action and perception; interestingly, mirror neurons seem to have both a congruency in terms of their visual and motor responses (196). Thus, past studies have demonstrated that there is a correspondence between observed actions and their internal motor representation (Calvo-Merino 198).

In a study performed by Calvo-Merino and her colleagues, fMRI scanning was used to measure brain activity of ballet dancers and capoeira performers when they viewed videos of ballet dancers and capoeiristas, with the outcome that when viewing movements, particularly familiar movements, one performs an internal simulation that is represented in the brain's AON (200).

Another point Calvo-Merino pursued was that viewing dance is an aesthetic pursuit distributed among three processes or networks which are perceptual, cognitive, and emotional (205). The researchers discovered that the brain activity of the subjects was different when they viewed videos of dance movements they liked compared to those they did not like as measures of the subjects' aesthetic evaluation of the movements. When the subjects liked the movements, two brain regions seemed to be active during the neuroaesthetic responses. These areas were in the early visual cortex in the medial region and premotor cortex of the right hemisphere; no significant brain responses were found when the subjects viewed videos of dance movements they did not like (Calvo-Merino 207–08).

In their article, Guido Orgs et al. described components of the communicative process which takes place during a dance performance as part of the aesthetic exchange. These components include the performer or dancer who conveys information to the audience via his or her movements; the message that is conveyed based on the visual, action, and social features of the dancer's movements; and processing and acknowledgment of the movements by the spectator (239–41). The neural structures responsible for aesthetic perception in dance involve the visual cortex and motor, premotor, and parietal brain areas (Orgs et al. 242).

It is interesting that the discoveries of Calvo-Merino and others parallel comments made at a much earlier date by *New York Times* dance critic John Martin when he attempted to describe how and why audience members experience and respond to a dance performance. It was Martin's contention that movement was the medium through which aesthetic and emotional content could be transferred between the consciousness of individuals (13). Martin wrote that it is by way of "kinesthetic sympathy you respond to the impulse of the dancer which has expressed itself by means of a series of movements" (12).

Learning by watching the movements of others is a basic human skill and integral to learning in dance technique class and choreographic rehearsals. However, identifying what happens in the brain of the learner is in its infancy of understanding what goes on during this type of learning; focusing on the human mirror neuron system has contributed much to the study of observational learning but has led to neglecting the role of other systems and their interactions, such as the motor system and brain regions associated with semantic processing, attention, and memory (Ramsey et al. 478–79).

Of particular interest in the preceding article was understanding the role of nonmotor brain systems in observational motor learning. One of the nonmotor systems is the brain's cognitive control system, which regulates other mental processes and guides attention to what is relevant in the environment; another concerns the human reward system, which tracks the value of a trial or task (Ramsey et al. 485–86). Other brain systems which will require further investigation to better understand observational motor learning are the processes by which meaning is extracted from interactions with the environment and discovering how such learning unfolds in the real world (Ramsey et al. 486).

Nonverbal Communication

There are many ways to communicate nonverbally or without words. Physical gestures, body postures, and works of art all communicate nonverbally. It is rare that anyone speaks without accompanying their words with physical gestures. In fact, one of my favorite endeavors is to watch people in airports and other public places while attempting to assess how they are thinking and feeling based on their facial expression, gestures, gait, movement speed, and posture.

Nonverbal communication is often referred to as body language; David Matsumoto et al. defined *nonverbal communication* as "the transfer and exchange of messages in any and all modalities that do not involve words" (4). This definition implies that nonverbal communication encompasses more than body language; it can include the distance between people as they converse, sweat stains on clothing, manner of dress, placement of furniture in a room, colors used when decorating, use of time, or bumper stickers placed on a car (Matsumoto et al. 4). Nonverbal communication is important because only about 35% of communication takes place through language, while 65% is based on the use of movement, posture, distance between those communicating, and other nonverbal behaviors (Samovar, et al. 155). However, since this book is about bridging the mind-body divide, the discussion here will be limited to the bodily or physical aspects of nonverbal communication.

The Historical Developments in Nonverbal Communication

The work of Françoise Delsarte in the nineteenth century can be historically connected to nonverbal communication because he was concerned with describing how humans moved in various situations for the purpose of imparting emotions to an observer. Genevieve Stebbins taught classes based on the Delsarte system and correlated the type of energy being used in each body region and the position of body parts to types of characters and their emotional states (Foster 105). "[W]ith Delsarte's theory of expression and Stebbins' application of his system, movement was seen as embodying types of energy and directions of energy flow that corresponded to types of feelings" (Foster 106).

Stebbins developed a series of exercises and published books based on these ideas in the first part of the twentieth century. The routines or pantomimes which Stebbins devised resembled artistic, statue-like poses that transitioned the body through different dramatic moments (Foster 106). A photo of some of the statue-like poses can be seen in Figure 4.1.

Delsarte's theories about movement and nonverbal communication connect as well with John Martin's ideas presented previously in this chapter. In a book based on a series of lectures presented in 1931–1932, Martin wrote there is no difficulty following the meaning of movements observed because you have performed them yourself, and through sympathetic muscular memory, it is possible to associate an observed movement with its purpose (12). When watching dance, Martin continued, "There is a kinesthetic response in the body of the spectator, which to some extent reproduces in him the experience of the dancer" (48).

In a giant step forward, psychologist Edward Titchener was one of the first to connect kinesthetic bodily responses to the mind of the mover. He argued that one's kinesthetic sensations, together with visual and auditory input, created images or traces in the mind related to bodily actions (Foster 111). Although often an unconscious phenomenon, Titchener believed kinesthetic sensations were a type of thinking (Foster 111).

Role of Body in Interpersonal Connections and Communications   127

FIGURE 4.1 Stebbins-based pantomime depicting grief by five women, each of which portrays a different aspect of grief. Photo determined to be in the public domain. Photo originally appeared in Wilbor, Elsie. *Delsarte Recitation Book*, 4th ed. Edgar Werner & Company, 1905.

Further developments by psychologists James Gibson in the 1960s and Alain Berthoz in the 1990s elaborated on the connection between kinesthetic input and the mind. In contrast to previous theories, Gibson proposed that perception was an active process in which information was extracted from the environment and that kinesthesia was a central aspect of that process by providing input concerning one's orientation in relation to gravity and progression through space (Foster 115–16). Like Gibson, Berthoz believed kinesthesia played an important role in orientation and organization of the senses, but that perception simulated action even though all observers did not share a common environment and each person could view the world differently (Foster 122). Berthoz proposed that attention had an anticipatory quality because the brain could simulate movement options based on previous kinesthetic knowledge (Foster 122).

Cultural Differences in Nonverbal Communication

Having spent some time in Hong Kong, Taiwan, and Japan, the author can attest to the differences in use of nonverbal communication between the East and West. When flying on a Korean airline, the flight attendants greet customers with a bow before they board a plane, and when parting from a meeting with friends, the same postural gesture is used.

Gestures often accompany speech, but the use of such gestures is more acceptable in some cultures than it is in others. For example, Latin and Middle Eastern cultures encourage the use of illustrative gestures when speaking; it is especially acceptable to use one's hands when speaking in Italy, while use of gestures while speaking, especially when in public, is discouraged in East Asian cultures and can be considered impolite and even aggressive (Matsumoto and Hwang 77).

Pointing is another common gesture that accompanies speech, but in the United States, the index finger is used to point, while the Japanese use the middle finger (Matsumoto and Hwang 77). Other examples of gestural differences are that in China, all the fingers are crooked in a beckoning gesture, but Americans use only the index finger when performing this gesture with the same meaning; in China, two fingers beside the head indicate the person is thinking, and circling the index finger by the head in America means someone may be a bit crazy (Cai 291–92).

There are also cultural differences in the use of posture which refers to the way a person carries or positions their body. In China, both men and women stand when they are introduced, but in America, the woman does not need to stand during an introduction, unless the man has a very high social status; it is also considered offensive in China for a student to remain seated when answering a question or for a person to lean back in their chair or put their feet up when talking to another person (Cai 292).

Intercultural communication has become increasingly important in a globally interconnected world, especially in the arena of international business. Jeffrey Sanchez-Burks et al. wrote that communication can be direct or indirect; based on previous research, indirect forms of communication go beyond words and include nonverbal bodily cues, such as looking down or avoiding eye contact. The hypothesis of the authors was that Americans would be less attuned to relational indirect cues in work settings compared to social settings (Sanchez-Burks et al 364). The outcomes of four studies done on indirect communication differences between Eastern and Western cultures provided mixed results but demonstrated that indirectness is relatively dynamic and dependent on context. Thus, East-West differences related to indirect communication seemed to be apparent in work settings but not as pronounced in social settings (Sanchez-Burks et al. 370).

A study was done on eight factors which could affect intercultural communication; a group of Japanese university students participated in the study by answering a questionnaire related to the eight factors (Munezane 1664). Although there were limitations to this study, various activities were believed to improve intercultural communication, including teaching the nonverbal aspects of communication (Munezane 1674). Michael Byram, who has researched foreign language education, suggested learners could research the nonverbal communication styles found in different cultures for the purpose of comparing them in a nonjudgmental way (Munezane 1674).

In a recent article, another author pointed out that movement patterns are learned and unconsciously represent cultural conditioning and one's identity; they reflect an absorbed value system (Larimer 24). Movement patterns have their origin in the body's muscular system and are intimately involved with kinesthesia. Recognition of cultural movement patterns can lead to interesting classroom discussions and perhaps lead to personal changes; "physical experience of a conceptual theory can give students a more personal relationship to the material and potentially energize them to pursue a more extensive inquiry as well as create new ways of moving" (Larimer 25).

Nonverbal Communication through Dance

It seems that all involved with dance would agree that dance communicates nonverbally, although there are different ways in which one can make use of and explain this property.

According to Edward Warburton, "[a] growing body of research suggested that the nonverbal art form of dance can be an effective medium for intercultural communication and exchange between people from different cultures" ("Dance Marking" 131). ArtsCross is an entity designed to produce a more productive debate between East and West; through observations and interviews, Warburton was able to examine the responses of dancers as they rehearsed works created by choreographers from Taipei, Beijing, and London ("Dance Marking" 131 & 133). One of his observations was that the dancers learned the choreography nonverbally through a process of marking or practicing the movements in a minimal manner; Warburton concluded that the marking process was a cognitive reduction process that distributed the weight of mental activity, making it less intense and a more digestible method of diplomacy ("Dance Marking" 137).

The role of dance as cultural exchange was also manifest in a qualitative study by Alfdaniels Mabingo, who sought to understand the intercultural meanings students at New York University attached to their experience of learning Ugandan dances, songs, rhythms, and stories; student performers with varied dance backgrounds participated in the study in which data included dancer interviews and journal reflections made by the researcher/choreographer (51). Student responses to learning the dances indicated that a different process was used to learn the African dances because the movements, songs, and rhythms were learned wholistically rather than in a piecemeal fashion, since the technique and dance are taught simultaneously; the students also experienced a constant feeling of being grounded rather than sensing weight shifts found in other dance forms (Mabingo 52). Overall, the students felt the movements, songs, and drumming connected them together as a group and created a communal feeling, in contrast to Western dance genres, in which the focus is on the individual, while Mabingo's use of storytelling supplied a contextual framework and helped supersede a purely imitative form of learning (54).

The nonverbal traits of dance, specifically Graham technique, have been used to enhance female empowerment—a teaching strategy which is based on self-discovery, ownership of movement, and exploring different aspects of the body as related to the psyche (Harrington 35). Some of the techniques used in these classes included discovering how the movements communicate nonverbally to avoid being seen as an object, helping students make accommodations when movements do not fit on their bodies, exploring the Laban efforts, creating an awareness of the social body by relating to other dancers, and understanding the social themes at the heart of many Graham works; the students also worked with partners, coaching each other as they practiced movements learned in class and experienced Graham's floor exercises with their eyes closed (Harrington 40–41).

The ability of dance to communicate nonverbally has also been used to generate peaceable behaviors. Somatic dance, in particular, can be used to reduce stress caused by conflict and return the body to homeostasis (Eddy "Dancing Solutions" 103). The dance-based strategies suggested by Eddy included performing expressive movement, engaging in deep breathing, developing a kinesthetic sensory awareness, exploring imaginary situations that trigger anger, and interacting with others peacefully through dance ("Dancing Solutions" 105). Eddy indicated that an appreciation of different movement styles builds tolerance by learning dances from other cultures ("Dancing Solutions" 107). In addition, conflict resolution can be resolved through active witnessing, in which pairs of students focus on a conflict situation by first describing it and then by telling the same story through movement, followed by having the other partner echo the essence or meaning of the first person's movements; the witnessing concludes by having each partner describe the feelings experienced (Eddy "Dancing Solutions" 108).

Closely connected to conflict resolution was a study in which a salsa dance class was used to teach participants about consent within the environment of a social dance class (McMains 1). One of the exercises described in the article was to help students recognize nonverbal cues exhibited when a dance partner feels uncomfortable. Such cues could be a partner's increased bodily tension or a facial expression, such as a grimace or nervous laughter (McMains 7). The other exercises used in the salsa classes included verbal comments about how to say no respectfully when asked to dance, or discussing whether movements such as dips might make a partner uncomfortable (McMains 5–6).

Symbolic Communication

Written and spoken words are a form of symbolic communication. In addition, visual images, sounds, or movement gestures are also a form of symbolic communication, but forms which are nonverbal.

In his book about symbols, David Fontana indicated symbols are an inherent form of human expression and have prevailed in all cultures throughout our history, with one of their first appearances in Paleolithic cave paintings (8). Fontana wrote, "[S]ymbols are more than just cultural artifacts: in their correct context, they . . . speak powerfully . . . simultaneously addressing our intellect, emotions and spirit" (8).

Symbols are distinguished from signs because *signs* are straightforward, may be a part of a language, and give one an immediate message which is of momentary importance; a symbol is an image that represents an idea which is deeper and an indicator of a universal truth (Hennessy 6). Although written and spoken words usually represent meanings in a direct way, some forms, such as metaphors, are not as directly understood. Visual symbolic images and gestures also transmit messages both directly and indirectly and can be considered forms of nonverbal communication.

Swiss psychiatrist and psychologist Carl Jung described symbols as implying something more than could obviously be understood (20). Jung's description of symbols clearly connects with symbolic communication in its indirect mode. In addition, representations Jung called natural symbols, as contrasted with cultural symbols, were derived, he believed, from the unconscious part of the mind (93), although he noted that the conscious part of the mind developed relatively slowly in the human evolutionary process (23)

In his book, Leonard Shlain presented a different and interesting take on nonverbal and verbal symbols as functions of the right and left brain, respectively. The right brain, he wrote, is nonverbal, connected with generating feelings, and provides an all-at-once or nonlinear experience; it is better at understanding imagery, recognizing faces, experiencing the emotional content of speech, appreciating music, and perceiving space, among other nonverbal functions (18–21). The left brain operates in a linear, nonholistic fashion and in connection with words and numbers; it analyzes, strategizes, and thinks in logical steps (21–22). One final point made by Shlain is that women seem to have more neuronal connections between the two sides of the brain, which could account for a higher level of integration between brain hemispheres and for the female ability to communicate emotions more readily (23).

Literal and Abstraction as Symbolic Processes

Literal symbols are a direct illustration of the content they represent. Some examples of literal symbols are the signs on restroom doors or those representing that you are about to enter a traffic circle on a roadway. Many literal symbols can be found in photographs because the objects seen are an attempt to represent the most perfect reproduction of the actual objects.

Abstraction is a process in art and in the symbol making process in which there is an attempt to capture the essence or core of whatever is represented. One way to understand abstraction and its indirect nature is to consider the feeling response to whatever is represented in the symbol as an abstraction (Minton *Using Movement* 39). For example, imagine you are hiking through a forest filled with evergreen trees and you can see the blue sky above framed by the trees. The path along which you are hiking is also surrounded by wildflowers in hues of pink, purple, red, yellow, and white. Then, consider your feeling response to this environment and how best to capture this response in a symbol. Would you feel joyous, nostalgic, or enclosed by what you experienced in the surrounding environment?

Abstracting can also be considered a process of elimination. This means that whoever created such a symbol eliminated all but a key element from their observations and thinking; the underlying goal in an abstraction can involve singling out one important feature of the inspiration on which to create the symbol (Root-Bernsteins 72–73). It was Picasso's belief that an abstraction can also reveal less-obvious properties of whatever is represented—a feature which requires one to think and find hidden properties—which is an important aspect of Picasso's paintings (Root-Bernsteins 73).

Artwork based on differing degrees of abstraction was the subject of a research project to determine the subjects' aesthetic preferences. In this study, a group of fifty-nine adults which included forty-nine females was asked to respond to a set of 150 images produced by lesser-known artists; subjects' responses were based on how meaningful and complex the paintings appeared as a basis for the subjects' aesthetic judgments (Ball et al. 240–41). The outcome of this study showed that the subjects preferred more complex works based on judgments of beauty, but only when these works were relatively easy to understand conceptually (Ball et al. 235).

In most circles, the belief is that symbols, whether they are literal or encompass abstraction, are of no use unless they can be interpreted and understood. Kerry Freedman and Robyn Seglem, who are concerned with visual literacy, proposed that understanding visual images, whether they are in the form of visual symbols or works of art, is becoming important today because there is an increased focus on the visual as a mode of communication, resulting in a need for a higher level of visual literacy; this means students need to be able to use images to make sense of their world (Beier 37–38). Thus, visual literacy is based on assumptions that such images can be read and known; instead, the recommendation in this article was to encourage tapping into the effect such imagery has on the body outside the prevalent concept of visual literacy and meaning making (Beier 49). It is important to note that this conclusion seems especially relevant to the mind-body dichotomy debate and the role of the body in learning.

Language as a Form of Symbolic Communication

According to Shlain, gestures as a form of person-to-person communication probably preceded speech, but when written words began to be used, the dominance of the human left brain increased; thus, in reading and writing, one primarily uses the left hemisphere of the brain, since, unlike with speech, the connection with one's emotions are less direct when understanding the written word (40).

However, there seem to be multiple theories as to how or why human language came to be, because there are no intermediate documented steps which describe its evolution (Ramachandran 165). One theory, developed by linguist Noam Chomsky, is the principle of emergence; a second theory is that language is connected to the development of thinking because it supplied a more sophisticated way to represent content; and a third theory, proposed by linguist Steven Pinker, is that language is instinctual and an adaptation which evolved through natural selection for the purpose of communication (Ramachandran 165–67).

Perhaps some light can be shed on the evolution of language by understanding how and why infants learn a language. Language is the first symbolic system children learn, but it is not the only one, because many children are exposed to numbers, maps, and other types of symbols early in life (Xu 848). Language enables infants to group objects which share perceptual features into categories and distinguish between object categories; as early as 3 months, words become symbols that go beyond perceptual similarities and which infants use to form beliefs about objects and categories of objects (Xu 849). This description of the development of language in infants seems to connect with the relationship between language and thinking.

While it is possible to sense the nonverbal elements that accompany speech, such as the tone of a speaker's voice, along with their gestures and postures, these aspects are missing from the written word. In addition, written words present content in a linear, sequential manner and lack the wholistic nature of nonverbal communication forms (Shlain 44).

However, some forms of written language do communicate nonverbally, as is true of metaphors. In addition, metaphor should be included in a discussion of symbols because it is a form of symbolic language. Metaphor is also related to abstraction because it is the use of a word or phrase to apply to an object or concept that it does not usually represent but which communicates a meaning as an essence. Some examples of metaphors are "a walk in the park," indicating a task was easy to accomplish, or "drowning in paperwork," meaning, that one is falling behind on the job. Metaphors are also connected to abstraction because the meaning behind a metaphor communicates how someone feels. Based on the previous examples, it is clear a metaphor cannot be interpreted literally and requires that listeners shift their focus from the literal meaning of the words used in the metaphor to a more feeling-oriented meaning; metaphors often require the listener to create a visual image in their mind as well to arrive at the correct interpretation (Baker 258–59).

In a discussion of the symbolic nature of language, Emmanuel Nzeaka pointed out that symbolic media languages, such as emoticons, emojis, and memes, are challenging more traditional languages by providing communication that overrides traditional methods of linguistic communication (190). To test this hypothesis, the author surveyed 267 Nigerian students aged 15 to 20 years concerning their use of symbolic media languages, with the outcome that over 92% understand and use the alternative forms, while 68% thought the symbols could be used to communicate with those who spoke different languages; the trend was toward a potential for using a blend of memes, emoticons, and emojis in written communications (Nzeaka 196 & 203).

Symbol Use in Western versus Eastern Cultures

Symbolic images can be connected to a particular cultural group. In fact, the same images have appeared in both Western and Eastern cultures but differ in the meaning communicated. One such symbol is the dragon, which was initially a Chinese creation; in China it represents glory connected with the emperor and sun, while in European Christian art, it has a negative connotation (Hennessy 8). Rats, snakes, and trees also have different symbolic meanings in the West compared to Eastern interpretations. In Asia, the rat represents good luck, while it is commonly associated with decay and destruction in the West; in Buddhism, the snake is seen in a more positive light, while Christians connect it with evil and corruption; and the tree of life, known in many Eastern cultures, represents immortality, but the tree of knowledge is associated with the Judeo-Christian tradition, combining elements of good and evil (Hennessy 53, 67 & 97).

More abstract visual symbols also provide East/West contrasts in their interpretations. For example, the triangle, sometimes framing an eye, represents God the Father in Christianity, while the equilateral triangle is a Hindu symbol of gender—male with the apex pointed up, and female when the apex is pointed down (Hall 7). In contrast, the circle, another abstract symbol, stands for the cosmos, heavens, or a supreme deity in both the East and West (Hall 1). The mandala is another abstract, symbolic image traditionally associated with Eastern cultures where Buddhism or Hinduism are practiced. The word *mandala* comes from the Indian Sanskrit and means circle or completeness and is a tool used in meditation (Hennessy 293).

There are also some basic differences in the symbols used in Western languages versus those used in Eastern languages. The first alphabet appeared when pictograms were transformed into symbols representing individual sounds; all current alphabets were derived from the North Semitic in about 1700 BCE and led to the Phoenician alphabet, the first one to be based on speech sounds, and later to the development of the Hebrew alphabet and European alphabets via Greece (Hennessy 306). Today, there are basically eight alphabet groups used in languages; these include Arabic, Aramaic, Armenian, Brahmi, Cyrillic, Georgian, Greek, and Latin (Worldfactsinc). From this list, it is easy to see that five of these alphabets are connected to Western cultures. Chinese characters, which date from about 1500 BCE, is one of the oldest writing systems in use today, but it is not considered an alphabet but a combination of pictograms and abstract symbols which represent whole words (Hennessy 309).

Symbolic Use of Gesture

In many instances, movements in the form of gestures are symbolic. There are many common gestures used daily, such as waving, pointing, or communicating *stop* by holding the arm up with a flexed wrist and the palm facing forward. Some of these gestures have become so common that they are used without thinking about them.

Research by Susan Golden-Meadow and others who have studied children's use of gestures when communicating ideas has shown their preference for gestures, especially when the children are too young to know the proper words (Macedonia and Klimesch 75). However, these two researchers wanted to discover whether the use of gestures supported memory when learning new words (Macedonia and Klimesch 76). Twenty-nine German-speaking college students participated in a study in which they learned thirty-six words that comprised an artificial vocabulary in which each word was assigned a meaning in German; learning the words was done under two conditions—one without the accompanying gesture, and one with it (Macedonia and Klimesch 76–78). An artificial language was used because there are recognizable connections between Western languages, such as those between English and German and English and the Romance languages.

The researchers concluded that accompanying learning words with more detailed sensory information makes retrieval more efficient; thus, the performance of a gesture along with learning a word enriches the brain network, producing deep coding along with enhancing retrieval from memory (Macedonia and Klimesch 82). In another study, the researcher investigated how to improve teaching and learning the Thai and Japanese languages by suggesting that a coordinated use of speech and gesture should be part of the teaching strategies (Kimura 675).

Those who have studied how children learn languages have hypothesized based on observations that there are common factors between children's early use of words and symbolic gestures (Suanda and Namy 143). Although previous researchers discovered there was a connection between the way infants learn words and use gestures, in two studies conducted by Suanda and Namy, it was concluded that the operation of this connection appeared to diverge at the age of 18 months (151). A review of literature on the topic of using gestures to help children learn language seemed to concur with the preceding conclusion; in their review, Elizabeth Fitzpatrick and her colleagues reported that there were no apparent benefits from adults' use of baby sign language, although no studies reported ill effects from its use (507).

Other researchers were interested in studying when and why gestures are imitated automatically from person to person during social interactions. Tanya Chartrand and Rick van Baaren, who have studied human mimicry, communicated that imitation is an interesting feature of human social interactions and may serve an important social function (Cracco et al. 187). One experiment conducted by the researchers included forty first-year psychology students with normal or corrected-to-normal vision at a Belgian university; this study demonstrated that automatic imitation of a gesture was weaker when the gesture was antisocial in nature (Cracco et al. 180 & 182). In a follow-up study including 120 participants similar to those in the first study, the researchers found that automatic gestural imitation is sensitive to context and "that imitative responses are inhibited when they could go against social norms" (Cracco et al. 183–84).

Symbols and Dance

Symbolic, pantomimic gestures have been a part of many choreographies. For example, the interplay between James and the Sylphide in the ballet *La Sylphide* aptly communicates the interplay between the two—his interest and desire and her tantalizing elusiveness. The use of gestures is also the focus of the ballet *Lilac Garden*, in which the tortured relationship between two former lovers is expressed through a brush of hands, hurried embrace, or the young woman holding the back of a hand to her forehead to express her agony at not being able to marry her lover (Terry 192).

One way to discuss the symbolic nature of a dance is to analyze the emotions communicated by specific movements. For instance, angular or diagonal actions can convey a threat, and rounded arms warmth (Gervasio 261). Different gestures typically communicate other feelings—joy with open or flat hands, or anger with crossed arms and hands in fists (Gervasio 268–69).

In her article, Henrietta Bannerman discussed the Graham contraction as a movement device which could be described as a symbolic icon. She noted that "the contraction draws the gaze to the visceral area of the body and connects with the sheer physicality of the sensation experienced by the dancer"; thus, this movement points to an emotional area of the body as defined culturally (24–25). In the same article, Bannerman also described Cunningham's symbolic use of movements which were animalistic in nature even though his work is usually described as nonliteral or without a communicative intent. She noted that in *Points in Space*, the dancers swoop and flap or soar and hover like a flock of birds (30).

Another example of a symbolic use of movement can be found in Kenneth MacMillan's one-act ballet *Winter Dreams*, based on Chekhov's play *Three Sisters*, which is about the sisters' dream of one day returning to their original home in Moscow (Kodera 109). The hero character in this ballet performs big steps and leaps to communicate his strength and nobility and is thus described as a symbol of hope; a second character in the same ballet represents fear through his performance of unattractive actions, which are described as awkward and angularly shaped (Kodera 113–14).

There are many culturally based dance genres which are organized around hand gestures which communicate symbolic meanings. Eastern Indian dance is an example of such a form. David Frawley, director of the American Institute of Vedic Studies, wrote that mudras, or hand gestures, are used traditionally in three ways in India—in yoga practice, religious rituals, and Indian dance and drama (Carroll and Carroll 9). "The Sanskrit word *mudra* means 'attitude,' 'gesture,' or 'seal'"; some of the mudras used in classical Indian dance are performed for the purpose of expression, while others are pure dance (Carroll and Carroll 18 & 25).

Some examples of specific mudras and their meaning as they are used in classical Indian dance follow. When the hands are positioned with the palms facing and the dancer forms two interlocking rings by touching the thumbs and forefingers of each hand, a gesture is performed which denotes a monkey; in a second mudra, the hand is held with the palm facing up and the little finger is brought as close as possible to the palm while the other fingers are fanned apart so the thumb is extended at ninety degrees to the index finger to perform a mudra known as the fully opened lotus (Carroll and Carroll 38 & 41). These mudras can be seen in Figures 4.2a and 4.2b, while Figure 4.3 shows an Odissi dancer as she performs a mudra.

Role of Body in Interpersonal Connections and Communications **137**

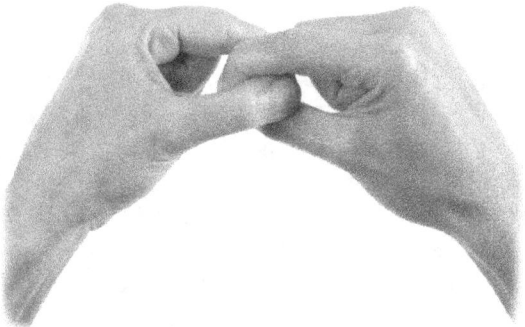

FIGURE 4.2A Adhomushti Mukula mudra denoting a monkey. Carroll, Cain, and Revital Carroll. *Mudras of India: A Comprehensive Guide to the Hand Gestures of Yoga and Indian Dance.*

Source: Singing Dragon, Jessica Kingsley Publishers, 2013, p. 38. Copyright © Cain Carroll and Revital Carroll 2012, 2013. Reproduced with permission of Licensor through PLSclear.

FIGURE 4.2B Alapadma mudra denoting a fully opened lotus. Carroll, Cain, and Revital Carroll. *Mudras of India: A Comprehensive Guide to the Hand Gestures of Yoga and Indian Dance.*

Source: Singing Dragon, Jessica Kingsley Publishers, 2013, p. 41. Copyright © Cain Carroll and Revital Carroll 2012, 2013. Reproduced with permission of Licensor through PLSclear.

Many movements performed in the hula are also symbolic. The earliest form of the Hawaiian dance, known as mele hula, was both a religious and public form; the religious form was performed in a temple under the direction of a priest and connected with a specific deity, and the public forms honored chiefs and royalty or were danced for pleasure (Lakainapali).

FIGURE 4.3 Odissi dancer performing the Mayura mudra denoting a peacock. Carroll, Cain, and Revital Carroll. *Mudras of India: A Comprehensive Guide to the Hand Gestures of Yoga and Indian Dance.*

Source: Singing Dragon, Jessica Kingsley Publishers, 2013, p. 25 & 154. Copyright © Cain Carroll and Revital Caroll 2012, 2013. Reproduced with permission of Licensor through PLSclear.

Every movement, expression, and gesture in the hula has a meaning, but the hands are of particular significance; the chants that accompany the dancing help tell the story (Lakainapali). The hula includes intricate combinations of footwork, movements of the hips, and gestures, all of which illustrate prayers, songs, and historical epics; some of the movements in the hula are the result of observing movements in nature (Uchiyama 1 & 5).

There are three basic types of gestures performed in the hula: (1) those in which the movements of the hands are a symbol of a specific object, such as flower or tree; (2) gestures which represent types of movement, such as wind, rain, or paddling a canoe; and (3) gestures which stand for more abstract concepts, like love, sorrow, or power (Uchiyama 60). Each hula is accompanied by a particular song, and the words are interpreted with the movements of the hands (Uchiyama 81).

Dance and Notation Symbols

A connection between dance and symbols can be found in notation systems which have been used to record dance steps and movements. One of the first of these was a system originally devised by Pierre Beauchamps in the 1680s and later described by Raoul-Auger Feuillet in 1700; in Feuillet notation, the musical notation was displayed across the top of the page, with the floor pattern or pathway the dancers were supposed to follow pictured below, along with markings for the musical bars shown on the diagram of the dancers' pathway (Beauchamps-Feuillet notation).

In 1955, another dance notation system was introduced by Rudolf Benesh. In this system, the dancer's movements are plotted from behind, as if the dancer were superimposed on a staff which extends from the head down to the feet. The five horizontal lines on the staff designate the top of the head, shoulders, waist, knees, and feet; other symbols are added to notate movement quality and dimension (Benesh Movement Notation). Additional symbols are included to represent movements performed in front, to the side, and behind the body, while a direction sign is placed below the staff when the movement direction changes (Benesh Movement Notation).

Labanotation, the most widespread movement notation system used today, was first described by Rudolf Laban in 1928. This system was further developed by Ann Hutchinson Guest in the United States and by Albrecht Knust in Europe, where it is called Kinetography Laban. Ann Hutchinson Guest became inspired to develop a more flexible body of notation that would be applicable to children. She based it on the prime actions of movement and called this framework the Movement Alphabet®, which became the inspiration upon which she developed a pedagogical system that has been used with adults and dance teachers worldwide to explore, create, perform, record, analyze, and teach movement and which is called the Language of Dance® (LOD) (Heiland "Personal").

The aforementioned writing system, or Motif Notation, developed over time to include numerous concepts. While a few symbols are related to those of Labanotation, the system is entirely independent of Labanotation and depicted with a less-formal staff which is read from the bottom of the staff upward to indicate how the movements progress over time, and horizontally from the center outward, to indicate the body part used to perform the movements (Guest and Curran 3–5). If metered timing is desired, musical bars and tick marks using short horizontal lines can be placed horizontally within the staff (Guest and Curran 13–15). For creative activities, the concept of relative time can be used. Motif Notation is flexible and allows choices in level of complexity in the writing of concepts. The concepts of body actions, space, time, energy, relationships, phrasing, and stillness can be represented and described using LOD in a basic or highly nuanced approach (Hutchinson Guest 1–14). The LOD approach to pedagogy developed to include sensing, observing, reflecting, identifying, interpreting, notating, and creating appropriate to many types of dance and activities for all ages (Heiland *Leaping*).

Edward Warburton was interested in studying the effect movement notation might have on learning in dance; in this study, ninety-six children aged 8 to 9 years participated in an eight-week dance program in which dance notation was integrated, along with a control group who participated in the dance program but did not experience the notation (193). The purpose and implication of this study was that learning the language of dance can have conceptional and cognitive effects (Warburton 196). This supposition was based on the study of symbolization by many in psychology, such as Gardner, Gardner and Wolf, Vygotsky and Werner, and Kaplan, that symbolizing activity can provide an organizing function (Warburton 196).

The outcome of the previous study indicated that in general children learned correct movement observation skills when they were involved in dance curricula emphasizing movement exploration and composition, although children exposed to movement notation improved more in this area—an accomplishment that was not affected by gender or academic ability (Warburton 206). One caveat concerning this phase of the study's outcome was that the use of notation may affect the children's general movement recognition ability, but not their more fine-grained discrimination abilities (Warburton 207). In conclusion, Warburton stated that approaching learning in dance via both verbal and notation methods helps children achieve a steady progression in their ability to read dance (209).

In a study dealing with dance notation, Tara Munjee was interested in investigating location as a variable when using movement notation (128). This author's contention was that movement notation systems need to accommodate both mobile and stable spatial locations (128). According to Munjee, Labanotation and Motif Writing can describe how a moving body engages with space in great detail, but the field in which the movements are performed is often a constant or discrete location (139). The author continued that Motation, created by Lawrence Halprin, accommodates the fact that in contemporary society environments, some factors are mobile and change (137). Examples of such environmental factors included people, cars, and even clouds (Munjee 139). To accommodate such mobile factors, Motation includes a central track and added tracks which provide information about pathways of travel, speed, and distance with rectangles off to the side which record sensory elements like sound or rain (Munjee 139).

In third study, Aspasia Dania and her colleagues evaluated the effectiveness of using the Language of Dance movement framework in combination with Motif symbols during a five-week program to teach Greek traditional dances to university students (71). The Language of Dance movement framework used in this study was designed to develop the students' psychomotor, cognitive, and affective abilities by focusing on their use of the body, space, shape, and effort in the movements (Dania et al. 74). One hundred six male and female students ages nineteen to twenty-two who were novice dancers participated in this research and were randomly assigned to two groups—one group was taught using the Laban movement analysis framework, while the other group learned the dances by mimicking a teacher's demonstration; each dancer's performance was evaluated pre and post using the Dance Performance Assessment Instrument (Dania et al. 76). At the conclusion of the study, the two groups did not demonstrate differences in improvement for all movement categories on which they were scored, although the group taught using the Language of Dance framework did demonstrate more improvement for rhythmic accuracy; the researcher thought perhaps the use of the motif symbols enabled these students to better perceive the timing of the movements (Dania 81).

Finally, Teresa Heiland was interested in the learning styles of those who use dance notation and those that do not. Two hundred seventy-two dancers aged 18 to 96 participated in this study, in which the researcher used the Kolb Learning Styles Inventory to assess the subjects' learning styles (Heiland "Kolb" 148). The learning modes based on the Kolb model of the experiential learning cycle include concrete experience, reflective observation, abstract conceptualization, and active experimentation—all of which constitute a dynamic understanding of learning (Heiland "Kolb" 149–50).

The assessment of learning styles for all the dancers in this study, whether they used notation or not, demonstrated that concrete experience was the main learning approach used (Heiland "Kolb" 158). Thus, all dancers made up a group who appeared to prefer concrete experiences more than abstract conceptualization, although this same group demonstrated less difference in active experimentation and abstract conceptualization (Heiland "Kolb" 159). The subgroups involved in this study included non-notation users, structured notation users, and Motif Notation users; based on these subgroups, there were more marked differences between the scores of the dancer subgroups (Heiland "Kolb" 158–59). Structured notation users' scores were moderate in all categories, except they had moderately high scores for abstract conceptualization, while non-notation users had significantly greater abstract conceptualization scores than both other groups (Heiland "Kolb"159). Heiland also indicated that non-notation users had high scores for concrete experience, and structured notation users were high for abstract conceptualization ("Kolb" 159). The Motif Notation users' scores were similar to the scores of the non-notation users (Heiland "Kolb" 159). In conclusion, Heiland noted that since most dancers prefer experiencing when learning, a recommendation would be to begin to learn notation by starting with the students' experiences ("Kolb" 171).

Exploration Experiences

The following movement explorations are again based on the content of the preceding chapter.

Basic Empathy Explorations

1. Think about a major cultural group to which you belong. Where would you place your cultural group on the continuum between the opposite poles of individualism and collectivism? Thus, is there more emphasis on the individual in your cultural group, or does the group see themselves as an interconnected community?
2. How would you describe the relationships or connections between people in your cultural group?
3. Imagine that you have just met someone who is from a different cultural group. What preconceived negative ideas might you have about this person? What might you do to change those ideas?
4. How would you describe similarities between your cultural group and the cultural group to which this individual belongs? What are some differences between your cultural group and the other person's cultural group?
4. Imagine that you have seen someone fall on the sidewalk in front of you. What would your first impulse be?
5. What is your initial emotional response to the previous situation in question 4?
6. What feelings do you think the person who has fallen is experiencing?
7. How would you describe some of their possible thoughts?

Questions 4 through 7 are adapted from the following site: Buffalmano.

More Complex Empathy Explorations

Select a specific cultural group that is different than your own cultural group. Then, do some research on this cultural group which will enable you to answer the following questions.

1. Describe some of the outward observable or superficial aspects of this cultural group. For example, what foods are popular with the people in this group? How would you describe their traditional costumes or holidays?
2. Next, discuss deeper characteristics of this same cultural group, such as their values, worldview, or typical practices.

3. Describe any changes you experienced in your ideas about the aforementioned cultural group following your research and attempt to answer the preceding questions. Did your appreciation and understanding of this cultural group change in any way?
4. New Mexico, in particular, is rich with legends which have Spanish or Mexican roots. One of the most famous of these is the Legend of La Llorona that is predominantly from Southern New Mexico.

    You can read Paul Harden's summary of this legend on the following site, https://www.caminorealheritage.org/articles/1207_llorona.pdf, followed by answering the questions which follow.
5. If you could empathize with La Llorona throughout this legend, how would you describe the different emotions she might have experienced from the beginning to the end of the tale?
6. If you could empathize with La Llorona's husband throughout this legend, how would you describe the different emotions he might have experienced from the beginning to the end of the story?
7. What traits or characteristics might you attribute to the culture that gave rise to this legend?
8. The Legend of La Llorona is often told to children to get them to obey their parents. Do you see any similarities between this cultural practice and practices in your own culture?

Basic Social Emotional Learning Explorations

1. Imagine that you are invited to a party or gathering where you are unlikely to know many of the people. When you arrive at the gathering, what are some of the emotions you might experience?
2. If you feel fearful about entering the gathering, how might you use your breathing to calm yourself?
3. How might you use your sense of empathy to strike up a conversation with some of the people you meet?
4. What would you do if a friend has said something that is a real blooper? How might you use your sense of empathy to help relieve this situation without being too obvious?
5. Suppose you become involved in a conversation with an individual whose views are opposite your own. What might you say to indicate you appreciate their diverse opinion or idea?

The exercises in this section are adapted from Calacoras and Buffalmano.

More Complex Social Emotional Learning Explorations

1. Self-awareness. Imagine you are temporarily stuck in an elevator with someone weird. What thoughts and emotions would run through your mind?

2. Self-management. What might you do to regulate your emotions in this situation?
3. Social awareness. Imagine you are on a public bus or train and somebody awkward wants to have a conversation with you. How would you handle this situation in an empathetic way?
4. Relationship skills. Suppose you are stuck talking to someone at a party who has a deep interest in a topic in which you are not interested or you know nothing about. How would you communicate with this person and then end the conversation in a polite way?

   Exercises 1 through 4 are adapted from the Calacoras.
5. Responsible decision-making. Consider the following situation. You see someone being punched by an attacker. Which of the following actions would you take? (a) Immediately call the police. (b) Run up to the attacker and punch him or her. (c) Run up to the attacker and try to restrain him or her from behind their body. (d) Get someone else to help you approach the attacker and restrain him or her.

Basic Nonverbal Communication Explorations

1. Do the following exploration when you are sitting in a location where you can observe people as they move about. Then, focus on one person and analyze their changing body shapes. For example, are their body shapes mostly rounded or angular?
2. Based on a continuum from strong to weak, how would you describe this person's use of energy?
3. Is the person moving continuously in only one direction, or does he or she change directions as they move?
4. Focus your attention on a different individual and describe their changing body shapes, use of energy, and movement direction.
5. Compare the movements performed by the two persons based on their use of body shapes, energy, and movement direction.
6. Observe another person as they move, but this time analyze how their use of body shapes, energy, and movement direction communicate nonverbally.
7. Analyze another person's use of body shapes, energy, and movement direction and how these actions communicate nonverbally. Then, compare the nonverbal communication of the two individuals.
8. Find two persons who are speaking to each other. Describe whether either individual is using gestures as they speak. Based on the gestures you observed, describe the possible meaning of the conversation between the two.

More Complex Nonverbal Explorations

1. Watch a video of a group of dancers in an ensemble, but focus on one of the performers. How would you describe this performer's use of body shapes, energy, and directional changes?

2. Watch a second video of a group of dancers who are performing a work that is much different in quality or tone from the first piece. Again, focus on one of the dancers and describe his or her use of body shapes, energy, and changes in direction.
3. Compare the performance of the two dancers based on the same movement components.
4. What meaning is communicated nonverbally based on the movements performed in the first dance? How would you compare this meaning to the nonverbal communication transmitted via the movements performed in the second dance?
5. Stand in front of a mirror and focus on a particular emotion. How would you shape your body and/or its parts to communicate this emotion nonverbally? What about your use of energy and movement direction?
6. Repeat the same exploration while focusing on an emotion which is totally different in tone or feeling. Then, compare the two experiences.

Basic Symbolic Explorations

1. Perform a common symbolic gesture, such as pointing or beckoning, and describe an instance in which you used this gesture along with words to clarify your meaning.
2. Was this use of gesture literal or an abstraction of the meaning communicated nonverbally?
3. Think of a common literal symbol which is visual. Then, explain the meaning of this symbol and how it has guided your behavior.
4. Focus on a common feeling and draw a symbol that you believe is an abstraction of this feeling. Carefully consider how you will use colors, lines, and shapes to construct your symbol.
5. Focus on a contrasting feeling and draw another symbol that could be used as an abstraction to represent it. Compare the two symbols based on your use of colors, shapes, and lines.
6. Describe how you would represent either of the aforementioned feelings as a movement abstraction. How would you describe the body shapes, movement direction, size, level, timing, and energy quality you would use in this movement abstraction?

More Complex Symbolic Explorations

1. "Life is a journey," "the crowd began to simmer down," and "a recipe for disaster" are common metaphors. Select one of these metaphors and explain its symbolic meaning.
2. How could the symbolic meaning of this metaphor be represented in movement?
3. View a video of a dance and select one of the movements in the video. Describe this movement in terms of the body shapes performed and how

movement direction, size, level, timing, and energy were used. Next, draw a symbol which you think represents one of the body shapes found in this movement. Draw additional symbols which you believe represent one aspect of the direction, size, level, timing, and energy used in this same movement.
4. View a video of a dance which is different in tone. Then, select one movement from this video and again draw symbols which you feel represent a body shape and one aspect of the direction, size, level, timing, and energy used in this second movement. Then, compare the two sets of symbols. How would you describe the similarities and differences between the two sets of symbols?
5. Do some research to find a choreography in which symbolic movement is used to convey the message. Based on your research, describe how movements are used in this work in a symbolic way.

References

Baker, Lynne. "Review Essay: The Art of Visualization: Understanding Metaphors." *International Journal of Disability, Development and Education*, vol. 54, no. 2, 2007, pp. 257–62.
Ball, Linden, et al. "The Effects of Stimulus Complexity and Conceptual Fluency on Aesthetic Judgements of Abstract Art: Evidence for a Default-Interventionist Account." *Metaphor and Symbol*, vol. 33, no. 3, 2018, pp. 235–52.
Bannerman, Henrietta. "Movement and Meaning: An Enquiry into the Signifying Properties of Martha Graham's *Diversion of Angels* (1948) and Merce Cunningham's *Points in Space* (1986)." *Research in Dance Education*, vol. 11, no. 1, 2010, pp. 10–33.
"Beauchamp-Feuillet Notation." Beauchamp-Feuillet notation—Wikipedia, accessed 16 Oct. 2021.
Beier, Jessie. "Visual Literacy and the Untimely Transmogrification of the Problem." *Visual Arts Research*, vol. 39, no. 1, 2013, pp. 35–51.
"Benesh Movement Notation." Benesh Movement Notation—Wikipedia, accessed 22 Jan. 2022.
Bialystok, Lauren, and Polina Kukar. "Authenticity and Empathy in Education." *Theory and Research in Education*, vol. 16, no. 1, 2018, pp. 23–39.
Brucker, Birgit, et al. "Watching Corresponding Gestures Facilitates Learning with Animations by Activating Human Mirror-Neurons: An fNIRS Study." *Learning and Instruction*, vol. 36, 2015, pp. 27–37.
Buffalmano, Lucio. "How to Help People Out of Awkward Social Situations: A Guide | TPM" (thepowermoves.com), accessed 17 July 2022.
Cai, Ming. "Reflection of Cultural Difference of the East and the West in Nonverbal Communication." *Advances in Social Science, Education and Humanities Research*, vol. 311, 2019, pp. 288–96.
Calacoras, Kate. "9 Awkward Social Situations—Search (bing.com)." accessed 17 July 2022.
Calvo-Merino, Beatriz. "Neural Mechanisms for Seeing Dance." *The Neurocognition of Dance: Mind, Movement and Motor Skills*, edited by Bettina Blassing, et al., Psychology Press, 2010, pp. 153–76.
Carroll, Cain, and Revital Carroll. *Mudras of India: A Comprehensive Guide to the Hand Gestures of Yoga and Indian Dance*, expanded ed. Singing Dragon, 2013.
Cetin, Zeynep, and Pelin Cevikbas. "Using Creative Dance for Expressing Emotions in Preschool Children." *Research in Dance Education*, vol. 21, no. 3, 2020, pp. 328–37.

Coleman, Allarie. "ELA + SEL." *English Journal, High School Edition*, vol. 111, no. 1, 2021, pp. 77–81.

Conz, Rosely, and Stephany Slaughter. "Dance Immigration: Eliciting Empathy." *Journal of Dance Education*, 2021, pp. 1–12, doi: 10.1080/15290824.2021.1906881.

Coudé, Gino, et al. "Mirror Neurons of Ventral Premotor Cortex Are Modulated by Social Cues Provided by Others' Gaze." *The Journal of Neuroscience*, vol. 36, no. 11, 2016, pp. 3145–56.

Cracco, Emiel, et al. "Automatic Imitation of Pro- and Antisocial Gestures: Is Implicit Social Behavior Censored." *Cognition*, vol. 170, 2018, pp. 179–89.

Cross, Emily. "Building a Dance in the Human Brain: Insights from Expert and Novice Dancers." *The Neurocognition of Dance: Mind, Movement and Motor Skills*. 2nd ed. edited by Bettina Blassing, et al., Routledge, 2019, pp. 215–37.

Dania, Aspasia, et al. "From Symbols to Movement: 'LANTD,' the Design and Implementation of a Laban Notation-Based Method for Teaching Dance." *Research in Dance Education*, vol. 18, no. 1, 2017, pp. 70–89.

de Souza, Marian. "The Empathetic Mind: The Essence of Human Spirituality." *International Journal of Children's Spirituality*, vol. 19, no. 1, 2014, pp. 45–54.

Detrick, Rebecca. "All the Feelings: Seeking to Understand Empathy." *California English*, vol. 23, no. 2, 2017, pp. 6–7.

Eddy, Martha. "Dancing Solutions to Conflict: Field-Tested Somatic Dance for Peace." *Journal of Dance Education*, vol. 16, no. 3, 2016, pp. 99–111.

———, et al. "Local -Level Implementation of Social Emotional Learning in Arts Education: Moving the Heart through the Arts." *Arts Education Policy Review*, vol. 122, no. 3, 2021, pp. 193–204.

Edgar, Scott, and Bob Morrison. "A Vision for Social Emotional Learning and Arts Education Policy." *Arts Education Policy Review*, vol. 122, no. 3, 2021, pp. 145–50.

Epstein, Rebecca. *Discovering Countries and Their Cultures Through Movement: Fifth-Grade Students Developing Awareness and Empathy toward Each Other*. MA Thesis, The University of Northern Colorado, 2018.

Fitzpatrick, Elizabeth, et al. "How Handy Are Baby Signs? A Systematic Review of the Impact of Gestural Communication on Typically Developing, Hearing Infants Under the Age of 36 Months." *First Language*, vol. 34, no. 6, 2014, pp. 486–509.

Fontana, David. *The Secret Language of Symbols: A Visual Key to Symbols and Their Meanings*. Chronicle Books, 1994.

Foster, Susan. *Choreographing Empathy: Kinesthesia in Performance*, Routledge, 2011.

Gandhi, Arti, et al. "Empathy Mind-Set Moderates the Association Between Low Empathy and Social Aggression." *Journal of Interpersonal Violence*, vol. 36, nos. 3–4, 2021, pp. 3–4.

Gervasio, Amy. "Toward a Psychology of Responses to Dance Performance." *Research in Dance Education*, vol. 13, no. 3, 2012, pp. 257–78.

Goodwin, Bryan. "Beyond Locks and Drills: Helping Students Feel Safe in School Requires a Soft Touch." *Educational Leadership*, Oct. 2019, pp. 82–83.

Green, Amy, et al. "Evaluation of the SPARK Child Mentoring Program: A Social and Emotional Learning Curriculum for Elementary School Students." *The Journal of Primary Prevention*, vol. 42, 2021, pp. 531–47.

Guest, Ann Hutchinson, and Tina Curran. *Your Move: The Language of Dance® Approach to the Study of Movement and Dance*. 2nd ed. Routledge, 2008.

Hall, James. *Illustrated Dictionary of Symbols in Eastern and Western Art*. Westview Press, 1996.

Hammond, Zaretta. *Culturally Responsive Teaching & the Brain: Promoting Authentic Engagement and Rigor Among Culturally and Linguistically Diverse Students*. Corwin, 2015.

Harden, Paul. "The Legend of La Llorona." accessed 1 Nov. 2021, https://www.caminorealheritage.org/articles/1207_llorona.pdf.

Harrington, Heather. "Female Self-Empowerment Through Dance." *Journal of Dance Education*, vol. 20, no. 1, 2020, pp. 35–43.

Heiland, Teresa. "Kolb Learning Styles of Dancers Who Do and Don't Use Dance Notation Compared to Other Fields." *Research in Dance Education*, vol. 20, no. 2, 2019, pp. 148–73.

———. *Leaping into Dance Literacy through the Language of Dance®*. Bristol, 2022.

———. Personal Communication. 2 Feb. 2022.

Hennessy, Kathryn, senior editor. *Signs and Symbols: An Illustrated Guide to Their Origins and Meanings*. 2nd ed. Penguin/Random House, 2019.

Jung, Carl. *Man and His Symbols*. Anchor/Doubleday, 1964.

Kimura, Daisuke. "Cooperative Accomplishment of Multilingual Language Tutorial: An Intercultural Pragmatics Study." *The Modern Language Journal*, vol. 105, no. 3, 2021, pp. 655–78.

Knust, Albrecht. *Dictionary of Kinetography Laban*, vol. 1&2. MacDonald and Evans, 1979.

Kodera, Ryota. "Living in the Fragments of Dreams: An Analysis of the Dual-Narrative Structure in Kenneth MacMillan's *Winter Dreams* from Narratological and Psychoanalytical Perspectives." *Research in Dance Education*, vol. 13, no. 1, 2012, pp. 107–19.

Lakainapali, Tracey. "Hula: The Soul of Hawaii." (huna.org), accessed 10 Dec. 2021.

Larimer, Amy. "Articulate Bodies: The Value of a Somatic Curriculum in a Virtual World." *Journal of Physical Education, Recreation & Dance*, vol. 87, no. 3, 2016, pp. 22–27.

Mabingo, Alfdaniels. "Intercultural Dance Education in the Era of Neo-State Nationalism." *Journal of Dance Education*, vol. 19, no. 2, 2019, pp. 47–57.

MacBean, Arianne. "Dancing into Diversity: A Curriculum for Self-Discovery, Empathy, and Creative Leadership." *Journal of Dance Education*, vol. 14, no. 3, 2014, pp. 117–21.

Macedonia, Manuela, and Wolfgang Klimesch. "Long-Term Effects of Gestures on Memory for Foreign Language Words Trained in the Classroom." *Mind, Brain, and Education*, vol. 8, no. 2, 2014, pp. 74–88.

Mai, Lan Thi Quynh. "Intercultural Competence as an Important Attribute for the Graduates in the Context of Globalisation: The Case of Young Vietnamese Working for INGOs." *Intercultural Education*, vol. 32, no. 5, 2021, pp. 562–77.

Martin, John. *The Modern Dance*, A. S. Barnes, 1933; reprinted by Dance Horizons, 1965.

Matsumoto, David, et al. "Reading People: Introduction to the World of Nonverbal Behavior." *Nonverbal Communication: Science and Applications*, edited by David Matsumoto, et al. Sage, 2013, pp. 3–14.

Matsumoto, David, and Hyi Sung Hwang. "Body and Gestures." *Nonverbal Communication: Science and Applications*, edited by David Matsumoto, et al., Sage, 2013, pp. 75–96.

McMains, Juliet. "Fostering a Culture of Consent in Social Dance Communities." *Journal of Dance Education*, 2021, https://doi.org/10.1080/15290824.2020.1851693.

Minton, Sandra. *Using Movement to Teach Academics: The Mind & Body as One Entity*. Rowman & Littlefield Education, 2008.

Munezane, Yoko. "A New Model of Intercultural Communicative Competence: Bridging Language Classrooms and Intercultural Communicative Contexts." *Studies in Higher Education*, vol. 46, no. 8, 2021, pp. 1664–81.

Munjee, Tara. "Single or Multiple? Looking at Location in Movement Notation." *Research in Dance Education*, vol. 16, no. 2, 2015, pp. 128–41.

Norris, Shannon. "Leadership from Ourselves and Respect from Others: Refining Interpersonal Skills and Social Emotional Learning Through FFA." *The Agriculture Education Magazine*, Sept./Oct. 2021, pp. 15–18.

Nzeaka, Emmanuel Ezimako. "New Media Semiotics and the Rise of Universal Symbolic Language: Digital Natives' Perspective Amidst Covid 19." *Journal of Higher Education Theory and Practice*, vol. 21, no. 1, 2021, pp. 190–206.

Olive, Caitlin, et al. "Promoting Social-Emotional Learning Through Physical Activity." *Strategies*, vol. 34, no. 5, 2021, pp. 20–24.

Omasta, Mark, et al. "Social Emotional Learning and the National Core Arts Standards: A Cross-Disciplinary Analysis of Policy and Practices." *Arts Education Policy Review*, vol. 122, no. 3, 2021, pp. 158–70.

Orgs, Guido, et al. "Knowing Dance or Knowing How to Dance? Sources of Expertise in Aesthetic Appreciation of Human Movement." *The Neurocognition of Dance: Mind, Movement and Motors Skills*. 2nd ed., edited by Betina Blasing et al., Routledge, 2019, pp. 238–57.

Payne, Helen, and Barry Costas. "Creative Dance as Experiential Learning in State Primary Education: The Potential Benefits for Children." *Journal of Experiential Education*, vol. 44, no. 3, 2021, pp. 277–92.

Qiao, Shubei, et al. "Role of Art Programs in Young Children's Social-Emotion Learning." *Thinking Skills and Creativity*, vol. 41, 2021, pp. 1–7.

Rabkin, Nick. "Learning and the Arts." *Putting the Arts in the Picture: Reframing Education in the 21st Century*, edited by Nick Rabkin and Robin Redmond, Columbia College Chicago, 2004, pp. 5–15.

Ramachandran, V. S. *The Tell-Tale Brain: A Neuroscientist's Quest for What Makes Us Human*. Norton, 2011.

Ramsey, Richard, et al. "Watch and Learn: The Cognitive Neuroscience of Learning from Others' Actions." *Trends in Neurosciences*, vol. 44, no. 6, 2021, pp. 478–91.

Root-Bernstein, Robert, and Michèle Root-Bernstein. *Sparks of Genius: The 13 Thinking Tools of the World's Most Creative People*. Houghton Mifflin, 1999.

Samovar, Larry, et al. *Understanding Intercultural Communication*. Wadsworth, 1981.

San-Juan-Ferrer, Barbara, and Pedro Hipola. "Emotional Intelligence and Dance: A Systematic Review." *Research in Dance Education*, vol. 21, no. 1, 2020, pp. 57–81.

Sanchez-Burks, Jeffrey, et al. "Conversing Across Cultures: East-West Communication Styles in Work and Nonwork Contexts." *Journal of Personality and Social Psychology*, vol. 85, no. 2, 2003, pp. 363–72.

Shlain, Leonard. *The Alphabet Versus the Goddess: The Conflict Between Word and Image*. Viking, 1998.

Shushok, Frank. "On Teaching Empathy." *About Campus*, vol. 20, no. 3, 2015, p. 2.

Suanda, Sumarga, and Laura Namy. "Young Word Learners' Interpretations of Words and Symbolic Gestures within the Context of Ambiguous Reference." *Child Development*, vol. 84, no. 1, 2013, pp. 143–53.

Terry, Walter. *Walter Terry's Ballet Guide*. Popular Library, 1977.

Uchiyama, Mahealani. *The Haumana Hula Handbook for Students of Hawaiian Dance*. North Atlantic Books, 2016.

van Zonneveld, Lissette, et al. "Affective Empathy, Cognitive Empathy, and Social Attention in Children at High Risk of Criminal Behavior." *Journal of Child Psychology & Psychiatry*, vol. 58, no. 8, 2017, pp. 1–22.

Wade, Rachel. *Embodying Empathy: Engaging High School Students in Social Awareness Through the Choreographic Process*. MA Thesis, The University of Northern Colorado, 2019.

Walker, Gabriela, and Jeni Venker Weidenbenner. "Social and Emotional Learning in the Age of Virtual Play: Technology, Empathy, and Learning." *Journal of Research in Innovative Teaching & Learning*, vol. 12, no. 2, 2019, pp. 116–32.

Warburton, Edward. "The Dance on Paper: The Effect of Notation-Use on Learning and Development in Dance." *Research in Dance Education*, vol. 1, no. 2, 2000, pp. 193–213.

———. "Dance Marking Diplomacy: Rehearsing Intercultural Exchange." *Journal of Dance Education*, vol. 17, no. 4, 2017, pp. 131–37.

Westbrook, Timothy. "New Reflections on Mirror Neuron Research, the Tower of Babel, and Intercultural Education." *Christian Higher Education*, vol. 14, no. 5, 2015, pp. 322–37.

Worldfactsinc. Eight Alphabet Groups—Search (bing.com), accessed 22 Jan. 2022.

Xu, Fei. "Towards a Rational Constructivist Theory of Cognitive Development." *Psychological Review*, vol. 126, no. 6, 2019, pp. 841–64.

Zull, James. *From Brain to Mind: Using Neuroscience to Guide Change in Education*. Stylus, 2011.

5
THE BODY, MOVEMENT, DANCE, AND LEARNING

Popular Learning Theories

Charles Bonwell and James Eisen wrote about active learning as part of the ASHE-ERIC Higher Education Report. They said, "Based on active learning theory, pedagogy that involves students in the learning process and encourages participation is more effective than passive listening" (qtd. in Howard 1). Thus, many educators believe children learn best when they are doing, because they become more engaged with the subject matter; this contrasts with traditional instructional methods in which teachers do most of the talking (Minton *Using Movement* 1). Students need to be able to move, squirm, discuss, and collaborate daily because our society is in constant motion and our brains help us survive through movement; this need is also present in the classroom (Boone 5). The teaching theories described next are student-centered instructional approaches which can involve problem-solving and integrate movement teaching strategies.

There are many learning theories which can use movement and dance as a teaching strategy to provide students with an active learning environment. Some of these theories include the zone of proximal development (ZPD), learning styles, multiple intelligences, experiential learning, cooperative learning, and brain-based learning, among others (Minton *Using Movement* (3–6). A brief description of each of these learning theories can be found in Table 5.1.

Zone of Proximal Development

As originally described by Lev Vygotsky, the zone of proximal development (ZPD) represents the space between a student's level of development and the degree of learning that can be accomplished, provided the student receives the proper teaching and guidance. There are factors that can impact individual variance in ZPD,

DOI: 10.4324/9781003258926-5

TABLE 5.1 Description of and Details Related to the Learning Theories Described in This Chapter

Theory	Description	Details
Zone of Proximal Development	Space between student's level of development and degree of learning possible.	Originally described by Lev Vygotsky • Proper teaching and guidance needed • Influenced by emotions, self-confidence, learning style, and attention span • Tasks should stretch ZPD
Learning Styles	David Kolb • Convergers, divergers, accommodators, and assimilators • Based on how learner thinks, feels, does, or observes Sensory-based • Visual • Auditory • Tactile-kinesthetic	Different approaches • Cognitive—patterns used to perceive and receive information • Theoretical—structure and cognitive connections • Sensory—how senses are used during learning
Multiple Intelligences	Howard Gardner • Linguistic—based on semantics, word sounds, syntax, and word order • Musical—sensitive to rhythms, tones, sound progressions • Logical-mathematical—enjoy working with numbers and have abilities with categorization, pattern recognition, problem-solving, and abstract thought • Visual/spatial—recognizes same object in different instances, recognizes elements, creates related images, produces graphic likenesses • Bodily/kinesthetic—mastery of body's movements • Intrapersonal—self-knowledge • Interpersonal—appreciates how others think	Further empirical evidence needed to support theory
Experiential Learning	Learning which • Takes place through experience • Is knowledge constructed through direct experience • Should match student's interests and be relevant	John Locke—knowing developed through senses John Dewey—one of early proponents David Kolb—Learning based on • Process • Relearning through examination • Cycle of conflict resolution • Holistic process • Interaction with environment • Connections with existing knowledge • Constructivist

Theory	Description	Details
Cooperative Learning	Learning in group based on • Lesson-related tasks • Active engagement • Face-to-face interactions • Learning social skills • Leaving time for reflection and review	Recommendations • Tasks should not be extensive • Students who can work together • Each member held accountable
Brain-Based Learning	Based on neuroscience principles • Brain adapts • Brain a social brain • Search for meaning innate and based on patterns • Learning focused and peripheral • Learning stimulated by challenges and discouraged by threats	Related to work of Renate and Geoffrey Caine • Creates neural connections in brain • Peer-based learning creates enriched environment • Problem-solving, role-playing, and discussions important • Information provided in meaningful chunks • Time for organization, integration, and memory storage • Distributed practice significant • Describing patterns in content encouraged • Trial and error and experimentation part of method • Positive experience important

such as emotional differences related to self-confidence, variation in learning styles, and attention span, all of which need to be considered when structuring lessons (Horowitz et al. 106). In response to these differences, lesson content can be adjusted or scaffolded to help students reach their uppermost ZPD level by providing them with appropriate choices and guidelines, carefully designed sequences of tasks, and timely adult interventions (Horowitz 106). In this context, scaffolding should be used sparingly to provide temporary support and extend the range of the learner, permitting students to accomplish tasks not otherwise possible (Schunk 335).

When working with ZPD, learners bring their own understanding to the problem to be solved and construct meaning by integrating their understanding with their experiences in the context of the learning situation (Schunk 333). Thus, in a creative movement lesson dealing with the water cycle, elementary school students would need to first understand steps in the water cycle. These include evaporation, condensation into clouds, precipitation in the form of falling rain or snow, and runoff on the ground. This understanding would be followed by instructions in how components of movement such as direction, level, timing, and energy/quality can be used to transform the stages of the water cycle into movement. The students would then integrate their understanding of the stages of the water cycle with their knowledge of the movement transformation process to create movements representing each stage in the cycle. Once they understand the dance-making process, older students could work together using basically the same process to create movement and then a dance based on a more sophisticated concept, such as climate change.

In an article based on a conceptual analysis, Rob Wass and Clinton Golding explored what works and what does not work in terms of the ZPD approach to teaching; the researchers wanted to learn what is involved in assisting students to do a task that is beyond their ability and thus one they could not do on their own. The researchers also were interested in the influence of the teaching environment and whether students will learn more when operating at the limits of their mental capacity (673). In conclusion, the researchers determined that teaching should begin by assigning tasks that stretch the students' ability with assistance, which are scaffolded, and in an environment that promotes learning; they also believed completing the hardest possible tasks will lead to the greatest gains (Wass and Golding 682).

Relationship to Dance

One clue to the relationship between ZPD and learning in dance was revealed by Miriam Giguere in her research. In the introduction to her study, she referred to comments by Barr and Lewin that novice dance students are more likely to evidence declarative knowledge of lesson content, such as memorization, while more experienced students demonstrate both declarative and procedural knowledge or knowing how to complete a task ("Dancing Thoughts" 10). The connection with these comments and ZPD is that younger students, while not as cognitively mature, are also more likely to be less experienced dancers and inclined to use memorization over understanding.

In 2012, the Governing Board of Brigham Young University (BYU) adopted a philosophical framework titled The Five Commitments, which addressed best teaching practices; in her article, Kori Wakamatsu, a BYU faculty member, outlined how these commitments support best practices in dance education (78). One of the commitments, titled "Engaged Learning through Nurturing Pedagogy," indicated that curricular choices must build on students' prior knowledge and speak to students' interests, pointing to the belief that the embodied nature of dance can be designed to support pedagogy in a significant way (Wakamatsu 80). Under another commitment, titled "Equitable Access to Academic Knowledge and Achievement," Wakamatsu noted that dance provides opportunities for learning which is differentiated in approach and recognizes diversity (81). Lessons which build on prior knowledge and offer differentiated instruction would mesh well with the learning abilities of students who have different levels of cognitive development.

In another article, Dale Johnston described how private speech might be integrated into ballet instruction to combat the traditional authoritarian nature of such classes (3). Johnston commented that students usually learn ballet technique through observation of the teacher's demonstration or from watching other students, an instructional method which bypasses the use of private speech or self-talk as part of the learning process (6). Johnston's belief in the use of private speech in teaching ballet was based on Vygotsky's learning theories, because such internalized speech "occurs frequently at various stages within a child's zone of proximal development when the child attempts to master challenging new competencies" (6). Vygotsky believed that merging speech and action generates intellectual development, and when students could not speak out loud, they were not accomplishing a task (Johnston 7–8). Thus, the author suggested the silence and obedience found in traditional ballet classes inhibit students from using private speech, which guides thoughts and actions (Johnston 7–8). A suggested method to encourage private speech was to use concept maps to organize loose thoughts into user-friendly knowledge structures (Johnston 11).

In light of Vygotsky's ZPD learning theory, movement-based teaching methods can be tailored to meet the needs of students who are at different levels of cognitive development (Minton *Using Movement* 3). Thus, it is possible to have younger students create single movements connected with concepts to be learned to help them better understand those concepts in a more concrete way, while older students can work together to create longer movement sequences and dances based on content they are learning in their academic classroom.

Learning Styles

The research concerning learning styles is large and rather messy, with numerous books, articles, research reports, and conference proceedings devoted to the topic (Ren 22). However, three broad approaches have been used to describe this topic, including (1) a cognitive approach based on an individual's behavior patterns used to perceive and receive information, (2) the theoretical method in which models such as those created by Dunn and Dunn and also Kolb are used to explain how different learning styles are structured and interconnected, and (3) a sensory-based approach which attempts to explain how a person uses their senses during learning (Ren 23).

Kolb's analysis of learning styles is a conceptual approach which describes how a person gathers and processes information; the first component has to do with thinking or feeling, and the second with doing or watching (Bolles and Chatfield 7). Kolb described four learning styles based on different combinations of these two factors: convergers, divergers, accommodators, and assimilators. Convergers think and do and like abstract conceptualization and active experimentation; divergers watch and feel, preferring reflective observation and concrete experiences; accommodators do and feel and gravitate toward active experimentation and concrete experiences; and assimilators think and watch and favor abstract conceptualization and reflective observation (Bolles and Chatfield 7).

The third approach to learning styles is most closely related to the bodily and sensory-oriented content already included in this text. A discussion of learning styles based on the human senses is a frequently cited approach among educators. The general understanding, based on content written by Laura Massa and Richard Mayer and also by Robert Sternberg and Li-fang Zhang, is that visual learners can process information faster and retain more content when the learning materials are presented in a visual or pictorial format (Marschark et al. 155). However, a recent study did not demonstrate connections between learning style preferences and immediate recall or working memory performance (Aslaksen and Loras 6–7).

Based on the sensory approach, learning styles are usually classified as visual, auditory, and tactile/kinesthetic. In truth, individuals learn using all three styles with probable emphasis on one learning modality. Professors Jamie Pinchot and Karen Paullet believed that although students prefer a key learning style, they can use multiple learning styles to understand information (Odom 13). Thus, teachers must use a variety of instructional strategies to relate to all students' learning styles, which are determined, in part, by their different ethnic backgrounds and cultures (Odom 13).

Visual Learning Style

According to some authorities, approximately 20% of students are assessed as being visual learners (Morrow 11). Visual representations can include photos, drawings, maps, diagrams, figures, graphic organizers, charts, or videos. In a study on the use of visually based teaching materials in technology teaching approaches using multiple types of college students, it was learned that the students were highly receptive to the use of graphic organizers and comic strips (Bryans-Bongey 47 & 54).

Dale Schunk, an education professor at the University of North Carolina, pointed out that having a visual learning style should not be confused with visual memory, because the former refers to a student's preferred mode of organizing and processing input, while the latter describes the mental representation of visual/spatial knowledge; all students with normal vision possess visual memories, but only some possess a visual learning style (233–34). An interesting fact concerning the visual modality is the idea that deaf individuals are usually visual learners based on the visual nature of sign language (Marschark et al. 153). However, in a study of 102 deaf college students using two self-report measures, the Individual Differences Questionnaire (IDQ) and the Index of Learning Styles (ILS), the researchers discovered the deaf students were not more likely to be visual learners in comparison to their hearing peers (Marschark et al. 159 & 167).

Many aspects of pictorial/visual representations can be transformed into movement to aid students' learning. For instance, students can use various movement components, such as direction, to help them understand the cardinal directions, position to connect with landmarks on a map, level, or size of to relate to different plants, shape to assess the overall configuration of a building, and pathway to understand the route of a river.

Auditory Learning Style

The auditory learning style is characterized by a preference for listening to content to be learned; auditory learners like to hear a lecture or instructions in comparison to reading a book or figuring out content through hands-on learning (Auditory Learning Style Explained). Another source indicated that auditory or aural learners are attuned to music, rhythms, sounds, and even movement (Morrow 11). In general, auditory learners excel in presenting information orally, have a good memory for spoken input, enjoy conversations, can process changes in the tone of words, and can explain their ideas easily, among other abilities (Auditory Learning Style Explained). About 18% of students are believed to be auditory learners (Morrow 12).

It is thought that difficulties with auditory perception can disrupt a student's ability to recognize words (Kidd et al. 1). In a research project, fifty-seven kindergarten children with language impairment and fifty-three language-typical age-matched children were studied to measure their ability to recognize words along with their auditory frequency detection and frequency discrimination skills (Kidd et al. 1). All subjects were Cantonese-speaking Chinese children. The outcome, as suspected, was that the children with language impairments lagged behind their language-typical peers in the ability to correctly recognize high-neighborhood-density words and had worse auditory tonal perception (Kidd et al. 30). The term *neighborhood-density* refers to the number of words that overlap with the target word (Kidd et al. 12). These are words which are very similar in sound to the target word; for example, *fleet*, *meet*, and *eat* bear a resemblance in terms of sound to the word *feet*.

Tactile/Kinesthetic Learning Style

Kinesthetic learning can refer to multiple approaches. It can include (1) using creative movement and dance to interpret and understand lesson content; (2) simply having students move around the class as they solve lesson problems; or (3) using classroom furniture which allows students to stand or move.

In terms of the first interpretation, Rao Zhenhui noted that kinesthetic or physical learners are responsive to the sense of touch and sensitive to the physical world; they want to jump right into learning and use hands-on tactics when encountering new information (Morrow 12). Such learners often use creative movement and dance to transform lesson concepts into actions. Harriet Tenenbaum and Martin Ruck indicated that approximately 18% of individuals are kinesthetic learners (Morrow 13). Other learning styles described in the same study included verbal 21%, logical 12%, social 8%, and solitary 3% (Morrow 12–15). The learning style percentages noted previously and in the preceding paragraphs were based on a dissertation about middle school students and their teachers.

Kim Campbell explained that one of the reasons kinesthetic teaching techniques can be effective is that stationary students are usually able to listen with attention only for the number of minutes which equals their age (McGlynn and Kozlowski 24). In their article, Kayce Mobley and Sarah Fisher described kinesthetic teaching techniques related to the second form of kinesthetic learning noted previously and which could be used in college social science classes. One suggestion was to post important quotations around the room, followed by having the students move around the room, responding to the quotations on a blank paper located next to the quotation; following this, the students stood by their favorite quotation and explained its significance to the class (306). Another activity described in the same article was to give the students a set of socially relevant questions, followed by having them go out on campus to poll and record other students' opinions; after about twenty minutes, the students would return to the classroom, congregate in groups, and discuss the responses (306).

Natalie Boone was interested in studying the impact of movement performed on balance seats, ski swings, and elliptical equipment, along with cross lateralization on student behavior and academic performance in two first-grade and two fourth-grade classes in which one class in each grade was the experimental group and one was the control (48–49). The researcher observed the classes to record the degree to which students demonstrated on-task behaviors, while the classroom teachers in the classes which included the movement inventions were interviewed; data was also collected which represented student achievement in the four classes (Boone 50–51). This study showed the most positive results for the fourth-grade class with the movement interventions; these students demonstrated a significant increase in their reading achievement and a 14% increase in on-task behaviors over their counterparts who did not experience the movement interventions (Boone 78).

Another study was conducted by Meghan Howard in three university classrooms to assess perceptions concerning the implementation of kinesthetic classrooms, (5) which could include moveable chairs, standing, stepper, glider, and cycling desks and wobble stools (1). One hundred sixty-one students and fifteen faculty were surveyed based on their interest in classrooms in which movement in the previously described formats would be incorporated; the outcome was that 65% of the students and 53.3% of the faculty were in favor of teaching in classrooms which included equipment that allowed students to move (Howard 10). These last two examples of kinesthetic learning are related to the third interpretation of tactile/kinesthetic learning described prior.

Relationship to Dance

Clare Guss-West emphasized the fact that when attempting to engage students' attention, it is important to address different learning styles through a visual movement demonstration which is enhanced by the desired movement quality, intention, use of breath, and accompanying emotions (154). In addition, the dance teacher's voice can appeal to those with an auditory learning style through its creative use, emphasizing the musicality, rhythms, and accents of the movements being learned (Guss-West 154).

The use of touch or tactile feedback has been used traditionally to teach ballet. In a study, Eric Assandri questioned his first- and third-year students about their response to the use of touch as a ballet teaching technique (198). As part of this study, the researcher explored the response to three different types of touch: light/short touch or brief contact, to guide an action to be performed; sensitive/occasional touch, in which a part of the body considered intimate, such as the inner thigh, is touched; or longer touch/manipulation, which involves more sustained contact, such as holding and manipulating a body part (Assandri 199–200). He also taught for one week without using touch, although when the researcher resumed using touch, the visual/aural learners responded differently than the tactile/kinesthetic learners (Assandri 201). All the students in the study felt the use of touch was an added teaching tool; the first-year students connected touch with technical understanding, and the third-year students believed the use of touch supplied a more holistic understanding and use of space (Assandri 201).

In a study previously described in Chapter 3, Bolles and Chatfield explored the relationship between a person's imagery ability, imagery use in studying and performing dance, and learning style. Based on Kolb's Learning Style Inventory-3 (LSI-3), the dance students in the study displayed varied learning styles. Of the thirty-four subjects, fifteen were identified as divergers, twelve as accommodators, four as assimilators, and three as convergers (9). Divergers use feeling to gather information and watching to process it; accommodators gather information through a feeling-based process but use doing to process it; assimilators prefer to use thinking to gather input but watching to process it; while convergers think when they gather information and doing during the processing phase (9).

Multiple Intelligences

While some practitioners promote multiple intelligences, others view this theory with reservations. Krasnow and Wilmerding noted that some research supports general intelligence, not multiple intelligences, while other studies have shown people excel in some forms of intelligence over others (179). Thus, this theory needs to be resolved with empirical evidence and definitive supporting research.

Intelligence, according to Howard Gardner, is "the ability to solve problems or create products, that are valued within one or more cultural settings" (xxviii). Gardner created the theory of multiple intelligences because he believed human cognition needed to include a far broader set of competencies than were usually considered when discussing the human intellect (xxviii). The intelligences initially encompassed in Gardner's theory included linguistic, musical, logical-mathematical, spatial, bodily-kinesthetic, and two personal intelligences (vii-viii).

Linguistic intelligence is based in semantics, or the meaning of words; the sounds of words; and syntax, or the order of words (Gardner 80–81); musical intelligence deals with sensitivity to rhythms, tones, and the progression of sounds (Gardner 114). Those who have a high level of logical-mathematical intelligence enjoy working with numbers and have abilities in terms of classification, categorization, pattern recognition, problem-solving, and abstract thought ("Logical-Mathematical Learning Style").

Spatial intelligence, or more correctly, visual-spatial intelligence, means being able to perceive the visual world with accuracy and perform modifications of one's initial perceptions (Gardner 182). The loosely related capabilities encompassed by spatial intelligence involve the ability to recognize the same object during multiple instances, the capacity to transform what is perceived and then recognize its elements, the mental skill to create images related to a perception and to transform those images and having the ability to produce graphic likenesses of spatial information (Gardner 185). Having well-developed spatial abilities are essential for a sculptor to understand how parts of the whole are related, or when using mental imagery to solve a problem which encompasses spatial relationships (Gardner 200).

Mastery over the motions of one's body and its skillful use involves a keen development of bodily-kinesthetic intelligence. Gardner pointed out that this form of intelligence contradicts the age-old dichotomy between mind and body, although in recent years psychologists have recognized there is a close link between using the body and other cognitive abilities (219–20). In many arenas, including the movement arena, a skilled performance is well-timed, involves translating intention into action, and also being able to discern what comes next (Gardner 220–21). Dancers, actors, athletes, and inventors, among others, have a refined bodily-kinesthetic intelligence.

The personal intelligences, intrapersonal and interpersonal, are to have self-knowledge and an appreciation of how others think and how one functions in a community (Gardner 252–53). In recent years, the naturalistic (capacity to identify and classify objects in nature) and existential intelligences (ability to take on deep questions about life's meaning) have been added to this list (Bates 84). While all the intelligences described previously can be connected to movement and dance in some shape or form, those most directly related include the spatial and bodily-kinesthetic intelligences.

It is possible to design lessons which integrate all or some of the multiple intelligences. For instance, the lesson topic might be a particular type of plant. Linguistic intelligence could be tapped by writing a short story or poem about the plant, while logical-mathematical intelligence could be introduced by relating the shape of the plant's flowers or leaves to geometric shapes. Students could carefully describe or draw the plant to tap into their spatial intelligence, copy shapes seen on the plant with body shapes using their bodily-kinesthetic intelligence, and discuss what they have discovered with other students to integrate interpersonal intelligence into lessons.

Relationship to Dance

Before multiple intelligences, academic learning was described largely in verbal or mathematical terms; being smart in the arts is validated by this theory because it relates to being able to solve problems and fashion products (McCutchen 78). Thus, when applied to dance, Gardner's theory means that students need foundation knowledge first and then can synthesize what they know into dances (McCutchen 79). In writing about the multiple intelligences, professor Pokey Stanford claimed this theory made its greatest impact on education because it suggested teachers should expand their repertoire of teaching techniques used in the classroom beyond the logical and linguistic approaches which previously dominated (Prichard 118).

Anne Green Gilbert wrote that the multiple intelligences theory supports brain compatible teaching; thus, brain research indicates students learn best through a multisensory approach ("Best Practices" 28). Green Gilbert pointed out that dance students' bodily-kinesthetic intelligence can be deepened by having them explore movement and by connecting with the musical, spatial, logical-mathematical, linguistic, interpersonal, and intrapersonal intelligences ("Best Practices" 29–30). For instance, learning to turn can be explored by practicing this skill with a variety of music, by turning in general space or around objects, or by speaking or writing the word *turn* in different languages (Green Gilbert "Best Practices" 29–30). Green Gilbert also wrote that "[a]pplying the concept of multiple intelligences to the practice of teaching can be a powerful tool for encouraging learning beyond simply dance technique" and could be a way to increase the dance student base ("Best Practices" 33).

A somatic approach to movement based on the multiple intelligences can be used to enhance students' technical, artistic, and personal growth. In her article, Denise Purvis described an approach which could be used at the secondary level to allow students to share their strengths yet develop skills in challenging areas in a safe environment (35). The use of the multiple intelligences in the dance classroom was recommended because although most dancers have a well-developed bodily-kinesthetic intelligence, this may not be their most accessible intelligence (Purvis 36). Some of the teaching strategies used to integrate a multiple intelligences approach in dance technique class were to draw the dance based on the energies or directions found in a combination, sing its rhythm, describe thoughts related to a movement sequence, imagine performing the movements, pay attention to points where the performance could be improved, and reflect and write about the movement experience (Purvis 36–38).

In another article, Robin Prichard described an approach to providing critical responses to choreography based on nonlinguistic methods—an approach which touches on the multiple intelligences by translating what one feels when watching a dance into a drawing or movement improvisation (121). Prichard was careful to point out that prior to introducing nonlinguistic feedback into her choreography classes, she establishes a rigorous system of verbal feedback for several weeks (121). The outcome of this approach was that when allowed to choose their method of reflection, half of the students used nonlinguistic methods because they believed these approaches could reflect the intensions and processes of their dances, although many students remarked that nonlinguistic feedback might be better suited for dances that would not be further revised (Prichard 123–24).

Experiential Learning

It has been established that learning takes place through experience, including practice, thinking, and observation (Schunk 4). British philosopher John Locke noted that knowledge or knowing is developed through sensory impressions of the outside world and being personally aware (Schunk 6). In experiential learning, students construct knowledge and skills through direct experience; they have a primary experience in which they are directly involved with a skill or its application (Johnson 128). In this form of learning, students are not provided with background information to provide understanding, but comprehension is gained from the experience first, followed by providing background related to theory and context (Johnson 128).

John Dewey, one of the early proponents of experiential learning, proposed that teachers should use students' experiences as a teaching strategy, although these techniques must be relevant and quality experiences; in this process, the teacher is responsible for providing guidance for the students' observations and judgments (Bates 20).

The Kolb experiential learning theory, developed by David Kolb, is based on work by Dewey, Lewin, Piaget, Jung, and others; it placed experience at the core of learning (Roberts 9). Kolb's theory is based on six premises: learning should (1) be based on process rather than outcomes; (2) involve relearning through examination and testing as the process continues; (3) include a cycle of conflict and resolution; (4) be a holistic process of cognition, along with thinking, feeling, perceiving, and behaving; (5) involve an interaction with the environment and assimilation into existing knowledge; and (6) be based on a constructivist theory that knowledge is created and recreated by the learner (Roberts 9–10). Learning games which include hands-on activities dovetail nicely with the experiential instructional approach (Roberts 14).

Relationship to Dance

Learning dance technique can be aided by using experiential anatomy, which is a learning approach in which movement, touch, and other art forms are used to embody and understand anatomical movement principles; in this process, focus is shifted to how a movement is performed rather than how it looks, using one's senses to experience movement within the body in order to reorganize habitual and ineffective patterns (Krasnow and Wilmerding 4).

An experiential anatomy lesson was described by Johanna Kirk, in which she led students through an exploration of their skin, one of the body's systems. The lesson included cellular breathing, information on the formation of the skin, interaction with props, exploration of touch with a partner, sensitivity to where the body touches the floor, improvisation based on points of contact with another person, a guided exploration of objects in the room, and ending with relaxation in stillness (Kirk 12–14).

An experiential approach can also be applied to teaching dance history for the purpose of enlivening the content. According to Tresa Randall, this approach is based on using primary dance history sources with undergraduate students by exposing them to posters, programs, notebooks, magazine articles, notation scores, lighting plots, costumes, musical scores, videos, and records, among other primary sources, so they can construct original interpretations (8). The author acknowledged that access to primary dance history sources can be a challenge, although dance archives are located in many major cities (Randall 9). The Dance Archive at the University of Denver is such a historical dance history repository. However, the largest of these collections is the Jerome Robbins Dance Division of the New York Public Library for Performing Arts, at Lincoln Center (Randall 9).

Randall described an example of an experiential dance history assignment. In this assignment, the students were asked to choose a year in the records of a famous dance company and then investigate several different sources connected with the company by answering professor-posed questions based on the sources; this assignment culminated by writing a fictional paper which described the experiences of a dancer in the company during the selected year (Randall 10).

Sixteen university dancers aged 19 to 30 participated in a study in which the researcher, Sarah Matzke, used an experiential learning approach to determine how the body forms an understanding of the environment and how that knowledge changes with the involvement of the participants (1 & 3). The researcher used observations and semistructured interviews to investigate the participants' movement patterns, spatial behaviors, and spatial memories (4). Some of the lesson activities included developing a heightened awareness of the dance studio space, performing tasks within a personal space in their home, and analyzing personal spatial behaviors, such as removing one's shoes before entering the house (Matzke 5–6). In conclusion, the researcher acknowledged the experiences created a kinesthetic comprehension of space which became familiar and fluid, and that memories form, layer, and are recalled based on bodily experiences (Matzke 8–9).

Internship programs can also provide invaluable experiential learning because students are directly in contact with what they are studying by doing rather than observing (Risner 63). Other authorities on such programs noted they must be carefully structured, have quality supervision, and have careful monitoring (Risner 64–66). High-quality formative and summative forms of evaluation were also recommended (Risner 66). The twenty students completing the author's internship program described a positive experience, although feeling overwhelmed at times in their attempt to balance the internship responsibilities with other commitments; an unforeseen outcome of this program was being able to capitalize on community resources (Risner 68).

Cooperative Learning

In cooperative learning, small groups of students work together to digest materials and solve problems using a variety of learning activities. There are five elements which are usually connected with cooperative learning: (1) a description of the task or tasks related to the lesson; (2) active engagement of all students in the group for successful learning; (3) interactions which take place in a face-to-face manner; (4) learning social or interpersonal skills if the group is to function successfully; and (5) time left for reflection and a review of what has been learned (Johnson 127).

However, cooperative learning tasks cannot be extremely extensive and should be those that can be easily accommodated with group work (Schunk 343). Those who have studied learning theories suggested students who engage in cooperative learning should be those who are likely to work well together; thus, high- and low-achieving students will probably not benefit from working with each other (Schunk 344). When using cooperative learning, it is important to hold each group member accountable by expecting them to make contributions to the group effort; two variations on cooperative learning are the jigsaw method, in which work is divided into parts, with each student bringing their ideas back to the group, and the student-teams-achievement strategy, which means students work together on the task but are tested individually (Schunk 344).

A group of Malaysian researchers was interested in studying the scientific creativity of 216 6-year-old children who were taught using different strategies (Siew et al. 100). The researchers were interested in scientific creativity since authorities believe it can produce products which are original and which have social or personal value (Siew at al. 100). In this study, group 1 experienced both cooperative learning and project-based learning, group 2 was taught using only project-based learning, and the third group practiced hands-on learning techniques (Siew et al. 100–01). Based on the Figural Scientific Creativity Test, which is mainly a drawing test used pre and post, the researchers found that the students in group 1 performed significantly better than the students in group 2, and those in group 2 performed significantly better than the group 3 students (Siew et al. 108). This was an outcome which could signify the effectiveness of cooperative learning on teaching creativity.

In another study, the investigators wanted to assess the effect of regulation on students in cooperative learning groups to avoid commonly experienced challenges to this mode of learning, such as difficulty understanding the reasoning of group members, group members who have different goals, or the use of dysfunctional communication (Hogenkamp et al. 1). Regulation of group work, known as socially shared regulation of learning (SSRL), includes planning in which students select their strategies and goals, become oriented to the problem, and activate prior learning; monitoring, during which students analyze their learning process and progress; and the evaluation phase, in which students assess their process and what they have learned (Hogenkamp et al. 2). Equal participation is also necessary for cooperative learning to be successful (Hogenkamp et al. 3).

One hundred four Dutch children in fourth, fifth, and six grades who participated in the preceding study were assigned to mixed-ability groups of four students; the regulated learning conditions were randomly assigned to some of the groups (Hogenkamp et al. 4). Outcomes of this study were that equal contributions did not affect the frequency of SSRL but did influence the SSRL processes observed; unequal contributions from group members created dysfunctional group interactions, and having students appreciate others' contributions is a significant aspect of creating effective group process. (Hogenkamp et al. 23).

Relationship to Dance

In a recent article, Miriam Giguere wrote that "cognitive activity is not centered in the brain alone but is dependent on embodiment and the environment in which it is functioning. A key component of that environment is the presence of others" ("Social Nature" 132). Thus, one way to stimulate cognition is through group choreography, in which the students choose the idea for the dance, have opportunities to think together as a group, and develop a tolerance for divergent solutions (Giguere "Social Nature" 136–37).

The ability to be able to work cooperatively or collaboratively is becoming increasingly important today, including in the world of dance. Karen Schupp pointed out that there is more collaborative work involved in the dance field than ever before in the form of working with other dancers and artists from other disciplines, interdisciplinary and community dance projects, and the growing role of dance in health care (157). Schupp suggested ways that collaboration could be encouraged in university dance classes. These ideas included establishing goals for group work, determining exactly what is to be explored by the group, listening to group members, taking turns when offering ideas, negotiating or coming to a consensus, and providing constructive feedback (154–56).

In a study conducted by the author and a colleague, it was learned that cooperative or group work in the form of collaborative choreography was a significant part of a high school International Baccalaureate dance class. The students indicated in their interviews that they learned to respect their peers, figured out how to describe movements to others, learned leadership skills, and became less judgmental and better acquainted with students in their class as an outcome of creating dances together (Minton and Hofmeister 71).

In another study, forty-six Welsh university dance degree students were taught Cunningham technique over a period of ten weeks, in which pair and small-group work was introduced to encourage the students to take more responsibility for the level and direction of their learning (Raman 79–80). The students were encouraged to change partners on a regular basis and worked with students of different technical levels while observing, comparing, providing feedback and suggesting technical solutions to each other, and evaluating their own learning (Raman 80). Nine students with low, intermediate, and advanced technical abilities were selected to be interviewed as a method of evaluating student responses to the classes, with the outcome that the class atmosphere became more relaxed, less isolating, and student-centered (Raman 81). Other benefits of the collaborative approach in the classes were more involvement in critical thinking, a higher level of motivation and engagement, and greater responsibility for one's learning (Raman 82–83).

Technology has also been used to aid collaboration and co-creation in dance classes. The goal in an action research project was to implement and investigate whether technology could improve student engagement and responsibility for their learning in a dance technique class (Huddy 180–81). The use of the technology led to having the students work in pairs, with one student performing the targeted movements while the other one filmed. This approach resulted in one student directing the other student as they filmed and sharing information about approaches or explorations (Huddy 182–83). Huddy concluded that the use of the technology led to a reflective form of pedagogy that empowered students to place learning dance technique in a wider arena and allowed them to become an active participant in their learning (187).

Brain-Based Learning

Brain-based learning is based on the work of Renate and Geoffrey Caine, in which they consolidated neuroscience discoveries into brain-based principles. According to the Caines, the brain adapts, which means thoughts, emotions, imagination, and physiology work in concert with the environment. Second, the brain is a social brain and changes as it responds to others. Third, the search for meaning is an innate need and is constructed by forming patterns between bits of information. Fourth, learning occurs through both focused and peripheral avenues and functions consciously and unconsciously. Fifth, learning proceeds developmentally based on a student's stage of maturity. Sixth, learning is stimulated with challenges but discouraged by threatening situations (Minton *Using Movement* 6).

Others have agreed with the brain-based learning principles described by the Caines. Allison Friederichs noted that learning is based on creating neural connections in the brain, and an enriched environment increases the likelihood the neural connections will form (45). In addition, peer-based learning tactics create an enriched environment because students not only rely on instruction from a teacher but also benefit from gaining information from other students through peer teaching and pair-and-share lesson strategies (Friederichs 46).

Other educational practices that support neuroscience research and brain-based learning include problem-based learning, role-playing, and active discussions (Schunk 70). The first of these practices is a search for meaning by thinking creatively and using knowledge in new ways; role-playing is a form of modeling in which students invest in the content emotionally; and active discussions engage the social brain because students cannot be passive observers (Schunk 70–72). Each of these educational practices can be designed to suit the development and maturity of students.

The following are some tips for structuring lessons that mirror how the brain learns. Thus, students will be able to process content more easily if it is presented in small, meaningful chunks and if adequate time is allowed to organize, integrate, and store new information (Johnson 20). Distributed practice helps students remain engaged, particularly younger students, but the timing used to present content should depend on when the students seem ready to move on (Johnson 20). Other tips included describing patterns in or the structure of lesson content; allowing time for trial-and-error experiences in which students experiment with content, getting feedback, and making corrections; and providing a positive learning environment by reducing the threat of failure (Johnson 20–21).

Zaretta Hammond outlined other suggestions for improving learning, especially for culturally diverse students. She indicated that, first, the brain needs to decide what part of the input it should attend to, such as an aspect of content that is important, relevant, or which encourages curiosity or a strong emotional response (125). The first phase is followed by elaboration, in which understanding takes place and the brain functions to organize content into patterns that aid memory; it is also during the second or elaboration phase in which teachers can introduce culturally relevant teaching strategies, such as movement, repetition, stories, metaphors, or music (Hammond 126). The elaboration stage also includes the brain's efforts to connect new content with previous knowledge as it cycles between elaboration and downtime to consolidate newly processed information (Hammond 126). Application is the final stage, in which the brain practices newly learned content or applies it to real-life situations through place-based learning or learning in which students complete a project or solve a problem (Hammond 126–27).

While educational neuroscience seems like the next logical step in the evolution of educational theory, Daniel Busso and Courtney Pollack expressed some concern with the interdisciplinary efforts to connect education and neuroscience discoveries (168). They defined *educational neuroscience* as "the dispersal of neurobiological language, imagery, symbolism and rhetoric within formal and informal learning environments" (169). Of a major concern were brain training products which claim to improve isolated cognitive functions, professional development workshops which focus on big ideas and create relationships between neuroscience and specific schooling practices, and the use of neuroimaging to diagnose and treat children with various educational difficulties (Busso and Pollack 170–71). To avoid using neuroscience knowledge indiscriminately in education, the authors suggested nonscientists should be taught to think critically about neuroscience approaches and products, learn which neuroscience discoveries are most important, know how they should be translated for use in education, and establish more opportunities for a dialogue between neuroscience researchers and teachers (Busso and Pollack 180).

Relationship to Dance

Batson and Wilson wrote that thinking and action are inseparable and linked; the intention in most cases is to communicate through movement (37). They noted:

> Thought and movement are one. Movement and mind work reciprocally within explicit contexts to become the dance. As a communicative, body-based art, dance engages all of cognition: perception, attention, intention, intuition, decision-making, memory and more. But rather than arbitrarily

168 The Body, Movement, Dance, and Learning

segregating mental processes from the kinesthetic dynamics of movement, body-and mind-in-motion are conjoined by the intention to communicate through movement.

(37)

Brain Functions and Dance

Figure 5.1 is provided to assist in understanding the location of different parts of the brain. Further information can be found in the glossary concerning the functions of some of the parts of the brain mentioned in the following content but not shown in the illustration.

Typical dance practices and brain functions are connected in many ways. In her book *Mapping the Mind*, Rita Carter clarified the concept that the visual cortex of the human brain is considered the center for human sight and that when an individual views an object, a neuronal pattern is created on its surface (Minton

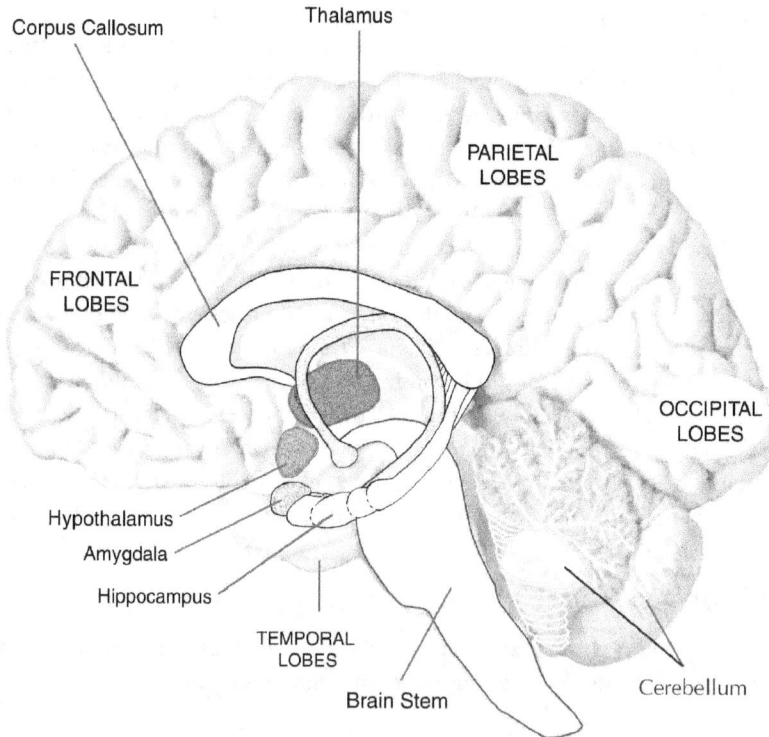

FIGURE 5.1 Medial view of the brain. From *Brain Matters: Translating Research into Classroom Practice*, by Patricia Wolfe, Alexandria, VA: ASCD.

Source: © 2001 by ASCD. Reprinted with permission. All rights reserved.

and Faber 22). Neuroscientist Ramachandran documented that research has shown mirror neuron activity in the brain resonates with patterns and mirrors incoming content (Minton and Faber 23). This means the eye encodes brain impulses for contours, angles, shapes, and lines, which are observed and constantly changing in the dancing body as it is observed. Ramachandran also believed the brain's mirror neurons activate connections in the brain which are associated with human sensory modalities and, as such, facilitate nonverbal communication, which is the motivating intent for creating many dances (Minton and Faber 31).

Paying attention and remaining motivated and engaged are integral factors in learning to dance. They also play a role in being able to maintain focus and motivation during the choreographic process and remain committed enough to see a dance through to its completion (Minton and Faber 46). Neuroscientist Adele Diamond and cognitive scientist Michael Posner observed that the brain function of attention is dependent on the prefrontal cortex, particularly the functioning of the rear part of the anterior cingulate, superior colliculus, and reticular activating system (Minton and Faber 39). According to John Ratey, professor of psychiatry at Harvard Medical School, motivation and attention involve the cerebellum as well, which updates and manages the flow of information, passing it to the basal ganglia and on to the prefrontal cortex; the basal ganglia can shift attentional resources, which are in line with demands of the cortex (Minton and Faber 45).

There are a number of higher-level thinking skills related to learning and creating in dance. Broca's area in the left-brain hemisphere is responsible for being able to sort incoming information into categories and is dominant in expressive language and the process of abstraction (Minton and Faber 51). Part of learning movement in technique classes is dependent on differentiating between movement types, and the process of abstraction plays a prominent role in creating movement for a dance. Laban's effort shape analysis system and Language of Dance Motif Notation have been used extensively in dance to analyze and categorize dance movement. Thus, planning a technique class is based on an organization of movement, which begins with a warm-up, leading to performing more demanding actions later in a class, and a choreography is organized to produce an orderly flow based on the type of movements used (Minton and Faber 53). Evaluation is the highest level of thinking described in Bloom's taxonomy, although Anderson and Krathwohl's revision names creating as the highest level. Nevertheless, evaluation and creating are prominent in dance education curricula in the form of creating dances and having students reflect on them through evaluation.

As indicated earlier, emotion and their connected meanings play an important role in dance. The brain's limbic system, especially the amygdala, a group of nuclei located deep in the cerebral hemispheres and hypothalamus, is responsible for producing emotions through either a direct or indirect pathway. Carter wrote that in the direct pathway, signals are sent by the amygdala to the frontal cortex, producing fear; whereas in the indirect pathway, signals are sent to the hypothalamus, releasing hormones which affect muscular contraction, blood pressure, and heart rate—changes which are relayed to the somatosensory cortex and then to the frontal cortex, where they are recognized as other emotions (Minton and Faber 63–65). Emotions can be the stimulating inspiration for creating a dance, which are, in turn, communicated nonverbally to the audience (Minton and Faber 67).

Dance students need to remember movements learned in technique class, while memory is important to dancers during rehearsals. Memory plays a role in choreographing a dance as well because the choreographer must, in many cases, but not all, remember movements he or she has created and then teach them to dancers. As indicated previously, Kandel has probed the chemical processes of memory (Minton and Faber 78). Memories are based on the formation of associations between neurons in the brain; when a neural pattern is strong or fired repeatedly, it is encoded and stored. A new memory is formed when the gap between two neurons is stimulated by thoughts, sensations, or perceptions (Minton and Faber 78).

However, memories differ and can be classified as either short- or long-term. David Sousa, an authority on educational neuroscience, professed that during short-term memory, information is held in the mind only while working on a problem. He also said research on the short-term system indicated that incoming information is processed for a few seconds during an intermediate phase and can later be consciously processed for a longer period but discarded if it no longer serves a designated purpose (Minton and Faber 80–81).

Authorities Kandel, Carter, Lynn Held, and Michio Kaku described the long-term memory process in the following way. Long-term memories are initiated in the hippocampus and are laid down in memory through an interplay between the hippocampus, cortex, and back, although there are different types of long-term memories associated with different brain areas; this means the hippocampus redirects long-term memories so those associated with emotions are stored in the amygdala, language memories in the temporal lobe, visual memories in the occipital lobe, and those associated with touch in the parietal lobe (Minton and Faber 83). Dancers use short-term memory when they first learn movements, to hold them in the mind before organizing them into sequences; improvement of long-term memory is a necessity for professional dancers (Minton and Faber 81 & 85).

The imagination is a necessary part of being a choreographer but is also an integral component of designing and implementing dance lesson materials. A mental image, as noted earlier according to Zull, is an electrical pattern imprinted on the cortex, which differs according to the experience (Minton and Faber 103). Research using fMRI technology demonstrated that the left brain encodes categories and creates images based on them; the right brain produces spatial images and the relationships between them (Minton and Faber 103). It goes without saying that the different types of imagery, such as visual or kinesthetic, can be used as inspirations for creating movement.

BrainDance created by Anne Green Gilbert is one of the most recognizable and accessible connections between dance and neuroscience discoveries about how the brain learns; BrainDance includes short sequences of exercises based on neurodevelopmental patterns that wire the central nervous system of a child in the first twelve months (*Brain-Compatible* 66). Based on the writing of authorities in physical education, neuroscience, and child development, Green Gilbert stated that current brain research has shown exercise can improve cognition and delay the onset of dementia because it increases the amount of protein in brain cells, along with improving the ability to pay attention and focus (*Brain-Compatible* 66).

The BrainDance movement sequences begin with deep breathing, followed by tactilely stimulating parts of the body, and then by performing movements which connect the periphery and center, head and tail, and upper and lower body. The last three movement patterns in BrainDance work the right and then left sides of the body, move across the body's midline, and stimulate the vestibular apparatus through turning and swinging actions (*Brain-Compatible* 70–73). Green Gilbert found that after using BrainDance, there was a difference in her students, because they were more focused and ready to learn (*Brain-Compatible* 67).

Green Gilbert also suggested the activities introduced in dance classes should be based on the respective level of brain development. From birth to age 3, when the brain is making synaptic connections, Green Gilbert recommended using crawling and creeping movement patterns, tactile and supportive activities, vestibular exercises, obstacle courses, and sensory-based movements with props, textures, and colors (*Brain-Compatible* 17–18).

From ages 4 to 12 years, the neuronal processes known as dendrites expand and students benefit from an enriched environment; some of the activities suggested for students aged 4 to 7 included ample movement in the form of partner work, expressing feelings through movement, use of imagery, and rhythms, practicing more advanced locomotor and nonlocomotory movements, and composing simple dances (Green Gilbert *Brain-Compatible* 18).

From age 12 to adult, activities should focus on protecting and stimulating the brain to encourage brain plasticity through collaborative activities, practicing more advanced skills, expressing deep, meaningful feelings, improvisation, introduction of varied dance styles, and the use of various forms of notation (Green Gilbert *Brain-Compatible* 19–20).

Research on Brain Functions and Dance

Researchers studying neuroscience and dance have collected evidence that motor control and thinking, along with imaging, seem to be produced by the same neuronal mechanisms (Cruse and Schilling 151). This explanation is based on the idea that the human brain contains neural networks which are simultaneously responsible for controlling movement, perception of those movements, and also enable the imitation, planning, and imagining of movements (Cruse and Schilling 165). In the words of Cruse and Schilling, "ability to plan ahead characterizes the system as a cognitive one; and the ability to imagine refers to the phenomenon of having subjective experience . . . an essential prerequisite for the system to be termed cognitive" (165). It seems this explanation can be applied to performing any movement, including those in a dance.

Various studies have been conducted in recent years to determine what goes on in a dancer's mind during common dance activities. This work resulted in the realization that different cognitive strategies are used during dance making and performing a dance because different tasks and their constraints are involved at various stages in these processes (Batson and Wilson 59). For example, when dancers are first learning movements in a work, there is a cognitive load on working memory. However, many movement tasks operate without conscious intervention (Batson and Wilson 59), which is probably what occurs when dancers reproduce movements they have already practiced and learned. Movement memory is aided by chunking movements together into rhythmic patterns or movement sequences and marking movements or performing minimally when first learning them, rather than dancing them full out; these techniques serve as codes for complex movement information and reduce the cognitive burden by assisting memory and reducing mental effort (Batson and Wilson 60).

Researchers have also studied other aspects of memory by analyzing the ability of dance experts and novices to remember ballet-like movements and nonsensical movements. The researchers found that the dancers had the ability to remember both types of movements for a longer time because they were able to use cognitive markers to bind the movements to other contents present in long-term memory (Schack 123). In another piece of research, it was discovered that dancers were better at recalling choreographically structured movement sequences than novices—the outcomes of these two studies emphasized the importance of mental representations in learning dance (Schack 123).

As stated previously, different cognitive strategies predominate during different dance activities. So how can cognition accompanying improvisation be described? In her article, Katia Savrami attempted to discuss the thinking-moving relationship which exists during improvisation which from a neuroscience perspective is an act of creating (284). Improvisation draws from a vast repertoire of possible movement responses to an inspiration but which are prioritized based on constraints, such as memories, logic, or emotions; this means that improvisation is both a conscious process based on the constraints and an unconscious process drawing from the repertoire of possibilities which could emerge (Savrami 284). The conscious and unconscious nature of improvisation means the underlying brain processes are difficult to study (284). While it is possible that the brain reorganizes itself during improvisation as new input is encountered—a process known as neuroplasticity (Savrami 283)—the researcher concluded, based on the opinion of a cognitive science authority, that a combination of personal experiences described by subjects and outside scientific observations might be the most promising way to understand how the brain operates during improvisation (Savrami 285).

Connections between the Learning Theories

Based on the previous descriptions, it is possible to identify similarities and connections between the learning theories and areas where they overlap. For example,

Learning Theories

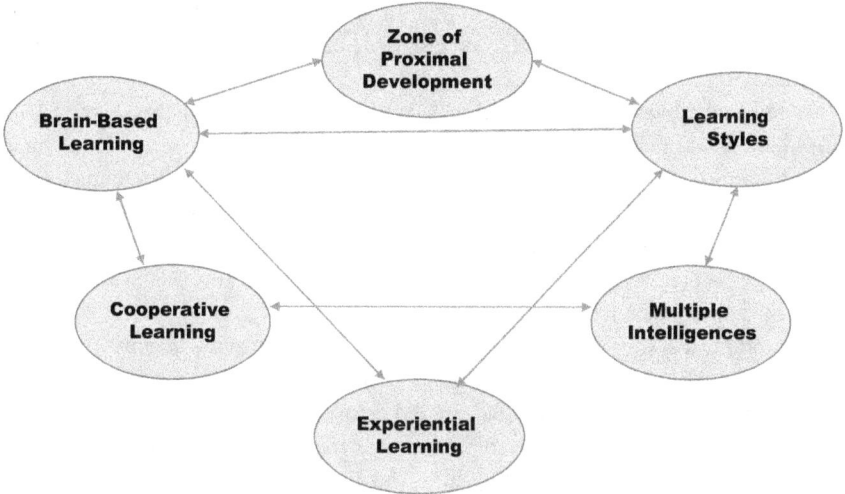

FIGURE 5.2   Diagram displaying similarities or connections between the learning theories.

Source: Illustration created by author.

tactile-kinesthetic learning, one of the learning styles, bears similarities to bodily-kinesthetic intelligence, a multiple intelligence; ZPD, which asserts that a student's developmental level determines the amount of learning possible, is related to the brain-based learning principle that learning is developmental; and cooperative learning can be connected to the principle of the social brain, also part of brain-based learning. Some of the connections between the various learning theories are displayed in Figure 5.2.

Creativity

An idea is considered creative if it is new and valuable, but to be really considered creative, it must pass a social evaluation (Csikszentmihalyi 23). Creativity indicates novelty and value (Schunk 291). Mihaly Csikszentmihalyi felt that the word *creativity* was used too widely because it could be applied in more than one way—to those who express unusual thoughts and appear uncommonly bright, to individuals whose experiences are unusual, or to those who, like Einstein or Edison, change the world in some significant way (25–26). Creativity can also be understood in terms of a system which integrates a domain, such as mathematics, a field, or the persons who are the gatekeepers to the domain, and to the individual who discovers a new idea or pattern using the symbols of the domain; sometimes, an entirely new domain can be established through creativity (Csikszentmihalyi 27–28).

Beth Hennessey and Teresa Amabile distinguished between different types of creativity, labeling them big C and little c (Schunk 291). Big C creativity is rare and generates a major idea or product that significantly affects society, while little c creativity occurs daily in the form of problem-solving and adapting to situations (Schunk 291).

A pertinent question in education is whether creativity can be learned. An important facet of creativity is to have an in-depth knowledge in an area, making it easier to connect ideas in new and different ways; group problem-solving also can enhance creativity, as does being motivated (Schunk 291). Creativity is important when teaching any subject because it provides learners with the confidence to solve problems, enables students to use knowledge in a meaningful way, and can lead to self-expression (Bates 102).

According to Donald Treffinger, who has studied creativity, creative problem-solving is an educational teaching strategy which involves three elements: understanding the challenge, generating ideas, and getting ready for action (Schunk 291). Understanding the challenge means collecting data and then formulating the goal or question to be solved; generating ideas involves divergent thinking to generate options; and getting ready for action includes analyzing the options and searching for assistance for solving the problem (Schunk 292). Brainstorming is an effective method when creative problem-solving is done in a group, since ideas can be developed from those generated earlier, but criticism of the ideas should be withheld until after all solutions are presented (Schunk 292).

Geoff Petty, a former teacher trainer, felt that creative work encompasses multiple steps, such as inspiration, clarification, distillation, incubation, perspiration, and evaluation. Petty described these steps in the following way. The inspiration is the starting point when doing creative work. It can be the exploration of new ideas in an uninhibited way, directing one to clarification, which leads to an improved understanding of the purpose or objective of a project; during the distillation phase, ideas generated are chosen for development or tossed aside. Incubation is more an unconscious than conscious process. During incubation, the creative problem to be solved is put aside and allowed to mature or ripen. Then, effort is required to move forward to a creative solution, which can be examined for its strengths and weaknesses through evaluation (Bates 102).

Csikszentmihalyi believed that anyone has the potential to be creative, although an individual can be exhausted by too many demands, be distracted from his or her goals, lack the discipline to pursue creative work, or cannot choose which creative projects to pursue (344). One of the most significant steps to becoming more creative is to adopt a curious attitude toward life; unfortunately, most people lose their curiosity as they age, so it is important to cultivate an attitude of awe, because without this attitude, life becomes routine (Csikszentmihalyi 346). Having a sense of flow also contributes to creativity. Flow is enhanced by having specific goals to look forward to, paying attention to the effects of one's actions, adjusting personal skills based on opportunities for action, and focusing on the task without being distracted (Csikszentmihalyi 348–49).

Relationship to Dance

The author conducted a quantitative study comparing the creative thinking skills of high school dancers to nondancers; 286 students were included in the study using the Torrance Test of Creative Thinking, Figural Form A (TTCT), as the basis for comparison of creativity between the two groups pre and post ("Creativity" 31 & 35). A mixture of dance genres with students at both the beginning and advanced levels were included in the study (Minton "Creativity" 34). Statistical adjustments were made to the data to correct for differences in time spent dancing between the classes and variations in the pretest scores for the dance and non-dance groups (Minton "Creativity" 38).

The TTCT consists of four subscales: originality, abstractness of titles, elaboration, and resistance to premature closure based on the subjects' responses to stimulus drawings found in the test. Originality was scored based on the uniqueness of a drawing created from a simple figure found in the test; abstractness of title indicated the student went beyond creating a generic title for their drawing; elaboration meant counting the details added to a simple figure that went beyond repetition; and resistance to premature closure indicated the subject's ability to leave stimulus figures open (Minton "Creativity" 36–37). The researcher attended formal TTCT analysis training to enable her to score the drawings created by subjects.

The researcher found there were significant differences between the dancers' and nondancers' scores for originality and abstractness of titles, meaning, dance may encourage participants to think outside the box and point to a connection between dance and literacy (Minton "Creativity" 47). The results of this study agreed in some ways with the outcome of earlier studies on the topic, although it differed in other ways from the results of earlier investigations dealing with dance and creativity (Minton "Creativity" 47).

The Root-Bernstein's Creative Thinking Tools

Robert and Michèle Root-Bernstein analyzed how creative people think and presented the outcome of their research in a book titled *Sparks of Genius*, in which they described the thirteen thinking tools of the world's most creative people. The thirteen thinking tools included observing, imaging, abstracting, recognizing patterns, forming patterns, analogizing, body thinking, empathizing, dimensional thinking, modeling, playing, transforming, and synthesizing. The Root-Bernstein's work cut across multiple disciplines and transformed the way we look at creative thought. Unfortunately, a traditional education does not always lead to creative thought, because "productive thought occurs when internal imagination and external experience coincide" (Root-Bernsteins 24)

Observing

Knowledge begins in observation, as does creative thinking, which demands active rather than passive observation; active observation means repeated observations by going beyond recognition and looking in a way that reveals details, such as the texture of an object (Root-Bernsteins 32–33). Observing is usually associated with the visual sense but can extend to other senses; it is possible to see textures, but one can also experience them through the tactile sense, while highly trained musicians have perfected their auditory observation skills (Root-Bernsteins 37–38).

Imaging

Imaging is the process of being able to visualize the solution to a problem in the mind and is a creative thinking tool used by artists and scientists alike (Root-Bernsteins 51–53). However, it is possible to create nonvisual images, such as those that accompany sounds, smells, tastes, and body feelings (Root-Bernsteins 56). In truth, most imaging is polysensual (Root-Bernsteins 59). For example, it is possible to visualize the appearance, smells, and sounds that accompany preparing a favorite food. The Root-Bernsteins also revealed that people have imaging preferences (62).

Abstracting

As the Root-Bernsteins wrote, abstractions "lack the full body of real things" (75). When artists create an abstraction, they eliminate everything from the image except a key element and engage in the act of considering an object from one viewpoint; according to Picasso, abstraction is the process of discovering properties hidden behind those that are most obvious (Root-Bernsteins 72–73). Abstractions are a simplification because they can reveal properties and hidden connections (Root-Bernsteins 75).

Recognizing and Forming Patterns

Recognizing patterns involves observing connections which at times can appear unrelated (Root-Bernsteins 94). Music contains many rhythmic/auditory patterns formed by connections between sounds, and a dance is made up of multiple movement/kinesthetic phrases or patterns, all of which can be recognized by the astute observer. Part of doing research is discovering the connections or patterns in collected data, while pattern recognition is an important aspect of playing chess or completing a jigsaw puzzle (Root-Bernsteins 105 & 111).

On the other hand, pattern formation is the process of arranging content to form connections that result in a pattern or patterns. Writers compose a work by forming patterns between words to form sentences, paragraphs, and then an entire story based on their diverse experiences; the process of forming patterns differs between disciplines, but understanding how to create patterns is the key to being an innovator in all disciplines (Root-Bernsteins 128 & 132).

Analogizing

In general, analogizing means finding a resemblance between things that are not alike (Root-Bernsteins 137). A poignant example of analogizing can be found in Helen Keller's ability to use her sense of touch, taste, and smell to learn about the visual and auditory world even though she lost the ability to see and hear at the age of 19 (Root-Bernsteins 141). Isaac Newton used analogizing when he created the theory of gravity, because he surmised the same force that causes an apple to fall to the ground draws the moon to its orbit around Earth (Root-Bernsteins 144).

Body Thinking

Numerous examples of body thinking have been described in this book. "Thinking with the body depends on our sense of muscle movement, posture, balance, and touch"; there is a heightened awareness of information from the proprioceptive senses when learning a new movement skill, although otherwise this sense seems to be hidden (Root-Bernsteins 161). There is a key connection between the movements performed, postures assumed, and one's emotional state, which can provide inspiration during the artistic process; sculptors are known to have feelings for the forms they create, and a composer often has a physical feeling for a piece of music (Root-Bernsteins 165 & 169–70). Body thinking seems important to thinking creatively in fields apart from the arts. Mathematician Norbert Wiener remarked that his mathematical thinking was accompanied by a physical bodily tension (Root-Bernsteins 173).

Empathizing

The meaning of empathy or empathizing has already been discussed, but it can also be applied to the creative process. For example, many writers have an empathetic identification with the characters they create (Root-Bernsteins 182). Numerous inventors have used empathy as a primary tool because it permits them to understand how an invention might function in a way that is not possible through other means (Root-Bernsteins 196–97). Empathizing also extends to connecting with animals. Temple Grandin, an American scientist/animal behaviorist, has been able to understand the feelings of cows and sheep, enabling her to successfully design humane animal restraint systems and facilities which handle livestock in a more caring way (Root-Bernsteins 191).

Dimensional Thinking

Dimensional thinking involves being able to transform information presented in one dimension into another; the process of scaling by altering the dimensions of an object is an example of such thinking, as is projecting one's shadow onto a flat surface, because it involves transforming a three-dimensional person into two dimensions (Root-Bernsteins 204 & 206). Perspective drawing and mapping are other examples of dimensional thinking (Root-Bernsteins 208).

Modeling

A physical model can be created by representing the characteristics of a real object, a functional model through capturing how a mechanism works, a theoretical model by capturing how an object operates, a theoretical model which embodies a process and its governing operations, while an imaginary model displays features of something which cannot yet be observed; models can also vary in size by being smaller, similar to, or larger than whatever they represent (Root-Bernsteins 229). War games and constructions created by architects are examples of models or the modeling process. The DNA double helix, created by James Watson and Francis Crick, is an example of a scientific model (Root-Bernsteins 238–39). The conclusion is that physical models are better than graphic models because they take time and space into consideration during their creation, and graphic models like equations do not (Root-Bernsteins 241–42).

Playing

Playing around can often result in scientific discoveries and creation of artistic works. In a sense, *playing* refers to fooling around with content or ideas and often results in novel observations and ideas (Root-Bernsteins 249). Sculptor Alexander Calder invented his circus figures and mobiles because it was fun; he loved to twist, bend, and tear wires, which were his favorite material (Root-Bernsteins 252). "The power of play is that it reveals the nature of worlds that might be . . . testing the limits of conventional practice by inventing alternatives" (Root-Bernsteins 260).

Transforming

When creating, the problem to be solved is defined using one set of tools, investigated with others, and presented in the form of a solution with a third tool set; such a process involves transformation (Root-Bernsteins 273). Practicing a mnemonic device such as the rhyme used to remember how many days there are in each month is a simple example of transforming; a more complex example is creating a drawing and paper and metal models which are later transformed into a sculpture (Root-Bernsteins 276–77). Unexpected transformations can sometimes have beautiful, and even useful results such as those discovered when data from neurology and physics was transformed into dance and dance notation (Root-Bernsteins 285).

Synthesizing

The result of transformational thinking is a synthesis of impressions, feelings, knowledge, and memories that are brought together in a unified way

(Root-Bernsteins 296). Synesthesia, which means describing content usually represented with one sensory modality with another, is integral to synthesizing because it is the key to a deeper level of understanding; thus, describing sounds in terms of proprioceptive or tactile sensations can lead to an enriched auditory experience (Root-Bernsteins 304).

The Root-Bernsteins noted that to fully comprehend the advances accomplished in the last century:

> [O]ne must be able to perceive the connections between mathematical calculations, logical constructions, patterns, visual images, and the technical processes of manipulating artistic media to produce electronic inventions. . . . [T]hose who become excited by such inspirations will have the desire to create the next synthesis.
>
> *(314)*

Individuals who can think in a way that incorporates synthesizing are needed today because major problems facing the world cannot be approached effectively from the viewpoint of a single discipline (Root-Bernsteins 314).

Relationship to Dance

There are numerous ways to draw relationships between the creative process of dance making and the creative thinking tools as described by the Root-Bernsteins. The discussion that follows is but a small sampling of these relationships.

Observing

Observing an inspiration can serve as the starting point for choreographing a dance, especially by using active rather than passive observation, which may require repeated surveillance attempts; the choreographer notices and becomes involved with something (object, idea, social issue) that sets the choreographic process in motion (Minton *Choreography* 3). Observing is also an integral part of watching a dance and providing feedback.

Imaging

Imaging is especially relevant to the creative choreographic process since it is common to imagine movements, costumes, and special effects when creating a work. In addition, visual, kinesthetic, and auditory imaging can serve as the basis for creating movement. In terms of dance making, the most vivid and meaningful images will prove to be the most effective inspirations; many forms of imagery discussed earlier in this book, such as visual, auditory, tactile, and kinesthetic imagery, can be used to inspire the creation of a work, although it is best to use imagery that fits one's learning style, as noted in Chapter 3 (Minton "*Choreography*" 6 & 8). One of the secrets of using imagery during the creative choreographic process is to turn away from the outside world and focus on the inner realm—a practice which can be aided by closing the eyes, at least when first working with this process; using deep, slow breaths can also increase the ability to focus on an image (Minton "*Choreography*" 8).

Vicky Fisher wrote that imaging often leads to exploring aspects of the world through movement in an embodied way (267). In her reflections on imagery use in dance, Fisher indicated that imagery is effective in helping dancers improve technically, can aid in understanding the multilayered effort to make meaning in dance, and often leads to exploring aspects of the world through movement in an embodied way (265–67). Images can engage different sensory modalities, often simultaneously, can change from an internal to external perspective, exist on a continuum from being body oriented to abstract, and relate to dance movement through a process of analogy (Fisher 259).

Nina Martin explained how imaging can be used with students who are beginning to learn how to improvise; in this technique, the student is required to move simultaneously when an image is generated in the brain (29). To begin with, students imagine a static image of their bodies and attempt to execute that image physically; then they wait in that pose for the next image to bubble up from their brain—a practice that encourages students to become aware of their mental imagery (Martin 29).

Abstracting

Abstracting targets aspects of an inspiration in a general way; it emphasizes the essence or semblance of the motivation for creating movement (Minton "*Choreography*" 111–12). During the process of creating movement for a dance, the choreographer can incorporate literal, pantomimic actions in a piece but can also create actions which are an abstraction of the inspiration by presenting its most essential elements.

Abstracting can be described as an indirect process as compared to moving like the inspiration or shaping the body like it. One way to internalize this indirect process is to consider and attempt to capture the feeling response to the inspiration; this feeling response is, in turn, transformed into actions in combination with mental images and memories (Minton *Using Movement* 39).

During her discussion of learning in schools, Judith Lynne Hanna pointed out that a way to test a student's knowledge could be to transfer nondance content into movement metaphorically by physically embodying written or spoken content ("Nonverbal Language" 499), with the understanding that a metaphor is used to highlight aspects of two dissimilar entities. In her argument to include dance in Pennsylvania's schools, Giguere observed that the creation of dances is imbued with symbolic abstraction, which means that choreography is metaphorical; however, the issue is how to connect the experience of making symbols with mainstream curricula in academic settings ("Revitalizing" 37).

Recognizing Patterns

A dance production titled *Move: A Seismic Journey* was created in response to earthquakes which rocked Christchurch, New Zealand, in 2011. The student dancers and professionals of the Hagley Dance Company recognized and used patterns typically experienced during earthquakes in the construction of this production (Egan and Quigley 162). Some of the earthquake-related traits experienced and used in the dances included surface fault rupture and land displacement, liquefaction, rockfall, and frequent aftershocks (Egan and Quigley 165).

In her article, Daniela Perazzo Domm described how choreographies "reflect on the . . . tensions, and contradictions that characterize the present moment" (67), which would mean the choreographer recognized these traits or patterns before being able to use them as an inspiration for creating a dance. In discussing choreography based on social justice themes, Randy Martin pointed out that such dances can be based on and reveal structures of power in society (Prickett 46–47).

Forming Patterns

The practice of forming movement into patterns can be an integral part of creating a dance. Elliot Mercer pointed out that minimalist choreographer Laura Dean's early dance and music creations were grounded in structure, pattern, and form (23). Dean herself acknowledged she was involved with rhythm, repetition, and patterns in her choreography (Mercer 27). The following are examples of patterns Dean used in some of her pieces. In *Stamping Dance* (1972), four dancers performed stylized walking while traversing four identical circular paths which were symmetrically superimposed over a larger circular path, followed by the entire group (Mercer 29). In *Walking Dance* (1973), two dancers were accompanied by two musicians as they performed Steve Reich's *Clapping Music*. This choreography is modeled on the structure of Reich's accompaniment so that one dancer remains fixed spatially while repeating the same twelve-beat clapping pattern as the other dancers progressively shift by one beat until all the performers again align (Mercer 33).

Forming movement into patterns can be an indispensable part of dance making, but it can also be used to help students understand academic concepts, such as those found in mathematics. Movement was used in an interdisciplinary college course for nondancers, titled Pattern Play, to help the students understand mathematics concepts by creating exercises in which choreographic patterns and mathematical patterns overlapped. By collaborating with each other, the students created choreographic patterns which were strongly embodied and understood mentally, and then available to be matched with mathematical patterns related to the choreographic patterns (Stern and Bachman 162).

Analogizing

The process of creating a dance based on a painting or piece of music is an example of producing a likeness in movement of nonmovement characteristics. For example, it is possible to duplicate shapes and lines found in a painting with the body or create movements that copy the rhythmic patterns found in a musical selection or are performed with a quality that mimics the musical tones. On a more complex level, Hanna described the metaphoric use of movement in dance or the act of expressing one thought or experience in the place of another idea which it resembles ("Nonverbal Language" 493).

In an assignment titled "Choreographing the Page," Renay Aumiller had her students reflect on their dance making by commenting on the content and context of their choreography through writing about it (12). "The purpose of this assignment . . . is to prompt students to think broadly about various elements of the creative process by conceptualizing reflective writing as a visual text that allows words to dance across the page" (Aumiller 12). Once the paper is written, the students were instructed to rearrange the words into a creative structure to discover how the written word might embody spatial patterns they used in their creative work (Aumiller 14). Aumiller commented that the students seemed to enjoy this project and had a higher level of motivation and engagement (16).

Body Thinking

In her discussion of 4E Cognition in relation to creative work in dance, Denise Purvis explained that this form of cognition is a complex process that is embodied, extended, embedded, and enactive; when discussing the meaning of *embodied*, she clarified that we think through the body and its interactions with the environment as part of an expressive process rather than as a mechanical process (150).

The following description is another example of body thinking. In the movement warm-up exercises to the interdisciplinary course Pattern Play, described previously, the students were led through a series of movement explorations to help them begin to feel comfortable working with movement as a learning strategy; the students also answered questions about how the movements felt in their bodies and described their personal responses to the explorations (Stern and Bachman 158–59). The two authors contended that this explorative process enabled the students to become aware that the body is thought and can lead to conceptual, affective, and personal, individual awareness (159).

Empathizing

Once a choreographer has selected an inspiration for the work, he or she can analyze their feeling response and empathize with the inspiration (Minton *Choreography* 3). In fact, the feeling response to an inspiration can, in many instances, provide the impetus for seeing a choreographic project through to completion.

Empathizing was one of the techniques used in an undergraduate university choreography course in which the students from multiple disciplines came together to solve an innovative design problem; the problem to be solved was to use a synthesis of dance, music, visuals, text, and technology to express feelings about an issue of concern (Lepczyk et al. 143). The model of design used in this study included empathizing in the first phase, which involved digging deep to discover stories, understand feelings, and solicit emotions related to the issue; for example, one student used a memory from her dance lessons to empathize with those who have body image issues (Lepczyk et al. 144 & 148). The study based on the aforementioned design techniques included ten nondance students whose projects were based on the following themes: bullying, body image, fallen soldiers, and relationships (Lepczyk et al. 145 & 147). The outcome of this project revealed thinking based on the design model, while the students' responses were optimistic and encouraging, expressing satisfaction and pride in their final products; each team in this project selected a topic which was relevant to them personally, although this was not a requirement (Lepczyk et al. 152).

In a choreography project based on gossip, a class explored ideas based on their personal experiences with the topic through discussion, improvisation, and reflection (Buck-Pavlick 24). In the second section of this dance-making project, the students investigated insider and outsider feelings that adolescents experience as they respond to gossip—a process which helped the students empathize by realizing that others experience similar feelings when responding to gossip (Buck-Pavlick 24).

Dimensional Thinking

Laura Dean's choreographic methods also encompassed dimensional thinking by transitioning from a two-dimensional drawing to a three-dimensional choreographic work. She often created minimalist geometric drawings that represented the floor patterns and rhythmic structures of a piece (Mercer 24). According to Dean, the drawings depicted her compositional ideas on paper rather than through use of her body and graphically represented her thought processes and concerns in creating minimalist dances. Although some of her drawings were created independent of her dances, they were a way to experiment with symmetry, repetition, pattern, and form (Mercer 24). An example of one of Dean's drawings can be found in Figure 5.3.

Modeling

Modeling was used in a long-distance choreography project. To begin, two duets were created separately at two different universities and uploaded to YouTube so they could be viewed by the students at each school; the modeling aspect of the project was introduced by sending floor plans of the dances through email along with suggestions concerning the appropriate movement quality of the dances (Donnelly and Trommer-Beardslee 23). The professors explained the original two duets created at each university were then combined to create a quartet at each school, with an outcome that was considered a success (23–24).

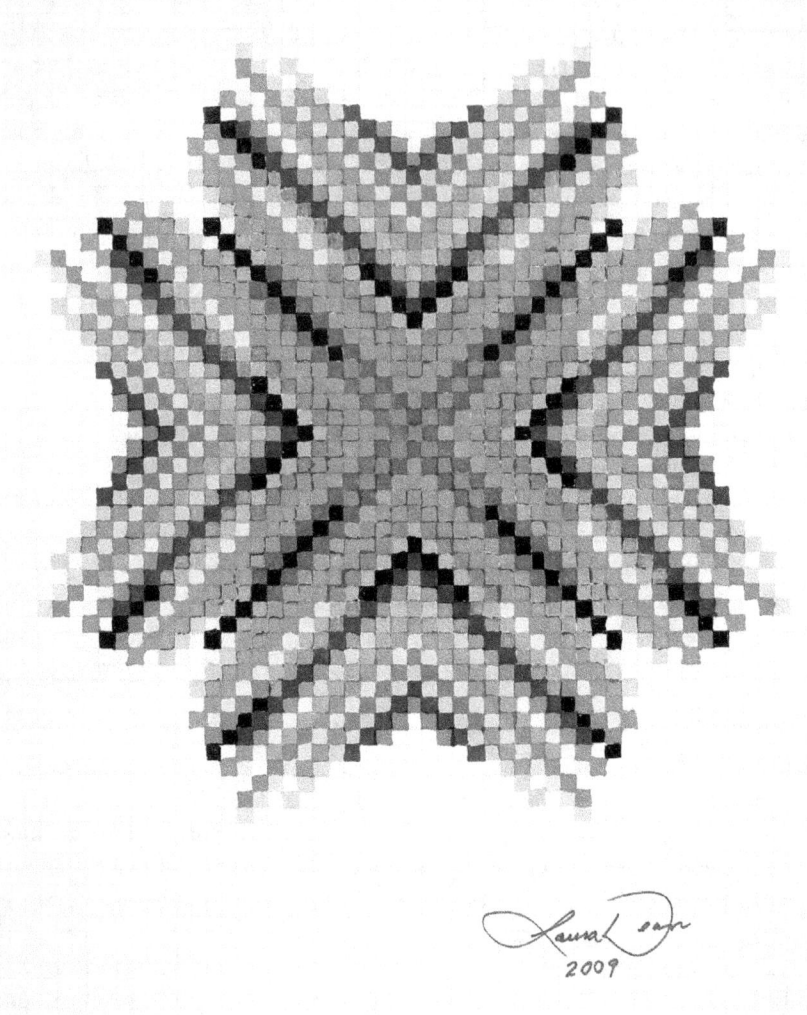

FIGURE 5.3 Laura Dean, Untitled, 2009. Felt marker on paper. Laura Dean Papers, American Dance Festival Archives, Duke University.

Shantel Ehrenberg explained how a dance can be created which explores activities and values found in a university library (97). As such, the dance would serve as a model of the library environment and the activities within it. The creation of this piece was based on an article by Broderick Chow indicating that "movement is a highly effective means through which to understand how social structures, such as political power, impact on public spaces . . . and thus impact on our lives in ways that can go unnoticed" (qtd. in Ehrenberg 99). The replication and exploration of movement observed at the library site led to questioning the extent to which movement was used or not used at this site, since the predominant activities were reading and writing, leaving embodied and procedural knowledge on the fringe (Ehrenberg 103).

Playing

Movement manipulation is a way to create and make more out of less. It is, in fact, a way to play around with movement. In describing Doris Humphrey's methods for teaching choreography, Myron Nadel pointed out that she often had students create a bite-sized movement phrase which they were expected to analyze and then manipulate or change seven or eight times by altering the use of position, pathway, timing, quality, or other aspects of the movements (14).

Choreographers can also play around with movement when creating a dance by organizing movements in a pattern or sequence and experimenting with the order of movements in the sequence. The same technique of playing around can also be used to order and reorder entire sections of a dance, change the location in which specific movements are performed, or experiment with having different dancers perform the same movement sequence to test the visual effect produced. Hanna commented that although in many instances the choreographic purpose may be to provide an emotional experience for the audience, the goal can alternatively be to play with form and create nonrepresentational movement ("Nonverbal Language" 492).

Transforming

There are many examples of transforming as part of the choreographic process. As such, transforming an inspiration into movement can lead to the embodiment of the inspiration in a dance. While examining choreography in her work *The Choreographic*, Jen Joy presented it as embodied thought (Domm 68), and thus a form of transformation.

Lynette Overby described how oral histories could be transformed into choreography as part of community engagement projects. In one of these projects, Susan Gingrasso collected oral histories from community members and transcribed them, which led to improvisations and the final choreography (39). Overby noted that the improvisation sessions brought Gingrasso closer to the participants and ultimately drove the direction of some of the pieces which were developed (39).

In addition to investigating the geological characteristics which accompany an earthquake in their production as noted in the preceding text, the Hagley Dance Company of Christchurch also explored the loss of life and psychological distress the residents experienced in response to the earthquakes (Egan and Qigley 161). Reviews of this production indicated that the process of transforming these calamitous events into a movement production was instrumental in recovery of the populace, leading to hope, healing, and empowerment (Egan and Qigley 161). Dances based on social justice themes are another example of the transforming process as described by Stacey Prickett in the article noted previously.

Synthesizing

The synthesis of the choreographic process results in a dance which has a sense of development and structure from beginning to end. This means the dance has a shape or form which develops through time, with each part fitting together to form a whole (Minton *Choreography* 94). There are many tried and true choreographic forms, such as the ABA, rondo, or theme, and variations (Minton *Choreography* 103–05), or the choreographer may choose to develop a dance that follows a personal and unique form.

Nadel also mentioned Louis Horst's technique for teaching dance composition based on preclassic dance forms. In Horst's classes, students were encouraged to follow the two- and three-part structure of early court dances through creative explorations, which led to understanding other compositional forms—a process which ultimately helped student choreographers organize chosen movement materials into a whole (Nadel 15–16).

Learning through the Arts

Dan Weissmann remarked that the strategies which are involved in work in the arts are skills students need in life, such as forming alternative solutions, working with others, being persistent, adjusting after making a choice, being responsible for decisions, and searching for options (24–25). A study by the US Department of Education showed low-income students who had a high level of participation in the arts did better in school and life than their peers who did not participate in the arts to the same extent (Rabkin 7).

Arts integration or interdisciplinary arts programs are another approach to including arts in schools. The following are comments on the effectiveness and success of such programs: "[A]rts integration presents itself as a strategy for engaging students more fully with the traditional academic curriculum, improving achievement without stinting aesthetics" (Weissmann 18).

An iteration of arts integration, dance integration, or interdisciplinary dance, refers to using movement and dance to help students understand nondance concepts. While some believe this use of dance is demeaning to the art form, it is an approach that has been used effectively to provide embodied learning for K-12 students and those in universities. Using movement and dance to teach nondance concepts is a way to make knowledge from multiple disciplines concrete and memorable. It is a process that first requires understanding the principles and components of the art of dance in order to use those components in a creative and transformative way to aid understanding. As Confucius said, "I hear and I forget. I see and I remember. I do and I understand" (goodreads).

Learning through Dance Curricula

Hanna explained that misconceptions about dance still continue to this day because a large portion of the "general public considers dance as only physical or emotional expression, a leisure activity—or merely frivolous" (*Dancing* ix). However, Hanna proposed this conception of dance should change because twenty-first-century research is beginning to question whether dance could be a tool for learning (*Dancing* x).

Humans learn initially through movement; dance is a system of communication different from speech and can impart information not transmitted through language (Hanna *Dancing* 47–48). Hanna described the ability of dance to communicate nonverbally in the following way: "Dance utilizes a multichannel led gestural system of various body parts . . . in addition to locomotion in time, space, and with effort, music, and costume" (*Dancing* 49). Thus, movement and dance can communicate meaning through multiple sensory systems, such as those which are visual and kinesthetic.

In addition, many of the abilities learned through dancing can contribute to the quality of life, success, and learning in other areas. Learning to dance requires perseverance—a skill that can contribute to being successful in other domains, while dance practice stimulates mental alertness and develops attention to detail and memory skills (Hanna *Dancing* 70). Hanna continued that the creative aspects of dance learning teach students to think critically, analyze, learn aesthetic appreciation, and differentiate between the literal and abstract (*Dancing* 70–71). Furthermore, in creative dance classes, young students learn to solve problems, and when older students work in groups to create dances, they are learning social skills and practicing different roles, such as being a leader (Hanna, *Dancing* 71 & 74).

Research Summaries of Learning through Dance

Susan Stinson examined two reports providing evidence for the value of dance education which were published by the National Dance Education Organization (NDEO) and the European-based Centre for Educational Research and Innovation (CERI), respectively (5). The NDEO report *Evidence: A Report on the Impact of Dance in the K-12 Setting* provided insights and evidence of how dance impacts teaching and learning, such as providing challenges, increasing self-confidence, and building both vocabulary and community for students, although Stinson pointed out she has observed situations in which dance produced opposite outcomes (7). This report also advocated for more dance education research offering proof of the value of dance in education in the form of quantitative, experimental studies (Stinson 8).

The CERI report *Art for Art's Sake? The Impact of Arts Education* asserted that most people, policy makers included, agree that arts education promotes creativity and perhaps other skills related to innovation (Stinson 8). However, the CERI report acknowledged there was little to no solid evidence of transfer between studying the arts and other skills; the positive evidence of transfer they did find was in arts areas other than dance, with the caveat that more research is needed, particularly in the relationship between habits of the mind, such as creativity and critical thinking, and arts education (Stinson 8–9).

In a more recent literature review, it was proposed creative dance can enhance divergent thinking and the ability to solve problems (Payne and Costas 283). In another article in this review, the writers remarked that creative dance could contribute to the invention of original ideas (Payne and Costas 283). The same authors continued, stating that dance can also be an instrument for transferring learning acquired in one situation to another through structured explorations, improvisation, reflection, and cooperative learning (284).

Cognition and knowing constituted a third area, described by Payne and Costas, in which dance could have a positive effect. Based on comments by John Ratey, the two authors wrote that, when used expressively, dance could stimulate brain areas which increase cognition (Payne and Costas 284). Payne and Costas also wrote that creating movement supplies a cognitive link between the original problem or intent and the outcome (284).

The fourth area discussed in this literature review was based on content written by Bettina Blasing, Marin Puttke-Voss, and Thomas Schack and described the physical attributes of dance which through the repetition and practice of movement can build an improved sense of one's physical self and better motor functioning (Payne and Costas 285). Dance as embodied learning was the final area included in this article, since engaging in the concrete experience of dancing affords opportunities for learning through bodily experiences (Payne and Costas 286).

Research Studies on the Value of Dance Education

Both qualitative and quantitative methods were used to assess the effects of a developmental dance movement (DDM) program on early-years students based on their accelerated learning and transfer (Golding et al. 235). Three early childhood practitioners were interviewed based on their classroom observations, while quantitative data were collected in the form of the Goodenough-Harris draw-a-person test as a measure of visual-motor integration, developmental maturity, accelerated learning, and transfer (Golding et al. 242–43). The movements introduced included dance games focusing on spatial/directional concepts and a developmental dance game which emphasized balance and proprioception (Golding et al. 245). Golding et al. found the qualitative assessment of the practitioners' observations indicated the students enjoyed the sessions, which appeared to have an impact on some students' physical skills, memory, and aural attention (250). The quantitative part of the study based on the children's drawings indicated that in fifteen instances out of twenty-one sets, the drawings improved; for example, some of the later drawings included more details and references from the environment (Golding et al. 256–57). Golding et al. concluded that the study demonstrated evidence of transfer based on the students' behavioral changes and the outcome of the drawing tests (262).

Geeta Sharma et al. were interested in learning whether dance affected students' literacy and ability to work with numbers; 187 New Zealand schoolchildren who were 8 to 9 years old participated in the study (1). The children were divided into two groups at four primary schools—the dance group with eighteen sessions over a period of six weeks, and a control group who did not participate in the integrated dance classes (Sharma et al. 1–2). The quantitative assessment procedures used included pre and post academic, behavioral, physical, and well-being evaluations and three qualitative measures—the children's journal writing, group interviews, and teachers' interviews of those whose students were in the dance classes (Sharma et al. 3). The pretest scores for mathematics and reading displayed no differences between the experimental and control groups, while posttest scores for those in the dance classes were not uniformly higher; however, the posttest math scores for the Maori/Pasifika children who danced improved, as did the reading scores for the special-needs children who danced (Sharma et al. 5). Nevertheless, the qualitative outcome of this study suggested the dance classes encouraged students to absorb, comprehend, and reflect on content, promoted cooperation, flexibility, and negotiation, with one child commenting that dance was a form of communication (Sharma et al 9).

In her quest to assess the value of dance in education, Giguere sought to examine children's thinking when they were involved in dance making and how this process might affect cognitive development ("Dancing Thoughts" 5). In the past, observations and interviews have been used to reveal what children experience when participating in dance that, according to Karen Bond, reveal these experiences are complex, interactive, and multimodal (Giguere "Dancing Thoughts" 9).

The subjects in Giguere's study were sixteen self-selected fifth graders who divided into four groups to create dances; their dance-making experiences were captured through interviews, daily journaling, brainstorming sheets, and videos of their dances (Giguere "Dancing Thoughts" 10–11). Seven categories of meaning emerged from reading the data accumulated in the study: making movement, organizing movement, knowing it's good, the group, how it feels, awareness of audience, and new experiences (Giguere "Dancing Thoughts" 12–19).

Further analysis of the four categories and subcategories within them enabled the researcher to describe the students' thinking as they created their dances. For example, under making movement, the students described how they used their bodies to translate thought into meaningful movements; the organizing movement category revealed how the students manipulated the physical symbols they created; the knowing it's good category reflected choices the students made during their creative process; and the group category illuminated roles in the group, social interactions/awareness, and ways of working together recognized by the students (Giguere "Dancing Thoughts" 20–21).

In a qualitative study, the author was interested in learning how middle school students connected meaning to their dance-making experiences. The eleven students in the study were electively enrolled in two choreography classes which met twice a week for nine weeks; data was collected through the researcher's class observations and the students' answers on two questionnaires (Minton "Middle School" 106–07).

Involvement in dance making and student communications comprised the two themes emerging from the data in the aforementioned study (Minton "Middle School" 108). From her observations, the researcher could see the students were discovering movements for dance-making, although many movements resembled codified dance steps; in terms of communication, the students were in discussions with each other and asked questions among other activities ("Middle School" 108–09). However, the students' answers on the questionnaires painted a more revealing picture because they claimed dance-making gave them feelings of ownership, identified personal talents, and enabled them to learn about choreographic craft, while in terms of communication and social parameters, it gave them a chance for self-expression, identification of their role in the group, and helped them think about the impression their dance might make on an audience (Minton "Middle School" 111–12). Overall, there was a difference in tone between the researcher's observations and the students' comments, leading the researcher to conclude that dance making meant more to the students than she was able to observe as an outsider; it was as if the researcher and students existed in two different but parallel worlds ("Middle School" 116).

Two hundred twenty-five high school students (dancers and nondancers) participated in a quantitative study on the relationship between studying dance and self-esteem (Minton "Self-Esteem" 63). The AD version of the Culture-Free Self-Esteem Inventory (CFSEI), which is appropriate for high school students, was used to test students pre and post; it contains four self-esteem subscales: general, social, personal, and lie items (Minton "Self-Esteem" 64). General self-esteem is the overall perception of a person's self-worth; social self-esteem refers to how an individual views the quality of his or her relationships with peers; personal self-esteem includes the most intimate feelings of self-worth; and the lie scale indicates defensiveness (Minton "Self-Esteem" 64). As a result, the dance students demonstrated slightly higher gains overall in their self-esteem scores in comparison to the non-dancers, but these gains were not significantly greater (Minton "Self-Esteem" 70). It is interesting to note that dancing seems to boost female self-esteem in comparison to its effect on male self-esteem, that the posttest social self-esteem scores were significantly higher at one school, and there was a positive correlation between hours spent in dance class outside school and the students' post social self-esteem scores (Minton "Self-Esteem" 71–72).

In a qualitative study, the authors wanted to learn how a class of International Baccalaureate dance students constructed meaning from their participation in dance (Minton and Hofmeister 67). The International Baccalaureate dance curriculum extends over a two-year period and is focused on dance making, world dance, research, writing, and performance (Minton and Hofmeister 68). To collect data for the fifteen-week study, the students completed a questionnaire, were interviewed, and the researcher observed, took notes on student interactions in the classes, and attended the culminating dance concert (Minton and Hofmeister 69). The themes which emerged from the data included the students' comments about their self-growth, interpersonal growth, understanding related to dance, and connections between dance and other areas of study and work (Minton and Hofmeister 69–72). The researcher also discovered connections between the data gathered in this study, especially comments made by the students in their interviews, and the twenty-first-century skills. For example, one student noted they learned problem-solving skills and to think quickly in the IB dance class, which can be related to the twenty-first-century skills of forming and finding solutions to problems and being adaptable and flexible (Minton and Hofmeister 73 & 75).

In her doctoral dissertation, Cheryl Halliburton used a case study to investigate how dance might restart the desire to learn in at-risk adolescent students (vi). Data in the study included semistructured interviews with six staff members, the researcher's journal notes, and observations along with historical and mission-based documents, visual images, and videos (Halliburton 95). Halliburton indicated the dance classes consisted of an orientation, trust exercises, content to encourage discipline and focusing, as well as technique, choreography, and learning and rehearsing a contemporary dance (88). Other strategies used in these classes included being consistent, providing individual attention and affirmations, immediate feedback, and connecting physical and cognitive learning through feedback and assessing portfolio assignments (122).

The aforementioned researcher concluded that the staff's skill sets of leadership, communication, collaboration, and listening contributed to advancements made by the adolescent students (125). Leadership style is important because it lets at-risk adolescents know the adults in their lives could see, hear, believe, and care for them; communication and collaboration between staff members created a culture of caring that could be sensed by the adolescents; and listening, often in individual sessions, offered the students a safe place in which they could talk (Halliburton 126–28). Halliburton realized as an outcome of her research that most of those not involved in dance are unaware of the value of dance but came to recognize that dance can offer an opportunity for re-engagement by promoting social-emotional and prosocial behaviors and learning, which can be achieved by connecting these behaviors to movement (128).

In another case study, Heather Warfel Sandler interviewed her former high school students to discover what they thought they had learned from participation in her dance classes. The comments made by the students indicated they believed they had learned a variety of skills from the classes, including learning to think outside the box, troubleshoot, and the ability to digest criticism and apply it, along with discovering how to use their body, especially in relationship to music; the students also indicated they came to know themselves better—knowledge which can be applied to navigating through life (NDEO 2021 virtual conference). Warfel Sandler indicated that creative work and production was emphasized in the classes and that the students' projects were self-directed, related to the students' interests, and included collaboration and taking on a variety of roles and responsibilities (NDEO 2021 virtual conference).

In a ninth study, Chinese researchers sought to investigate and differentiate between creativity and innovation of choreographers during dance making and distinguish the role played by the two forms of thinking during the choreographic process (Dou et al. 3). According to the researchers, *creative thinking* refers to creating something out of nothing to formulate something new, while *innovative thinking* is used to integrate dance elements and elements outside of the dance, such as space and costuming (Dou et al. 3).

The forty female undergraduate students who participated in the preceding study were not professionally trained in dance improvisation and had never participated in similar previous studies (Dou et al. 5). According to the researchers, the subjects were divided into two groups (limited and unlimited improvisation) (6). The subjects received four sessions in the two versions of improvisation training, with the limited improvisation group focusing on rhythm, the body, music, and a dance theme, while the unlimited group was freer and experienced yoga meditation, physical movement, and relaxation techniques to create a state of mindfulness, followed by improvising (Dou 6). The outcome of this study showed that both types of improvisation affected innovative creativity in a positive way, although the unlimited improvisation group demonstrated what the researchers called pure dance, which they thought was dominated by creative thinking and supported by innovative thinking (Dou et al. 7).

Lisa Wilson and Ann-Thomas Moffett used mixed methods of qualitative research techniques and artistic dance practices to study the phenomenon of racism in the United States and South Africa (135). This study included a racially mixed group of twenty-nine dancers from the two countries who were either dance professionals in some capacity or student dancers (Wilson and Moffett 138). To support triangulation of data, the researchers collected data from multiple sources, which included (1) the participants' personal and family stories, documents related to the targeted topics, and reflective writing; (2) observations of movement exploration, improvisation, and embodied storytelling; and (3) one large group reflective discussion in which the participants shared their experiences during the collaborative project (139).

The themes which emerged from this study included connectedness, transformation, and empowerment toward future practices in dance (Wilson and Moffett 141–43). The researchers noted that the layers of connectedness inspired empathy and greater understanding of differences and generated an understanding of how self and others are connected, which is crucial to combatting racial injustices (141). In terms of transformation, the subjects experienced a shift in how they saw themselves as dancers and world citizens, while the empowerment theme challenged them to think differently about their work in the future (Wilson and Moffett 142–43).

The various skills and abilities revealed in the different dance education studies previously described are summarized in Table 5.2.

Research on Learning through Dance Integration and Interdisciplinary Work in Dance

Dance has been used to teach concepts from multiple academic disciplines through integration and interdisciplinary approaches. The studies summarized next are descriptions of some of this work and its possible effectiveness.

TABLE 5.2 Partial Summary of Positive Effects of Dance Participation

Skill or Ability	Evidence from Studies
Quality of life skills	• Perseverance, mental alertness, attention to detail—Hanna, *Dancing* • Provides challenges—Stinson
Cognitive skills	• Critical thinking—Hanna, *Dancing* • Problem-solving—Hanna, *Dancing* • Problem-solving—Payne and Costas • Cognition and knowing—Payne and Costas • Embodied learning—Payne and Costas • Improved memory—Golding et al. • Improved comprehension—Sharma et al. • Embodied thinking—Giguere, "Dancing Thoughts" • Organizing and manipulating—Giguere, "Dancing Thoughts" • Making choices—Giguere, "Dancing Thoughts" • Improved problem-solving—Minton and Hofmeister • Thinking quickly—Minton and Hofmeister • Improved aural attention—Golding et al. • Drawings with increased detail—Golding et al. • Learned troubleshooting—Warfel Sandler
Creativity	• Originality—Minton "Creativity" • Divergent thinking—Payne and Costas • Original ideas—Payne and Costas • Encouraged flexibility—Sharma et al. • Thinking outside the box—Warfel Sandler • Positive effect on creativity—Dou et al.
Interpersonal skills	• System of communication—Hanna, *Dancing* • Role-playing—Hanna, *Dancing* • Builds community—Stinson • Role of self in group—Minton, "Middle School" • Student communications—Minton, "Middle School" • Encouraged negotiation and trust—Sharma, et al. • Ways of working together—Giguere, "Dancing Thoughts" • Interpersonal growth—Minton and Hofmeister • Promotion of prosocial behaviors—Haliburton • Connectedness—Wilson and Moffett • Increased empathy—Wilson and Moffett • Understanding differences—Wilson and Moffett
Intrapersonal skills	• Aesthetic appreciation—Hanna, *Dancing* • Increased self-confidence—Stinson • Feelings of ownership—Minton, "Middle School" • Identified personal talents—Minton, "Middle School" • Chance for self-expression—Minton, "Middle School" • Nonsignificant gains in self-esteem—Minton "Self-Esteem" • Self-growth—Minton and Hofmeister • Take and digest criticism—Warfel Sandler • Come to know self—Warfel Sandler • Empowerment—Wilson & Moffett • Shift in how see self in world—Wilson and Moffett

(Continued)

TABLE 5.2 (Continued)

Skill or Ability	Evidence from Studies
Dance knowledge	• Involvement in dance making—Minton, "Middle School" • Learn choreographic craft—Minton, "Middle School" • More dance understanding—Minton & Hofmeister • How to use body in relation to music—Warfel Sandler
Physical skills	• Improved sense of physical self—Payne & Costas • Better motor functioning—Payne & Costas • Improved physical skills—Golding et al.
Transference to other areas	• Building vocabulary—Stinson • Ability to create abstract titles for drawings—Minton, "Creativity" • Connections to other academic areas and work—Minton and Hofmeister • Improved reading and math scores for minority and special-needs children—Sharma, et al. • Transfer between situations—Payne and Costas The CERI report acknowledged there was little to no solid evidence of transfer between studying the arts and other skills, and the positive evidence they found was in arts areas other than dance (Stinson 8–9).

A study dealing with learning math was conducted with 117 second-grade children at a Portuguese primary school, with the children divided into experimental and control groups; the creative dance content experienced by the experimental group was based on Laban's framework of body, space, energy (movement qualities), and relationship (Leandro et al. 76–77). Some of the math concepts studied in both groups included addition, subtraction, decimals, money, and measurement of time, with dance exercises developed for the experimental group exploring connections between movement elements and math concepts (Leandro et al. 78). A statistical analysis of the pre-, post-, and retest data showed creative dance interventions had a positive impact on learning math concepts in comparison to outcomes for the control group (Leandro et al. 87).

An action research project was conducted with US elementary school children over a five-year period, with a maximum of 138 kindergarten through fifth-grade students and six lead teachers, six assistant teachers, the principal, the researcher, and two student research assistants as participants during the study (Valls et al. 118). The goal of the study was to learn about the teachers' perspectives on the integration of science and dance as it related to constructivist teaching practices (Valls et al. 119). Constructivist teaching, used by the teachers in this study, focused on student autonomy, interest, cooperation, play, and experimentation (Valls et al. 119–24). One positive outcome of this study was that the teachers identified parallels between their constructivist teaching strategies and methods used to teach creative dance (Valls et al. 124). The teachers also thought that, by composing dances, the students had a personal experience with the science concepts (Valls et al. 124). The teachers valued dance making because it deepened the students' understanding of science concepts and seemed to support the elements of constructivism, although a challenge was balancing the integration of dance and science experiences (Valls et al. 125).

The goal of another research project was to learn about the effects of a dance- and transportation-integrated curriculum on the learning and engagement of fifth-grade students (LaMotte 23). Megan La Motte noted that although transportation is not traditionally considered an academic subject, it does have roots in science and social studies (25). There were twenty-two students in the experimental group, and eighteen in the control group in this study (LaMotte 25–26). The groups were tasked with finding solutions to transportation issues, culminating in learning plans based on these issues, such as climate change; dance was integrated into the experimental group in the form of locomotor and nonlocomotor movements, movement components such as pathways and levels, different choreographic forms, and creating dances (LaMotte 26). The research instruments were pre-/posttests on transportation knowledge gained by the students in both groups, while the two groups of students also made journal entries (LaMotte 26–27).

Quantitatively, although both groups displayed no significant difference in transportation knowledge on the pretest, the experimental group did significantly better on the posttest (LaMotte 29). The journaling or qualitative portion of the study was included to assess student engagement and feeling responses to the lessons; assessment of the journal entries was based on coding the responses as falling in the cognitive, affective, or psychomotor domain (LaMotte 30). The outcome showed that the control group's responses fell mostly in the cognitive domain, with few coded as affective, while there was more diversity in the responses from the experimental group based on the three domains; the researcher concluded that positive feedback from the experimental group was consistent with the outcome of earlier studies on arts integration (LaMotte 29–31).

In a master's thesis study, Toni Duncan examined the possible effects of creative movement and dance on middle and high school students' understanding of poetry. The data from pretests and posttests on poetic knowledge, students' journal entries, and an audience survey were analyzed to produce the conclusions described by the researcher (Duncan iii). Based on the students' journal reflections, the researcher concluded that there was some growth in understanding poetic meaning by using creative movement, because it helped interpret what the author of the poem was trying to express (Duncan 36). In particular, the students found that taking each line in a poem and connecting it with movement ideas was especially helpful and contributed to a dramatic understanding of the poem (Duncan 36).

In the final portion of the previous study, the researcher involved the audience by assessing their responses to choreography created by the student subjects; these dances were based on the two poems used in the classes during the study. To assess the audience members' responses to the performance, the researcher distributed copies of the two poems so each could be read preceding the performance (Duncan 37).

In addition, the first three lines of one poem were read at the beginning of the performance, followed by reading the last three lines of this same poem at the end of this same dance (Duncan 37–38). The other targeted poem was recited by the second group of students as they performed their dance (Duncan 38). The outcome of the audience survey demonstrated that eighteen out of nineteen audience members thought the movements in the performance mimicked the energy of the words in the poems, while fourteen audience members found the movements portrayed the rhythm and tempo of the poems and helped them discover a deeper meaning from the words (Duncan 38).

Dance was also used to teach science concepts at the university level. One hundred fourteen American students participated in a course which included both lecture and dance with scientific content drawn from biology; in the classes, the dance faculty chose and presented scientific content which was combined with dance technique to produce a group dance (Swanson and Ostersmith 2). The effect of the classes was assessed through a review of journal reflections, poster presentations, and a dance performance with most of the knowledge of the students' metacognition and impressions gathered from the journals and answers to assessment questions (Swanson and Ostersmith 3–4). The researchers believed the classes were effective because the students engaged with the material physically and mentally, often had to struggle with unfamiliar activities, and were expected to discover and create (Swanson and Ostersmith 4–5). The conclusions were that dancing the interpretation of science concepts helped the students understand them in new ways and made the concepts more accessible; in addition, research projects designed by the students often assessed the effect of dancing on physiology or psychology (Swanson and Ostersmith 5).

The initiation of the Common Core State Standards led to the creation of a dance class in which English language arts content was integrated into the dance curriculum (Bashaw 26). Based on a book about how to teach thinking skills, the author of the article, Barbara Bashaw, asserted that there is an opportunity for integrating writing into dance classes because certain thinking skills spiral throughout the Common Core learning standards from kindergarten to high school and are already inherent in artistic processes in dance, including critical, creative, complex, comprehensive, collaborative, and communicative thinking and cognitive transfer (Bashaw 27).

The following are examples of critical, creative, and complex thinking which can be integrated into a traditional dance class through the use of writing. To employ critical thinking, the dance students can write down their analysis of movement in a sequence taught in class; to employ creative thinking, the students could describe in writing how they might alter a movement phrase learned in class to include locomotion; and for complex thinking, they could explain what they did to refine their performance of a movement sequence (Bashaw 28–29).

As mentioned previously, in some circles the use of dance to teach nondance content is considered demeaning to the art form. A carefully designed assessment is one way to ensure that the artistic and creative aspects of dance are retained in such integrative/interdisciplinary lessons. In an article, Overby et al. described a rubric that promoted such an assessment approach using a zero to four-point scale. The scoring in the rubric is based on four components: understanding of the lesson theme, demonstration of understanding of the art form, creation of an original work, and the connection between the art form and lesson theme (25). For example, in terms of art form, a score of 0 would be awarded to an integrated arts project if the "students do not construct or demonstrate their understanding of the art form," while a score of 4 means that the "students have full understanding of the art form and are engaged in constructing and demonstrating their art form without assistance" (Overby et al. 25).

The Author's Approach to Interdisciplinary Teaching through Dance

Having done numerous workshops with teachers of all varieties, the author felt it was necessary to devise a way to help nondance teachers use movement and dance to teach nondance concepts. To solve this issue, it was decided that a movement components approach might be effective. Thus, the author decided to use eleven movement components that could be matched with aspects of the concepts to be taught. These movement components included direction, level, size, timing, duration, rhythm, quality, shape, pathway, position, and starting and stopping (Minton "Using Movement" 13–23). Some examples of this matching process included pursuing a meandering pathway that follows the route of a river, shaping the body or a body part like a geometric shape, copying the tone of a spoken word using a particular movement quality, or moving rapidly or slowly to interpret the meaning of a timing-based word, such as *rapid*.

However, the previous examples are literal, because the dancer moves like the concept, shapes their body like it, or assumes its position. In contrast, abstraction, a more indirect movement transformation process which was described prior, can be used to relate to concepts based on a feeling response to the concept (Minton 39 *Using Movement*). An example of the abstraction process is to move in response to one's feelings about a color, although the same process can be used to transform the feeling response to characters in a story, various environments, or different types of music (Minton *Using Movement* 39–43).

Exploration Experiences

The following experiences are again provided to help the reader explore the content in the preceding chapter.

Basic Learning Theory Explorations

1. Zone of proximal development. Many shapes can be formed with the body based on different inspirations. What would be an appropriate inspiration that

could be used with first- or second-grade students to motivate creating body shapes? What type of inspiration would you use with middle school students as a basis for creating body shapes?
2. Learning styles. Try learning a movement from a particular dance genre in each of the following ways. First, watch a visual demonstration of a movement, and then attempt to perform the action. Next, read a description of the correct performance of a different movement, followed by attempting to perform it. Finally, consult information about how a third movement should feel in your body when it is performed correctly, and attempt to duplicate these bodily feelings while performing the movement. Which method of learning a movement was most effective for you?
3. Multiple intelligences. Create a simple movement with one arm.

- Then, describe this movement with words related to the qualities used.
- What type of music would be best to accompany this movement?
- Next, use counts to describe this movement, and add them together to determine the total length of the movement based on the total number of counts.
- Try to visualize the same movement in your mind. Then, describe its spatial attributes, such as its size, pathway, or direction.
- How did this movement feel in your body when you performed it?
- What message do you think this movement would communicate when it is observed by another person?

4. Experiential learning. Select a simple academic concept and describe this concept with words. Then, explain how you would use movement or hands-on activities to help students understand this concept.
5. Cooperative learning. Choose a movement to be learned and explain how you would work with a partner to help them perform the movement correctly.
6. Brain-based learning. Return to the movement you created in response to question 3. Then, develop the single movement into a phrase which includes at least three movements and describe the rhythmic pattern found in this phrase.
7. Brain-based learning. Perform the movement phrase in front of a mirror while focusing on the center of your body. Second, perform the same phrase again in front of the mirror, but this time focus more peripherally by extending your attention beyond your body. Did you perceive any differences in what you noticed in the movements in each of these two experiences?

More Complex Learning Theory Explorations

1. Zone of proximal development. Find two dance videos—one in which the movement would be appropriate for younger children, and another which is more challenging and appropriate for older students. Based on the movement

content in the videos, explain why each is appropriate for students in a different age group.
2. Learning styles. Choose one of the videos you used to answer question 1 in this section and explain how you would differentiate your instruction of the movement to accommodate visual, auditory, and kinesthetic learners. In other words, what would you emphasize to teach each type of learner?
3. Multiple intelligences. Using the same dance video you used to answer question 2, describe how two of the multiple intelligences might be used to aid in learning the movements.
4. Experiential learning. Find a video in which there is a description of how to learn academic concepts through the arts. Focus on one of the concepts described in the video, and describe how you could use creative movement to help students better understand the concept.
5. Cooperative learning. Use the same video as the one you used to answer question 4, and work with a partner to transform some of the concepts in the video into movement. What techniques could you use to create a well-coordinated and fruitful experience when working with a partner?
6. Brain-based learning. There are many different types of poetry. Three of these include limerick, sonnet, and haiku. Each of these types of poetry is based on a different organizational pattern. Learn the pattern found in each type of poetry and interpret the pattern in creative movement.
7. Brain-based learning. The following is a haiku poem. Read the poem and describe how and why its pattern and organization contribute to its meaning.

Traffic is insane.
Can I just go back to bed?
It must be Monday ("20 Funny Haiku Poems").

Basic Creativity Explorations

1. Observing. What are two contrasting images you observed in Figure 5.4?
2. Imaging. See if you can look away from the figure and imagine one of the shapes from the figure in your mind.
3. Abstracting. How would you describe the essence or essential quality of the entire design in Figure 5.4?
4. Recognizing patterns. Describe a relationship you see between two aspects of Figure 5.4.
5. Forming patterns. Why do these two aspects of Figure 5.4 form a pattern? What is their relationship?
6. Analogizing. How is one image in Figure 5.4 similar or like another part of the figure even though the two images are not exactly the same?
7. Body thinking. Select one of the images in Figure 5.4 and describe the bodily feeling to which it seems to connect.

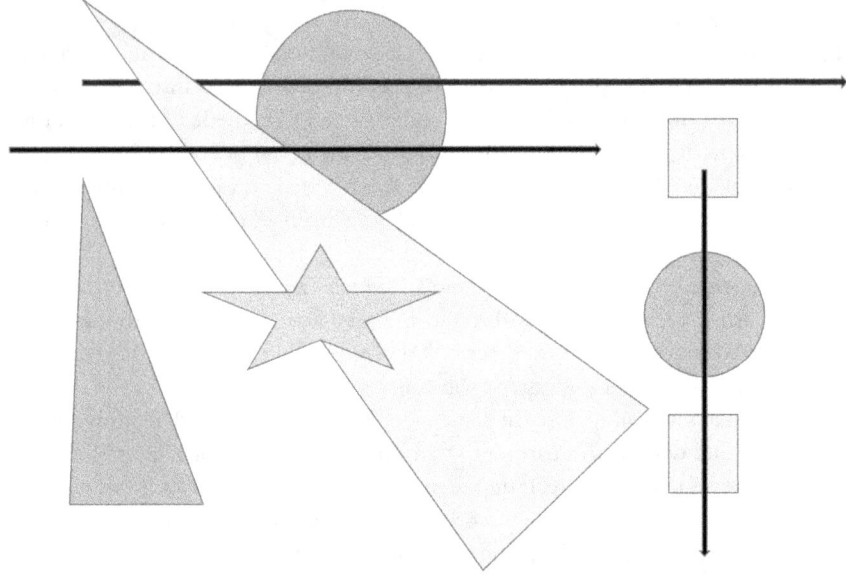

FIGURE 5.4 Figure is to be used in the explorations in this section.

Source: Illustration created by author.

8. Empathizing. What types of emotion or feeling do you connect with the same image?
9. Dimensional thinking. The images in Figure 5.4 are presented in two dimensions. How would you describe one of these images if you could create it in three dimensions?
10. Modeling. How would you describe a three-dimensional model of the relationship between two images shown in Figure 5.4?
11. Playing. What would Figure 5.4 look like if you could rearrange it in some way?
12. Transforming. How might you use your body to transform one image in Figure 5.4 into movement?
13. Synthesizing. What is your overall impression of Figure 5.4? How do its parts fit together?

More Complex Creativity Explorations

1. Observing. Return to the two contrasting images from Figure 5.4 which you identified in your answer to question 1 in the preceding section. Study each of these images and describe details which contribute their contrasting nature.
2. Imaging. See some of these details in your mind.
3. Abstracting. Create several movements which are based on these details and which capture their essence.

4. Forming patterns. Connect the movements you created in number 3 together to form one longer sequence.
5. Recognizing patterns. Practice the previous movement sequence several times and then describe any patterns or relationships you find, such as rhythmic patterns.
6. Analogizing. Compare the same movements you created to dissimilar objects, and describe any similarities you notice between the movements you created and the objects.
7. Body thinking. Perform the movement sequence again and describe how it feels kinesthetically in your body. What did you learn about the movement sequence using body thinking?
8. Empathizing. Do any of the movements in the sequence you created bring feelings to mind? If so, describe those feelings.
9. Dimensional thinking. Why is the process of creating the movement sequence based on Figure 5.4 an example of dimensional thinking?
10. Modeling. Draw a diagram or model of the movement sequence you created by copying the pathway through which you moved in space when performing it.
11. Playing. Rearrange the movements in your sequence several times and decide which arrangement you prefer and explain why you prefer one arrangement over another.
12. Transforming. Analyze the rhythmic pattern found in your movement sequence, and transform it into sounds played on percussion instruments.
13. Synthesizing. Describe how you might develop the movement sequence you created to form a section in a dance. Thus, how might you vary the movement sequence to create added movements.

Basic Interdisciplinary Explorations

1. Interdisciplinary or integrative methods were used in the studies and approaches described previously in the section titled "Learning through Dance Integration and Interdisciplinary Work in Dance." The academic concepts included in these studies and approaches were from math, science, writing, and transportation. Select a concept from one of these disciplines and describe it.
2. In the next section previously titled "The Author's Approach to Interdisciplinary Teaching through Dance," eleven movement components were described—direction, level, size, timing, duration, rhythm, quality, shape, pathway, position, and starting and stopping. These movement components can be used to transform concepts into actions using a literal transformation method. This means moving like the concept, shaping your body like it, or positioning your body in a similar way. How might you transform the concept you selected to answer the previous question into action using the literal method?
3. Continue by selecting additional concepts from the same discipline, and transform them into movements using the literal method.

4. Finally, connect the movements you created together to form a short dance. How would you describe the overall form or shape of this dance?

More Complex Interdisciplinary Explorations

1. Next, you are going to work with abstraction as the movement transformation method. Use the same concepts you worked with previously or choose new ones from a different academic discipline and describe those concepts.
2. The movement transformation process using abstraction is based on one's feeling response to the inspiration—in this case, academic concepts. Describe how you could use the same movement components to transform your selected concepts into movement using abstraction. Create your movement response to each of the concepts using abstraction and describe them.
3. Finally, combine the movements you created together to form a dance. How would you describe the shape or overall form of the dance? How does it compare to the first dance you created in the preceding section?
4. Which process—literal movement transformation or abstraction—provided a more in-depth understanding of the selected concepts?

References

Aslaksen, Karoline, and Havard Loras. "Matching Instruction with Modality-Specific Learning Style: Effects on Immediate Recall and Working Memory Performance." *Education Sciences*, vol. 9, no. 1, 2019, pp. 1–11.

Assandri, Eric. "Is 'Touching' Essential When Teaching Ballet?" *Research in Dance Education*, vol. 20, no. 2, 2019, pp. 197–207.

"Auditory Learning Style Explained." Western Governors University Blog, accessed 7 Nov. 2021, Auditory Learning Style Explained (wgu.edu).

Aumiller, Renay. "Choreographing the Page." *Dance Education in Practice*, vol. 4, no. 3, 2018, pp. 11–16.

Bashaw, Barbara. "Thinking Skills Writing Prompts for Dance—Negotiating Common Core Instruction." *Dance Education in Practice*, vol. 1, no. 1, 2015, pp. 23–32.

Bates, Bob. *Learning Theories Simplified*. 2nd ed. Sage, 2019.

Batson, Glenna, and Margaret Wilson. *Body and Mind in Motion: Dance and Neuroscience in Conversation*. Intellect, 2014.

Bolles, Gina, and Steven Chatfield. "The Intersection of Imagery Ability, Imagery Use, and Learning Style: A Exploratory Study." *Journal of Dance Education*, vol. 9, no. 1, 2009, pp. 6–16.

Boone, Natalie. *On the Move: A Mixed-Methods Study to Examine the Impact of Kinesthetic Learning Tables on Student On-Task Behavior and Academic Growth*. EdD Dissertation, Gardner-Webb University, 2016.

Bryans-Bongey, Sarah. "Tech-Based Approaches to Supporting and Engaging Diverse Learners: Visual Strategies for Success." *Contemporary Issues in Education Research*, vol. 11, no. 2, 2018, pp. 45–56.

Buck-Pavlick, Helen. "Using Empathy and Somatics in Dance Class to Engage Early Adolescent Learners from Low Socioeconomic Communities." *Dance Education in Practice*, vol. 6, no. 1, 2020, pp. 20–24.

Busso, Daniel, and Courtney Pollack. "No Brain Left Behind: Consequences of Neuroscience Discourse for Education." *Learning, Media and Technology*, vol. 40, no. 2, 2015, pp. 168–86.
Cruse, Holk, and Malte Schilling. "Getting Cognitive." *The Neurocognition of Dance: Mind, Movement and Motor Skills*. 2nd ed., edited by Bettina Blasing, et al., Routledge, 2019, pp. 150–68.
Csikszentmihalyi, Mihaly. *The Psychology of Discovery and Invention*. Harper Perennial Modern Classics, 2013.
Domm, Daniela Perazzo. "Im/possible Choreographies: Diffractive Processes and Ethical Entanglements in Current British Dance Practices." *Dance Research Journal*, vol. 51, no. 3, 2019, pp. 66–83.
Donnelly, Laura, and Heather Trommer-Beardslee. "Long-Distance Choreography, Learning, and Student Engagement: A Model for Connecting Students and Faculty Despite Geographic Location." *Dance Education in Practice*, vol. 2, no. 4, 2016, pp. 20–25.
Dou, Xinyu, et al. "The Linkage Cultivation of Creative Thinkng and Innovation Thinking in Dance Choreography." *Thinking Skills and Creativity*, vol. 41, 2021, pp. 1–10.
Duncan, Toni. *Understanding Poetry: Integrative Movement and Dance to Enhance the Learning Process for Middle and High School Students*. MA Thesis, University of Northern Colorado, 2016.
Egan, Candice, and Mark Quigley. "Dancing Earthquake Science Assists Recovery from the Christchurch Earthquakes." *Research in Dance Education*, vol. 16, no. 2, 2015, pp. 161–83.
Ehrenberg, Shantel. "Choreographic Practice and Pedagogy as Embodied Ideological Critique of the Labour for Knowledge" *Research in Dance Education*, vol. 20, no. 2, 2019, pp. 97–112.
Fisher, Vicky. "Unfurling the Wings of Flight: Clarifying 'the What' and 'the Why' of Mental Imagery Use in Dance." *Research in Dance Education*, vol. 18, no. 3, 2017, pp. 252–72.
Friederichs, Allison. "Peers Teaching Peers." *TD*, Jan. 2019, pp. 42–47. Peers Teaching Peers (peerlearninginstitute.com).
Gardner, Howard. *Frames of Mind: The Theory of Multiple Intelligences*. 3rd ed. Basic Books, 2011.
Giguere, Miriam. "Revitalizing Pennsylvania Through Creativity: Dance in Education." *Arts Education Policy Review*, vol. 106, no. 4, 2005, pp. 34–40.
———. "Dancing Thoughts: An Examination of Children's Cognition and Creative Process in Dance." *Research in Dance Education*, vol. 12, no. 1, 2011, pp. 5–28.
———. "The Social Nature of Cognition in Dance: The Impact of Group Interactions on Dance Education Practices." *Journal of Dance Education*, vol. 21, no. 3, 2021, pp. 132–39.
Golding, A., et al. "Investigating Learning Through Developmental Dance Movement as a Kinesthetic Tool in the Early Years Foundation Stage." *Research in Dance Education*, vol. 17, no. 3, 2016, pp. 235–67.
Goodreads, accessed 10 Nov. 2021, goodreads Confucius—Bing.
Green Gilbert, Anne. "Toward Best Practices in Dance Education Through the Theory of Multiple Intelligences." *Journal of Dance Education*, vol. 3, no. 1, 2003, pp. 28–33.
———. *Brain-Compatible Dance Education*. 2nd ed. Human Kinetics, 2019.
Guss-West, Clare. *Attention and Focus in Dance: Enhancing Power, Precision, and Artistry*. Human Kinetics, 2021.
Halliburton, Cheryl. *Re-Engaging Dis-Engaged Adolescent Students Through Dance*. EdD Dissertation, Long Island University, 2016.
Hammond, Zaretta. *Culturally Responsive Teaching & the Brain: Promoting Authentic Engagement and Rigor Among Culturally and Linguistically Diverse Students*. Corwin, 2015.
Hanna, Judith Lynne. "A Nonverbal Language for Imagining and Learning: Dance Education in K-12 Curriculum." *Educational Researcher*, vol. 37, no. 8, 2008, pp. 491–506.

———. *Dancing to Learn: The Brain's Cognition, Emotion, and Movement*. Rowman & Littlefield, 2015.

Hogenkamp, Loes, et al. "Analyzing Socially Shared Regulation of Learning During Cooperative Learning and the Role of Equal Contribution: A Grounded Theory Approach." *Education Sciences*, vol. 11, 2021, pp. 1–26.

Horowitz, Frances Degan, et al. "Educating Teachers for Developmentally Appropriate Practice." *Preparing Teachers for a Changing World: What Teachers Should Learn and Be Able to Do*, edited by Linda Darling-Hammond and John Bransford, Josey-Bass, 2005, pp. 88–125.

Howard, Meghan Kelly. *Transitions in University Learning Environments: Moving Towards a Kinesthetic Model*. EdD Dissertation, University of North Carolina, 2019.

Huddy, Avril. "Digital Technology in the Tertiary Dance Technique Studio: Expanding Student Engagement Through Collaborative and Co-Creative Experiences." *Research in Dance Education*, vol. 18, no. 2, 2017, pp. 174–89.

Johnson, Andrew. *Essential Learning Theories: Applications to Authentic Teaching Situations*. Rowman & Littlefield, 2019.

Joy, Jenn. *The Choreographic*. The MIT Press, 2014.

Kidd, Joanna, et al. "Auditory Perception and Word Recognition in Cantonese-Chinese Speaking Children with and Without Specific Language Impairment." *Journal of Child Language*, vol. 44, 2017, pp. 1–35.

Kirk, Johanna. "Experiencing Our Anatomy: Incorporating Human Biology into Dance Class vis Imagery, Imagination, and Somatics." *Journal of Dance Education*, vol. 14, no. 2, 2014, pp. 59–66.

Kosslyn, Stephen. "Stephen Kosslyn." accessed 1 Nov. 2021, Stephen Kosslyn—Wikipedia.

Krasnow, Donna, and Virginia Wilmerding. *Motor Learning and Control for Dance: Principles and Practices for Performers and Teachers*. Human Kinetics, 2015.

LaMotte, Megan. "The Integrated Approach Versus the Traditional Approach: Analyzing the Benefits of a Dance and Transportation Integrated Curriculum." *Journal of Dance Education*, vol. 18, no. 1, 2018, pp. 23–32.

Leandro, Cristina Rebelo, et al. "Interdisciplinary Working Practices: Can Creative Dance Improve Math?" *Research in Dance Education*, vol. 19, no. 1, 2018, pp. 74–90.

Lepczyk, Billie, et al. "Choreography as Design." *Journal of Dance Education*, vol. 18, no. 4, 2018, pp. 143–53.

"Logical-Mathematical Learning Style." Logical-Mathematical Intelligence: Logical Learning Styles (verywellfamily.com), accessed 30 Jan. 2022.

Marschark, Marc, et al. "Don't Assume Deaf Students Are Visual Learners." *Journal of Development and Physical Disabilities*, vol. 29, 2017, pp. 153–71.

Martin, Nina. "Spontaneous Dancemaking with Beginning Improvisers: Foundational Practices in Presence, Stillness, and Problem Solving." *Journal of Dance Education*, vol. 17, no. 1, 2017, pp. 27–30.

Matzke, Sarah. "Traversing the Succession of Space to Place to Home: A Kinesthetic Comprehension of the Body as It Forms an Epistemology of Space." *Research in Dance Education*, 2021, pp. 1–11, https://doi.org/10.1080/14647893.2021.1879774.

McCutchen, Brenda Pugh. *Teaching Dance as Art in Education*. Human Kinetics, 2006.

McGlynn, Kaitlyn, and Janey Kozlowski. "Kinesthetic Learning in Science." *Science Scope*, Summer 2017, pp. 24–27.

Mercer, Elliot. "Conceptual Systems: The Dances, Music, and Drawings of Laura Dean." *Dance Research Journal*, vol. 52, no. 3, 2020, pp. 22–41.

Minton, Sandra. "Assessment of High School Dance Students' Self-Esteem." *Journal of Dance Education*, vol. 1, no. 2, 2001, pp. 63–73.

———. "Assessment of High School Students' Creative Thinking Skills: A Comparison of Dance and Non-Dance Classes." *Research in Dance Education*, vol. 4, no. 1, 2003, pp. 31–49.

———. "Middle School Choreography Class: Two Parallel but Different Worlds." *Research in Dance Education*, vol. 8, no. 2, 2007, pp. 103–23.

———. *Using Movement to Teach Academics: The Mind & Body as One Entity*. Rowman & Littlefield Education, 2008.

Minton, Sandra, and Judi Hofmeister. "The International Baccalaureate Dance Programme: Learning Skills for Life in the 21st Century." *Journal of Dance Education*, vol. 10, no. 3, 2010, pp. 67–76.

Minton, Sandra, and Rima Faber. *Thinking with the Dancing Brain: Embodying Neuroscience*. Rowman & Littlefield Education, 2016.

———. *Choreography: A Basic Approach Using Improvisation*. 4th ed. Human Kinetics, 2018.

Mobley, Kayce, and Sarah Fisher. "Ditching the Desks: Kinesthetic Learning in College Classrooms." *The Social Studies*, vol. 105, 2014, pp. 301–9.

Morrow, Vanessa. *The Relationship Between the Learning Styles of Middle School Students and the Teaching and Learning Styles of Middle School Teachers and the Effects on Student Achievement of Students' Learning Styles and Teachers' Learning and Teaching Styles*. EdD Dissertation, University of Mississippi, 2011.

Nadel, Myron. "Everything Old Is New Again: Reviving the Traditional Choreographic Pedagogy of Louis Horst and Doris Humphrey." *Dance Education in Practice*, vol. 5, no. 4, 2019, pp. 11–16.

Odom, Bonzell. *The Effect of Teaching Styles and Learning Styles on Achievement in a College Classroom*. EdD Dissertation, University of St. Francis, 2019.

Overby, Lynette Young, et al. "Formative and Summative Assessments for Dance Interarts/Interdisciplinary Projects." *Journal of Dance Education*, vol. 13, no. 1, 2013, pp. 23–29.

———. *Public Scholarship in Dance: Teaching, Choreographing, Research, Service, and Assessment for Community Engagement*. Human Kinetics, 2016.

Payne, Helen, and Barry Costas. "Creative Dance as Experiential Learning in State Primary Education: The Potential Benefits for Children." *Journal of Experiential Education*, vol. 44, no. 3, 2021, pp. 277–92.

Prichard, Robin. "Nonlinguistic Feedback in Critical Responses to Choreography." *Journal of Dance Education*, vol. 19, no. 3, 2019, pp. 117–26.

Prickett, Stacey. "Constrained Bodies: Dance, Social Justice, and Choreographic Agency." *Dance Research Journal*, vol. 48, no. 3, 2016, pp. 45–57.

Purvis, Denise. "Meeting Students on Their Own Ground: Best Practices in Teaching Dance Technique, Grades 9–12." *Journal of Dance Education*, vol. 14, no. 1, 2014, pp. 35–38.

Rabkin, Nick. "Learning and the Arts." *Putting the Arts in the Picture: Reframing Education in the 21st Century*, edited by Nick Rabkin and Robin Redmond, Columbia College Chicago, 2004, pp. 5–15.

Raman, Tanja. "Collaborative Learning in the Dance Technique Class." *Research in Dance Education*, vol. 10, no. 1, 2009, pp. 75–87.

Randall, Tresa. "Enlivening Dance History Pedagogy through Archival Projects." *Journal of Dance Education*, vol. 12, 2012, pp. 7–13.

Ren, Guanxin. "Which Learning Style Is Most Effective in Learning Chinese as a Second Language." *Journal of International Education Research*, vol. 9, no. 1, 2013, pp. 21–32.

Risner, Doug. "Research, Design, and Implementation of an Internship Course in Dance: Turning Student Knowledge into Professional Know-How." *Journal of Dance Education*, vol. 15, no. 2, 2015, pp. 60–71.

Roberts, Frederic. *Experiential Learning in a Traditional Classroom: Experiential Pedagogy, Traditional Pedagogy, and Student Preference*. MA Thesis, Prescott College, 2016.

Root-Bernstein, Robert, and Michèle Root-Bernstein. *Sparks of Genius: The 13 Thinking Tools of the World's Most Creative People*. Houghton Mifflin, 1999.

Sandler, Heather Warfel. "Redefining Success in Dance: How Dance Education Can Impact Diverse Communities." Oct. 10, 2021, NDEO National Conference, virtual presentation.

Savrami, Katia. "A Duet between Science and Art: Neural Correlates of Dance Improvisation." *Research in Dance Education*, vol. 18, no. 3, 2017, pp. 273–90.

Schack, Thomas. "Building Blocks and Architecture of Dance." *The Neurocognition of Dance: Mind, Movement and Motor Skills*. 2nd ed., edited by Blassing et al., Routledge, 2019, pp. 117–38.

Schunk, Dale, and Maria Dibenedetto. "Self-Efficacy Theory in Education." *Handbook of Motivation at School*. 2nd ed., edited by Kathryn Wentzel and David Miele, Routledge, 2016, pp. 34–54.

———. *Learning Theories: An Educational Perspective*. 8th ed. Pearson, 2020.

Schupp, Karen. "Teaching Collaborative Skills through Dance: Isolating the Parts to Stengthen the Whole." *Journal of Dance Education*, vol. 15, no. 4, 2015, pp. 152–58.

Sharma, Geeta, et al. "Impact of a Curriculum-Integrated Dance Program on Literacy and Numeracy: A Mixed Methods Study on Primary School Children." *Journal of Dance Education*, 2021, https://doi.org/10.1080/15290824.2020.1864379.

Siew, Nyet Moi, et al. "The Effects of Problem-Based Learning with Cooperative Learning on Preschoolers' Scientific Creativity." *Journal of Baltic Science Education*, vol. 16, no. 1, 2017, pp. 100–12.

Stern, Erik, and Rachel Bachman. "Pattern Play: The Case for Dance in College Mathematics and Beyond." *Journal of Dance Education*, vol. 21, no. 3, 2021, pp. 158–67.

Stinson, Susan. "Search for Evidence: Continuing Issues in Dance Education Research." *Research in Dance Education*, vol. 16, no. 1, 2015, pp. 5–15.

Swanson, Brook, and Suzanne Ostersmith. "Moving toward Engagement: Teaching Collaborative Dance and Science Classes to First Year College Students." *Journal of Dance Education*, 2021, pp. 1–8, https://doi.org/10.1080/15290824.2021.1876237.

"Twenty Funny Haiku Poems." 20 Funny Haiku Poems: Examples for All Ages (yourdictionary.com), accessed 3 Dec. 2021.

Valls, Rebecca et al. "Five Years of Integrating Science and Dance: A Qualitative Inquiry of Constructivist Elementary School Teachers." *Research in Dance Education*, vol. 20, no. 2, 2019, pp. 113–29.

Wakamatsu, Kori. "The Five Commitments: A Philosophical Framework Manifested through Dance." *Journal of Dance Education*, vol. 13, no. 3, 2013, pp. 78–83.

Wass, Rob, and Clinton Golding. "Sharpening a Tool for Teaching: The Zone of Proximal Development." *Teaching in Higher Education*, vol. 19, no. 6, 2014, pp. 671–84.

Weissmann, Dan. "You Can't Get Much Better than That." *Putting the Arts in the Picture: Reframing Education in the 21st Century*, edited by Nick Rabkin and Robin Redmond, Columbia College Chicago, 2004, pp. 17–48.

Wilson, Lisa, and Ann-Thomas Moffett. "Building Bridges for Dance through Arts-Based Research." *Research in Dance Education*, vol. 18, no. 2, 2017, pp. 135–49.

Zull, James. *From Brain to Mind: Using Neuroscience to Guide Change in Education*. Stylus, 2011.

6
IN CONCLUSION . . .

Further Evidence

In her master's thesis project, Ann Moradian used survey research to find out how those in interdisciplinary fields that are not largely involved with movement-based practices engaged with body studies and learned about the body (43). Eighty-nine individuals initially participated in this part of the study (Moradian vi). Of the individuals surveyed, only 37% considered body studies to be a core focus of their research, while 29% considered this area of study to be of only general interest; 5% of those surveyed replied that the body was outside their field's interests (Moradian 43). The interdisciplinary participants in this study were primarily from the fields of education, psychology, neuroscience, medicine, philosophy, and the performing arts other than dance.

It is common knowledge that one way in which those in other fields could learn about the bodily basis of knowing is through interdisciplinary work with those highly involved in body and movement-based work. However, Moradian discovered there was institutional resistance to doing interdisciplinary work, with such efforts sometimes limited by the fact that knowledge is isolated into various silos; one respondent noted that there was a lack of understanding and appreciation between fields, with fifty-four out sixty respondents indicating there was no common language to deal with body-based content (45).

Nevertheless, Moradian discovered there was hope based on interest among those outside the dance and dance education fields. Those surveyed indicated areas of interest related to the human body and its movement and suggested exploring the mind as it relates to the body by researching mindfulness, consciousness, the generation of meaning, agency, anxiety, trauma, emotion, dementia, neuronal degeneration, neuroscience content, accelerated learning, and ecopsychology, among other proposed topics (Moradian 48).

208 In Conclusion . . .

Another issue uncovered by Moradian was how the interdisciplinary individuals surveyed focused on their bodies. This is also a significant issue because it seems those who are more concerned with their bodies and who regularly participate in movement practices would be more inclined to study or do research on body- or movement-based content. Moradian found that the respondents' awareness of their bodies ranged from being very unaware to having a refined awareness (50). Based on Moradian's research, thirty-seven of the respondents were most aware of their bodies when exercising or engaged in an activity like mediation or teaching; twenty-seven connected bodily awareness with a particular time of the day, such as the first thing in the morning; fifteen respondents were aware of their bodies throughout their day; another fifteen became aware of their bodies during discomfort or pain; and three participants acknowledged they were generally disconnected from their bodies (50). Only a few of the respondents were more aware of their body as it was related to other people or the environment (Moradian 50).

Future Considerations

Based on the content of Moradian's thesis and the content in the preceding chapters of this book, it is apparent there is interest in the bodily basis of knowing and in the mind-body connection among those in other fields. Figure 6.1 was created to display the basis for this interest and why it is believed the mind and body are connected.

The following is an attempt to explain Figure 6.1 in greater detail. Learning, creating, and problem-solving begin with some type of input, whether it is an inspiration, some type of sensory stimulus, or an attempt to decipher the answer

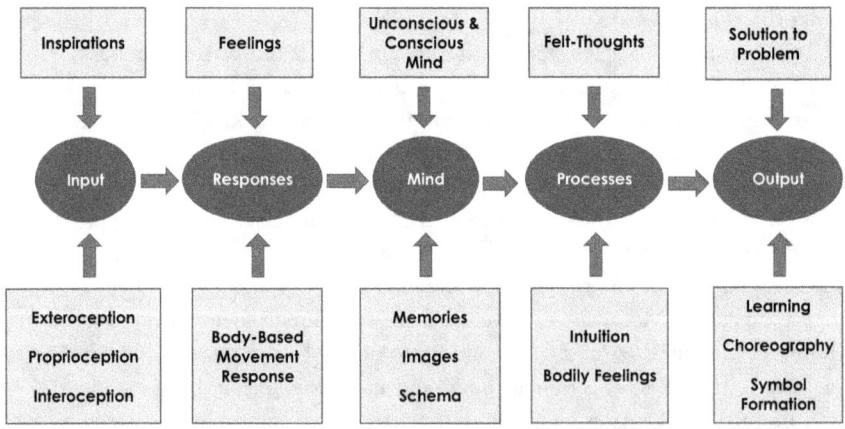

FIGURE 6.1 Diagram illustrating mind-body connections occurring during learning and creative problem-solving.

Source: Diagram created by author.

to a question. Thus, this process must be initiated in some manner. Following this initiation, a person responds whether with emotions or through movement, among other possibilities. Then, it is the job of the mind, either consciously or unconsciously, and usually both, to connect with memories, images, or other content which might aid the creative thinking/problem-solving process. These revelations, in turn, are guided by the individual's mental processes, felt-thoughts, intuition, and bodily feelings, resulting in finding a solution to the problem in the form of learning, solving the problem, or by creating art.

However, it is important to consider the fact that the processes featured in Figure 6.1 do not usually take place in a straightforward, linear fashion because at most points along the way, the person involved in solving a problem or creating art reverses course by returning to an earlier stage in the process. For example, the researcher or creator may begin to respond to the inspiration or problem to be solved and then return to the initial stage to re-evaluate the problem anew or reinspect the inspiration. There could also be a need to compare the processes experienced as thoughts, intuitions, felt thoughts, or even the final output to one's initial responses.

The overriding importance of this diagram, though, is that the body and movement can be connected to each step along the way as featured in the diagram. This fact was emphasized in the preceding chapters based on comments made by educators, dancers, dance educators, choreographers, somatics practitioners, psychologists, neuroscientists, and phenomenologists alike. While the research studies and comments described in the preceding chapters were made at different points in time, they uniformly point to the importance of the body and movement to cognitive processes and their connection with the human mind. Table 6.1 is an attempt to highlight some of the body- and movement-based comments made by various authorities and how those comments connect with the diagram in Figure 6.1.

Recommendations

So the question is where to go from here if movement and dance are to be considered integral components of education.

- First and foremost, it is imperative to make the information existing in multiple disciplines as noted in the previous chapters more available to the public in general. This end can be partially accomplished by publishing articles on the pertinent content in journals that are the purview of allied disciplines, such as other arts disciplines, education, psychology, philosophy, and even the neurosciences.
- Second, such articles should be published in popular magazines which are outside the scope of dance and dance education.
- Third, the content of such articles should be written in a way that is easy to understand by stakeholders outside the field and devoid of technical terms and jargon.

TABLE 6.1 Evidence of Movement in the Creative Thinking/Problem-Solving Process Based on Figure 6.1

Input	Responses	Mind	Processes	Output
Washburn: "Muscle sensations enter … into perception, ideas, sentiments, emotions … into the whole psychic life" (Cerny 17).	Two of the most important characteristics of emotions are that they are grounded and experienced in the body (Menon 44).	Bull: The unconscious is where the motor part of mental processes is conserved (Cerny 18-19).	Kant: "[M]athematical truths were forms of synthetic *a priori* knowledge, which means they are necessary and universal, yet known through intuition" ("Imanuel Kant" Wikipedia).	Piaget: Emphasized the role of the body and movement in the process of acquiring knowledge early in human life (Marmeleira & Santos 413).
Sacks: We do not see objects but instead view them as shapes, contours, and boundaries (73).	Schilder: Inner bodily tensions or motions created during perception and the resulting motor impulses were connected, but he could not explain how the two worked together (Cerny 13-14).	Piaget: Consciousness involved a subjective awareness that "is constructed; it was an active process that goes beyond exposure to the environment, requiring deliberate action" (Ferrari et al. 196-97).	Rugg: "These first physical movements … are the sources of the first flashes of meaning, for there is no 'mind' except in reactions of the body" (100).	H'Doubler: Physical movements can promote learning (George 17).
Merleau-Ponty: Humans come to know their world through personal experience and the lived body (Paparo 489).	Werner and Kaplan: Symbolic knowledge is transformed during one lifetime because an infant initially knows the world through his or her affective sensorimotor patterns (Cerny 12-13).	Dewey: The body represented a crucial component of consciousness (George 16).	Gendlin's felt sense is "an embodied experience of a whole situation … that exists before words or other symbols" (Cornell & McGavin 30).	Dewey: "Men are afraid … to recognize the most wonderful of all the structures of the vast universe—the human body" (Buono 150).
Wofflein: Content seen is internally modeled based on a hardwired sympathy (Pashman 20).	Gestalt practitioners: Believe the body holds a history of adjustments a person makes in his or her life based on muscular tensions held in the body (Grossman 84).	Todd: Advocated new investigations of the body by studying the unconscious (*Thinking Body* 3).	Sheets-Johnstone: "the felt on-going presence … the lived body's experienced hereness [is] … grounded in the tactile-kinesthetic body" ("Lived Body" 50).	Sheets-Johnstone: "Moving and thinking in movement eventuate in knowledge because they eventuate in learning" ("Kinesthesia" 157).
Arnheim: Experiences play a crucial role in conceptual development (Antovic & Stamenkovic 386).	Damasio: Common emotions are "a complex collection of chemical and neural responses forming a distinctive pattern" (*Looking* 53).	Damasio: Mental processes "[are] based on how the brain maps the body to produce a parallel demonstration of the mind-body connection" (*Looking* 12).	Ramachandran: "Human thought is deeply shaped by its interconnection with the body" (143).	Clark: Much of human higher cognition appears based on the human embodied perceptuomotor capabilities (xxvi-xxvii).
Sheets-Johnstone: "[T]actility and movement [are] not simply … sensorimotor pathways but … ways of knowing the world" (*Roots* 16).		Kandel: Conscious thought is a biological process explained by "molecular signaling pathways used by interacting populations of nerve cells" (*In Search* 9).		The processes of teaching and learning continue to be based on cognitive approaches despite the fact that holistic and embodied techniques might better serve educational goals (Rodríguez-Jiménez & Carmona 229).
		If the distinction between inside and outside the body is negated, one recognizes mind is in a world of the brain, body, objects, and other people (Bailey 287).		

- Fourth, the connections between movement, dance, and cognition should be written in a way which is broadly applicable and usable.
- Fifth, as Moradian indicated in the summary of her study, there needs to be a unified use of terms and language to accommodate understanding between different disciplines.
- Sixth, more research—both qualitative and quantitative—needs to be completed which connects directly with the substantial link existing between movement, dance, and learning, creative problem-solving, and cognition.
- Seventh, it appears that the results of good, solid quantitative research is more likely to convince school administrators and school district personnel of the value of including dance in education.
- Eighth, those outside the fields of dance and dance education need to be provided with techniques and methods they understand so they can use movement- and dance-based teaching methods in their own work. For instance, the educational viability of body- and movement-based content can be increased by providing stakeholders with lesson plans and step-by-step descriptions of how to use movement and dance to connect with academic content and students' cognitive processes.

Discussion

Based on the previous statements, it appears there is a need for research on the how and why of the bodily basis for cognition and learning. The question, then, is how the outcome of such research can be made credible for those outside the field. In a conference paper, John Mendy referred to this issue as the problem of depersonalization or "detaching oneself from the outcome of one's research such that the knowledge that is produced is seen to be un-biased . . . or convincing to other people" (274).

In answer to the preceding question, Mendy suggested that research outcomes are depersonalized when collaboration is involved among the stakeholders, and they become active researchers, so to speak, by strengthening their presence and the quality of the contributions made by each person involved (274). In the dance education arena, this could mean involving teachers and others involved in education who are not dance educators as active participants in such research—an approach which could ultimately lead to a change in teaching techniques and strategies which incorporate more movement and dance.

Content written by John Bransford, a professor of psychology and education, and his colleagues is pertinent to this discussion because they pointed out the importance of describing the mind-body connection in a way that provides understanding in comparison to merely remembering facts based on such content (19). Understanding, in turn, means explaining why something occurs or happens as it does (Bransford et al. 19). Thus, the point is to describe the mind-body connection in an understandable way so this information might lead to changing teaching and learning strategies in education. Learning which integrates the body and which incorporates creative movement-based problem-solving strategies in the process could fit such goals and encourage cognition which illuminates the why of learning. The emergence of such a new body of knowledge could help promote the why aspect in this learning paradigm and provide evidence for the creation of new and differentiated teaching strategies.

Assistance with the aforementioned goals might be found in the discipline of educational neuroscience. In his book *Mind, Brain, & Education*, David Sousa explained that this discipline has emerged in recent years based on the development of various imaging technologies (2–4). Some of these imaging technologies were described in previous chapters. Of importance to the current discussion, however, is that the many authorities who contributed chapters to Sousa's book discussed the relationship between the body, movement, and cognition. Some examples of these relationships follow.

Judy Willis, a neurologist with experience teaching elementary and middle school, wrote that learning includes recognizing patterns and matching new information to memories and established neural networks—processes which are closely allied with pattern recognition and formation (59) and integral to the creative problem-solving processes in dance. Cognitive neuroscientist Mary Helen Immordino-Yang and educational doctoral student Matthias Faeth recommended that teachers should encourage students to use their intuition while learning and solving problems (80). Based on discussions in previous chapters, intuition is closely connected to the bodily way of knowing. Diane Williams, a professor of speech and language pathology, suggested that interpreting language involves theory of mind or understanding the thoughts and intentions of the speaker (91). The thought process described by Williams appears connected with empathy, which was previously established as a body-based process which could be refined through creative movement practices. Finally, Mariale Hardiman, who has an extensive background in education, noted that involvement in the arts can teach persistence, symbolic understanding, resilience, absorption in content, and provide opportunities for collaboration (253). The studies by dance educators and others described in previous chapters demonstrated that dance can and does provide these benefits.

Researcher Bri Miller was interested in probing the perception nondance familiars (those associated with schools but who were not dance educators) had with respect to participating in dance; in other words, what benefits, if any, did this group attribute to involvement in dance (iii). In the outcome of this study, 100% of the nondance familiars believed participation in dance could improve the students' communication/social skills, 58.33% thought dance developed the ability to adapt, and 91.6% of this same group felt dance taught the ability to observe details (Miller 48).

A positive note can also be found in a doctoral dissertation study conducted by Patricia Reedy. In one part of this study, seventy-four classroom teachers who taught primarily in public elementary schools were asked to describe their beliefs about creativity (Reedy 82). The Teacher Perceptions of Creativity in Dance Instrument, created by the researcher, was used to assess the teachers' beliefs about creativity in dance (Reedy 111). The researcher found that the classroom teachers thought all children have the capacity for creativity in dance and that creativity can be improved upon (134). They also thought that the creativity, improvisation, and opportunity for expression often found in dance are important, while defining creativity as a form of self-expression, emotional freedom, and the opportunity for self-determination (Reedy 134).

References

Antovic, Mihailo, and Dusan Stamenkovic. "Vision, Space, and Embodiment: Interpretation of English Idioms by Serbian Students." *Selected Papers from UK-CLA Meetings*, vol. 1, 2012, pp. 385–400.

Bailey, Richard. "Educating with Brain, Body and World Together." *Interchange*, vol. 51, 2020, pp. 277–91.

Bransford, John, et al. "Introduction." *Preparing Teachers for a Changing World: What Teachers Should Learn and Be Able to Do*, edited by Linda Darling-Hammond and John Bransford, Jossey-Bass, 2005, pp. 1–39.

Buono, Alexia. "Interweaving a Mindfully Somatic Pedagogy into an Early Childhood Classroom." *Pedagogies: An International Journal*, vol. 14, no. 2, 2019, pp. 150–68.

Cerny, Sandra. *Analysis of Movement Resulting from Experiences Structured to Produce Involvement*. MA Thesis, University of California at Los Angeles, 1967.

Clark, Jonathan, and Taku Ando. "Geometry, Embodied Cognition and Choreographic Praxis." *International Journal of Performance Arts and Digital Media*, vol. 10, no. 2, 2014, pp. 179–92.

Cornell, Ann Weiser, and Barbara Mc Gavin. "The Concept of 'Felt Sense' in Embodied Knowing and Action." *The Art and Science of Embodied Research Design: Concepts, Methods and Cases*, edited by Jennifer Frank Tantia, Routledge, 2021, pp. 29–39.

Damasio, Antonio. *Looking for Spinoza: Joy, Sorrow, and the Feeling Brain*. Hartcourt, 2003.

Ferrari, Michel et al. "Piaget's Framework for a Scientific Study of Consciousness." *Human Development*, vol. 44, no. 4, 2001, pp. 195–213.

George, Doran. *The Natural Body in Somatics Dance Training*. Oxford UP, 2020.

Grossman, Susan. "Empirical Evidence of the Embodiment Awareness Changes in Somatic Focused Gestalt Psychotherapy." *The Art and Science of Embodied Research Design: Concepts, Methods and Cases*, edited by Jennifer Frank Tantia, Routledge, 2021, pp. 76–85.

Hardiman, Mariale. "The Creative-Artistic Brain." *Mind, Brain, & Education: Neuroscience Implications for the Classroom*, edited by David Sousa, Solution Tree, 2010, pp. 227–46.

"Immanuel Kant." Wikipedia, Immanuel Kant—Wikipedia, accessed 19 Dec. 2021.

Immordino-Yang, Mary Helen, and Matthias Faeth. "The Role of Emotion and Skilled Intuition in Learning." *Mind, Brain, & Education: Neuroscience Implications for the Classroom*, edited by David Sousa, Solution Tree, 2010, pp. 69–83.

Kandel, Eric. *In Search of Memory: The Emergence of a New Science of Mind*. Norton, 2006.

Marmeleira, José, and Graça Duarte Santos. "Do Not Neglect the Body and Action: The Emergence of Embodiment Approaches to Understanding Human Development." *Perceptual and Motor Skills*, vol. 126, no. 3, 2019, pp. 410–45.

Mendy, John. "Conference Proceedings: European Conference on Research Methodology for Business and Management Studies." 274–81, June 2015, www.proquest.com/docview/1721001687/?pq-origsite=primo.

Menon, Usha. "Analyzing Emotions as Culturally Constructed Scripts." *Culture & Psychology*, vol. 6, no. 1, 2000, pp. 40–50.
Miller, Bri Michelle. *Barriers to Dance Education: An Exploration into the Beliefs of Dance Educators and Non-Dance Familiars on Dance and Its Place in the Public School System*. MA Thesis, The University of Northern Colorado, 2021.
Moradian, Ann. *Missing in Action: Locating the Body in Interdisciplinary Studies*. MA Thesis, The University of Northern Colorado, 2020.
Paparo, Stephen. "Embodying Singing in the Choral Classroom: A Somatic Approach to Teaching and Learning." *International Journal of Music Education*, vol. 34, no. 4, 2016, pp. 488–98.
Pashman, Susan. "Dancing with Damasio: Complementary Aspects of Kinesthesia, Complementary Approaches to Dance." *Journal of Aesthetic Education*, vol. 51, no. 4, 2017, pp. 26–43.
Ramachandran, V.S. *The Tell-Tale Brain: A Neuroscientist's Quest for What Makes Us Human*. Norton, 2011.
Reedy, Patricia. *An Investigation of California Classroom Teachers' Beliefs and Ratings of Creativity in Dance*. Doctoral Dissertation, University of San Francisco, 2020.
Rodríguez-Jiménez, Rosa-Maria, and Manuel Carmona. "Mixed Methods for Evaluating Embodied Processes in Higher Education." *The Art and Science of Embodied Research Design: Concepts, Methods and Cases*, edited by Jennifer Frank Tantia, Routledge, 2021, pp. 229–41.
Rugg, Harold. *Imagination*. Harper and Row, 1963.
Sacks, Oliver. *The Mind's Eye*. Vintage/Random House, 2010.
Sheets-Johnstone, Maxine. *The Roots of Thinking*. Temple UP, 1990.
———. "Kinesthesia: An Extended Critical Overview and a Beginning Phenomenology of Learning." *Continental Philosophy Review*, vol. 52, 2019, pp. 143–69.
———. "The Lived Body." *The Humanistic Psychologist*, vol. 48, no. 1, 2020, pp. 28–53.
Sousa, David. "Introduction." *Mind, Brain, & Education: Neuroscience Implications for the Classroom*, edited by David Sousa, Solution Tree, 2010, pp. 1–7.
Todd, Mabel Ellsworth. *The Thinking Body*. Dance Horizons, 1975.
Williams, Diane. "The Speaking Brain." *Mind, Brain, & Education: Neuroscience Implications for the Classroom*, edited by David Sousa, Solution Tree, 2010, pp. 85–109.
Willis, Judy. "The Current Impact of Neuroscience on Teaching and Learning." *Mind, Brain, & Education: Neuroscience Implications for the Classroom*, edited by David Sousa, Solution Tree, 2010, pp. 45–66.

GLOSSARY

abstract a type of dance or other work of art that has no message but which is frequently created through a process of playing around or experimenting with movement

abstracting the process of emphasizing one aspect of an inspiration which is considered especially important (Root-Bernsteins 72–73)

abstraction process of removing, separating from, or condensing something to its essence; also, a method of changing concepts into actions by moving, like the basic feeling or essence of the concept

active learning gaining understanding or knowledge by doing or solving a problem

amygdala a brain area concerned with emotions, especially fear; part of the limbic system

analogizing process of finding a resemblance between two otherwise-unlike things (Root-Bernsteins 137)

anatomical imagery mental imagery that employs anatomical terms and which is metaphoric (Krasnow and Wilmerding 277)

anterior cingulate part of the brain's cortex that helps focus and awareness of thoughts; located at the middle of the frontal lobe in front of the corpus callosum

basal ganglia a group of cells found in the inner layers of the cerebrum of the brain that have a role in controlling movement and some cognitive functions

biomechanical the application of mechanical principles to entities which are alive; related to laws governing the movements or structure of living organisms

body image the image or picture one has of their body in their mind

brain-based learning lesson content based on how the brain/mind functions in organizing and understanding input (Caine and Caine 11)

Broca's area the brain area, located in the left frontal lobe, responsible for expressive language and the ability to use abstract thought

Cartesian duality a theory of thinking that asserts mind and matter are separate; that mind and body are nonidentical and the mind can continue to exist in the absence of the body

cerebellum part of the brain located beneath the occipital lobe that is responsible for movement control, coordination, and learning new motor skills

cognition the process of knowing; something which is perceived

conscious an awareness of one's existence, surroundings, or thoughts; having fully active mental faculties

constructivist an approach to learning in which the students actively attempt to interpret their world based on existing skills, knowledge, and developmental level (Bransford et al. 52)

control group the group of subjects who receive no treatment in terms of the variable or treatment being studied

cooperative learning a form of learning which, in many cases, may be too great for a single student to complete and which has an objective of developing the ability to work collaboratively (Schunk 516)

corpuscles of Ruffini nerve receptors in the skin which are sensitized when the skin is stretched (Schenkman et al. 208)

cortex the most superficial aspect of a bodily structure or the brain in this context

cutaneous pertaining to the skin

dance integration the use of dance to help teach nondance concepts

dimensional thinking using mental processes to move from 2D to 3D or vice versa; one of the thinking tools used by creative people (Root-Bernsteins 204)

direct imagery a nonverbal representation of an actual movement (Krasnow and Wilmerding 280)

divergent thinking cognition which leads into various directions; some original, and others conventional

dynamometer a device for measuring mechanical force such as grip strength

embody the process of giving content, such as an idea, a physical form or manifestation

emotion a state of mind based on one's circumstances, mood, or relationship with others

emotional intelligence the process of being sensitive to your feelings or to the feelings of others

empathy being able to see and understand the world as others see and experience it.

empathizing the process of being able to see the world through other peoples' eyes (Root-Bernsteins 187)

encode the process of analyzing sensory input and storing it

epistemology a branch of philosophy which is concerned with knowledge, belief, and truth; the theory of knowledge based on its methods, validity, and scope; an investigation of knowledge that differentiates beliefs from opinion;

a classic epistemological question concerned with what humans are able to know and how we know it

executive functions mental skills such as working memory, flexible thinking, and self-control used on a daily basis to manage life in an effective way; problems with executive function make it difficult to focus, follow directions, and handle emotions among other issues

experiential learning a type of curriculum centered on practical activities and hands-on projects (Bates 276)

experimental group the group of subjects who receive a treatment in terms of the variable being studied

explicit knowledge the conscious recall of people, places, things, events, and facts; the same as declarative memory or knowledge

external focus the effects of movements; general outcome (Krasnow and Wilmerding 281)

exteroception related to stimuli that come from outside the organism; sensitivity to stimuli which originate outside the body

felt sense a mechanism of inner knowing, or internal awareness, originally described by Eugene Gendlin

felt thought the concept that every human creative act is both felt and thought (Rugg 44)

force platform a small surface or platform which is used to measure variations of downward force on its surface

functional magnetic resonance imaging (fMRI) a device used by doctors, other medical personnel, and researchers to measure brain activity and track cognitive processes

Gestalt therapy a form of psychotherapy in which the emphasis is on the present moment; Gestalt therapists believe people are linked to and influenced by their environment and cannot be understood without understanding their context

global imagery a form of imagery which creates an overall state or feeling (Krasnow and Wilmerding 282)

Golgi tendon organ a mechanism of proprioception located at the junction of a muscle and its tendon, which is stimulated by muscle tension when the muscle is stretched or contracts (Schenkman et al. 213)

gyrus one of many inward folds on the surface of the cerebral cortex

haptic relating to the sense of touch, especially when perceiving and manipulating objects

hippocampus a part of the brain located deep within the temporal lobe that is necessary for forming explicit memories

holistic a belief that the parts are interconnected and explainable only by referring to the whole

hypothalamus a part of the brain located below the thalamus which controls autonomic, endocrine, and visceral functions

ideokinesis a somatic practice created by Mabel Todd in which the focus is on imagery which is used to create an anatomically balanced body (Eddy 28)

inferior parietal lobule a posterior area of the brain which is important to visuospatial processing; one of the divisions of the parietal lobe of the brain

inspiration the starting point for movement exploration and the creation of movement; can be used interchangeably with motivation or stimulus

instinct a fixed response to certain stimuli which is not learned

interdisciplinary dance a teaching strategy in which movement and dance are used to help students understand nondance concepts

internal focus the act of concentrating on specific movements that are part of a task (Krasnow and Wilmerding 282)

interoception a sensory system that enables one to understand what is going on inside one's body; the perception of internal body states

intrafusial fibers the muscle spindles consist of between two and ten slender and specialized muscle fibers known as intrafusial fibers; these fibers are surrounded by a thin capsule which is attached at both ends to the striated muscle fibers (Schenkman et al. 210)

intuition the ability to understand something without using conscious reasoning

isokinetic exercises in which the muscles move at a constant pace

joint receptor a part of the body's proprioceptive system located in the joint capsules and ligaments; function is more limited than that of the muscle spindles (Schenkman et al. 214)

kinesthesia the act of consciously sensing the body's movements (Krasnow and Wilmerding 283)

kinesthetic imagery a mental representation or inspiration that describes a body feeling which accompanies an action

Laban effort shape a method of analyzing human effort based on movement direction (direct or indirect), weight (heavy or light), speed (quick or sustained), and flow (bound or free)

Language of Dance Motif Notation a method of creating, exploring, and recording movement and dance

learning style the different ways individuals understand information, such as visual, auditory, or tactile/kinesthetic

limbic system a group of brain structures which regulate emotion located in the middle of the brain; includes the hypothalamus, hippocampus, amygdala, and a few other brain structures

lines of movement imagery mental representations which designate a specific movement direction required in the relative position of body parts (Krasnow and Wilmerding 283)

literacy the ability to read and write; in this context, also refers to the ability to understand and appreciate visual art, music, and dance

literal the most usual or basic meaning of words; not metaphorical; in the context of creative movement, means moving like an inspiration, shaping the body like it, or assuming its position

long-term memory a process in which connections between brain neurons are strengthened, resulting in continued ability to recall content or experiences

Meissner's corpuscles   receptors in the skin which adapt rapidly and contribute to fine tactile discrimination (Schenkman et al. 206–7)
mental image   a psychological activity which can evoke the characteristics of an absent object or event (Krasnow and Wilmerding 283)
mental practice   rehearsing a movement skill or sequence mentally without physically executing the movements (Krasnow and Wilmerding 283)
metaphoric imagery   representing the targeted movement with a figure or likeness; also called indirect imagery (Krasnow and Wilmerding 283)
mindfulness   the ability to be fully aware and present by waking up one's mental, physical, and emotional processes
mirror neuron   brain cells involved in empathy which become active when observing facial expressions, energies from, or movements of another person
modeling   a representation or physical entity that displays characteristics of the real object (Root-Bernsteins 229); in this context, can refer to movements or a dance
motor imagery   mental execution of movements without overt actions or muscular activation; similar to mental rehearsal
motor skill   precise movement of muscles, with the intent to perform a specific movement act
motor theory   a system of ideas related to human movement
movement literacy   having the ability to discriminate between slight differences in movements
multiple intelligences   a theory of human intellect that described diverse ways of thinking and knowing; challenged the traditional viewpoint at that time
muscle spindles   sensors scattered throughout skeletal muscles which respond to stretching or lengthening of the muscle (Schenkman et al. 209–10)
neuroimaging   a branch of medical imaging technology that can be used to assess brain health, discover how the brain works, and learn how different activities impact brain functions
neuromatrix   a network of neurons in the brain that connects the cerebral cortex, thalamus, and limbic system
neuromuscular   relating to the nerves and muscles; jointly affecting the nerves and muscles
neuron   the fundamental unit or cell of the brain and nervous system which receives input from the external world, sends motor commands to the muscles, and transforms and relays electrical impulses
neuroplasticity   the ability of the brain to form and reorganize connections between neurons, especially in response to learning experiences or following an injury which affects the brain
neuroscience   the scientific study of the nervous system
nociception   the process by which specific receptors in the body detect potentially damaging stimuli
nonverbal communication   communication which does not involve speech or words

occipital lobe one of the four divisions of the brain located at the back for processing visual input

organic a form that is developed naturally and not based on artificial rules

orbital frontal cortex the prefrontal region of the front brain lobes involved in decision-making

Pacinian corpuscles egg-shaped structures in the subcutaneous tissues of the hands and feet which respond to rapid changes in pressure; also occur in other tissues (Schenkman et al. 207–8)

paradigm a set of assumptions, theories, or beliefs that serve as the foundation of concepts, like identity, or for institutions

parietal lobe part of the cerebral cortex located at the top and back of the brain which processes spatial input and produces sensory integration

pedagogy the function of teaching; can also refer to instructional methods

perception becoming aware of something through the senses

perceptual motor processes in which a person takes in information through the senses and then organizes, interprets, and responds to it

phenomenological focuses on the study of consciousness and direct experiences; in the phenomenological approach, there is an effort to create conditions for the objective study of experiences and topics usually considered subjective

pictogram a chart or graph in which data is displayed using pictures

positron-emission tomography (PET) a form of technology in which radio tracers are used to assess the functioning of organs and tissues

posture how the body is positioned or held

premotor cortex a part of the frontal cortex which plans and creates movements

proprioception the sensory system in which receptors below the surface of the body provide the brain with information about muscular stretch, joint position, and tension on tendons; these receptors are found in muscles, fascia, tendons, ligaments, joints, and even in the skin (Krasnow and Wilmerding 286)

reticular activating system a group of nuclei at the top of the brain stem which trigger arousal; it is a primary contributor to paying attention

rhythm a repeated pattern in movement or sound

schema an underlying structure connecting information together in the mind based on a relationship to a theme

sensation an awareness of stimuli through the senses or to an internal bodily change

short-term memory information retained in the mind for only seconds or minutes

sign an object, quality, or event which indicates the probable occurrence of something else

social emotional learning an approach to teaching and learning which focuses on soft skills, such as self-awareness and control, and interpersonal skills, in addition to acquiring academic knowledge

somatics a field within body work and movement studies which emphasizes internal physical perception and experience; the Alexander technique, the Feldenkrais Method, and Ideokinesis are examples of somatic practices

somatosensory system   part of the sensory system which provides awareness of sensations from muscles, joints, skin, and fascia

spatiotemporal   relating to both space and time; attempting to merge into traffic on a freeway is both a spatial and temporal experience

stimulus   something which incites or excites, resulting in an organism's response

student-centered teaching   a form of instruction in which students are active participants in their learning and during which teachers recognize and accommodate different modalities without being overly directive

superior colliculus   part of the mental apparatus located deep in the brain which searches for and tracks movements and is attuned to sounds

symbol   something that stands for or suggests something else based on a relationship, association, convention, or resemblance

synesthesia   a sensory impression related to one sense when another sense is stimulated

synthesizing   a result in which sensory impressions, feelings, knowledge, and memories are brought together in a unified manner (Root-Bernsteins 296)

tacit knowledge   understanding that is gained from personal experiences and often not based on words or speech

teaching cue   a word or phrase that communicates critical features if a movement skill

temporal region   one of the brain lobes in the lower part of the brain near the ears which is responsible for audition and some types of memory

test-retest reliability   a way to determine whether a procedure or test produces the same results over time

thalamus   a point of processing in the brain for sensations and location and for relaying motor information to muscles

thematizing   the act of making an idea, experience, or emotion into the main topic; the thematic idea is placed at the beginning of a sentence so that attention is focused on it; the following is an example of a thematic sentence: "Evil can be punished in surprising ways"

transforming   creative work and problem-solving in which one set of tools is used to define a problem, another set to investigate it, and a third set to find a solution (Root-Bernsteins 273)

unconscious   part of one's mental life that does not enter into awareness

vestibular   a sensory system located in the inner ear responsible for balance and orientation in space

viscera   organs located in the body's cavities, especially those in the abdominal cavity

visual imagery   a mental representation of objects, events, or movements as they are perceived using vision (Krasnow and Wilmerding 290)

visual literacy   the ability to discriminate between slight differences in line, shape, color, and pattern that are seen

Wernicke's area   a portion of the left parietal lobe concerned with language comprehension

working memory a type of short-term memory in which moment-to-moment perceptions are integrated over a relatively short time period and combined with memories

zone of proximal development a learning theory presented by Lev Vygotsky in the early twentieth century which represents the space between a child's developmental level and the amount of learning possible when students are provided with proper teaching techniques and guidance (Minton *Using Movement* 3)

References

Bates, Bob. *Learning Theories Simplified*. 2nd ed. Sage, 2019.

Bransford, John, et al. "Theories of Learning and Their Role in Teaching." *Preparing Teachers for a Changing World: What Teachers Should Learn and Be Able to Do*, edited by Linda Darling-Hammond and John Bransford, 2005, Jossey-Bass, 2005, pp. 40–87.

Caine, Renate Nummela, and Geoffrey Caine. *Education on the Edge of Possibility*. Association for Supervision and Curriculum Development, 1997.

Eddy, Martha. *Mindful Movement: The Evolution of the Somatic Arts and Conscious Action*. Intellect, 2017.

Krasnow, Donna, and Virginia Wilmerding. *Motor Learning and Control for Dance: Principles and Practices for Performers and Teachers*. Human Kinetics, 2015.

Minton, Sandra. *Using Movement to Teach Academics: The Mind and Body as One Entity*. Rowman & Littlefield, 2008.

Root-Bernstein, Robert, and Michèle Root-Bernstein. *Sparks of Genius: The 13 Thinking Tools of the World's Most Creative People*. Houghton Mifflin, 1999.

Rugg, Harold. *Imagination*. Harper and Row, 1963.

Schenkman, Margaret, et al. *Clinical Neuroscience for Rehabilitation*. Pearson Education, 2013.

Schunk, Dale. *Learning Theories: An Educational Perspective*. 8th ed. Pearson, 2020.

INDEX

abstraction 131–132, 169, 176, 180
addiction 21, 83
African dance 56–57, 68, 99, 129
Alexander, Frederick Matthias 14, 35, 56, 58–59, 61, *61*, 86, 178
Amabile, Teresa 174
Ando, Taku 96–97
anorexia 81
Aristotle 2
Arnheim, Rudolf 27
arts education programs and analyses: Arts Education Partnership (AEP) 119; Art for Art's Sake? The Impact of Arts Education 187–188; ASHE-ERIC Higher Education Report 151; Common Core State Standards 196; Developmental Mental Dance Movement (DDM) program 188; Evidence: A Report on the Impact of Dance in the K-12 Setting 187; Interacting Cognitive Subsystems (ICS) 97; National Core Arts Standards (NCAS)119–120; Teaching Personal Social Responsibility Model (TPSR) 117; Twenty-First Century Skills 191; The Safe, Positive, Accountable, Respectful and Kind Program (SPARK) 117; value of dance education, research on 188–192
assessment instruments: Abbreviated Torrance Test for Adults (ATTA) 97; Basic Needs Satisfaction in Sports Scale (BNSSS) 93; Body Esteem Scale (BES) 94; Bulimic Inventory Test Edinburgh (BITE) 95; Cash 69-Item Body Self-Reliance Questionnaire 93–94; Collins Body Image Silhouettes Questionnaire 95; Creativity in Dance Instrument 212; Culture-Free Self-Esteem Inventory (CFSEI) 190; Dance Imagery Questionnaire (DIQ) 78; Dancers' Perceptions of the Creative Process Questionnaire (DPCPQ) 93; Dance Performance Assessment Instrument 141; David Kolb's Learning Style Inventory-3 (LSI-3) 92; Eating Attitudes Test (EAT-26) 95; Figural Scientific Creativity Test 164; Flexible Thinking Test (FTT) 97; Goodenough-Harris Draw-a-Person Test 188; Individual Differences Questionnaire (IDQ) 156; Movement Imagery Questionnaire-Revised (MIQ-R) 92; Multidimensional Assessment of Interoceptive Awareness (MAIA) 30; Multidimensional Inventory of Perfectionism in Sport (MIPS) 93; Perfectionistic Cognitive Inventory (PCI) 93; Physical Education Teacher Assessment Instrument (PETAI) 37; Short Physical Performance Battery (SPPB) 57; Spatial Kinesthetic Awareness Test (SKAT) 36; Sport Imagery Questionnaire (SIQ) 78; Subjective Movement Imagery Questionnaire-3 (MIQ-3) 87; Test of Ability in

Movement Imagery (TAMI) 87; Torrance Test of Creative Thinking, Figural Form A (TTCT) 175
attention: automatic 70; control 70; external focus 74; importance in learning to dance 74–76; importance to creative process 73; internal focus 74–75
autism 34

Barr, Sherrie 95, 154
Bartenieff, Irmgard 14–15, 56, 59, 72, 86
Batson, Glenna 37–38, 55, 58, 62, 167, 172
Beauchamps, Pierre 139
Beaunis, Heni-Etienne 5
Berthoz, Alain 127
body awareness 15, 25, 30–31, 37, 54–62, 63–68, 69–70, 98–102, 113
Bond, Karen 189
brain functions: executive function 67; neuroplasticity 172; relation to dance 168–172
brain structure: amygdala 169–170; anterior cingulate 169; basal ganglia 169; Broca's area 169; Cerebellum 169; hippocampus 170; hypothalamus 169–170; inferior parietal lobule 122, 124; limbic system 169; prefrontal cortex 122, 169; reticular activating system 169; somatosensory cortex 169–170; superior colliculus 169; Wernicke's area 122
Bransford, John 211–212
breath 71, 90, 116, 130, 158, 162, 180; Integrative Breathing Therapy 72
Bruner, Jerome 9
bulimia 81
Bull, Nina 7–8, 12

Caine, Renate and Geoffrey 166
Calder, Alexander 178
Calvo-Merino, Beatriz 124–125
Carter, Rita 21–22, 27, 168–170
Cattell, Raymond 73
Cerny, Sandra 5–9, **210**
Chappell, Kerry 76
characteristics of dance: social nature 69, 165
Chatfield, Steven 92, 155, 159
child development 1, 171
Chomsky, Noam 132
choreography 76, 78, 88, 94, 96–97, 120–122, 129, 146, 161, 165, 169, 179–183, 185–186, 189, 191, 195

cognition 9, 12, 26–30, 34, 54, 63–64, 73, 159, 162, 165, 171, 182, 188, 211–212; children's cognitive development 13; cognitive approach to learning 1, 155; 4E Cognition 68–69, 182
cognitive psychology 67
Cohen, Bonnie Bainbridge 31, 48, 56, 72
Confucius 186
consciousness: basis in biology 13; relationship to body 16, 62
creativity: brain storming 119, 174, 189; creative process 63, 73, 76, 93, 96, 177, 179, 182, 189; creative thinking 8, 175–176, 179, 192, 196, 209; different forms 25, 81; divergent thinking 73, 174, 188; problem solving 65, 77, 117, 151, 160, 174, 212; relationship to dance 154–155, 158, 160
Crick, Francis 178
Cross, Emily 124
Csikszentmihalyi, Mihaly 173–175
cultures, analysis of: archetypes 113; collectivism 113, 142; individualism 113, 142

Damasio, Antonio 10–12, 38, 66–67
Damasio, Hanna 66–67
dance studio mirrors, use of 33, 42, 93, 94
dance teacher behaviors 37
Dean, Laura 181, 183–184, *184*
Delsarte, Françoise 126–127, *127*
depression 31, 67
Descartes, René 3
Dewey, John 1–2, 8, 14, 29–30, 65, **152**, 162
Diamond, Adele 169
Doidge, Norman 11, **12**
Dowd, Irene 59, *60*
Dunn, Jan 86–89, 155

eastern movement practices: tai chi 56, 71, 102; chi kung 56, 71; judo 56; Katsugen Undo 56; yoga 56
embody: brain maps of body 10; body basis of knowing 4–12; body thinking 15; embodied cognition 9, 63–64, 68; embodied knowledge 185; embodied language 68; embodied learning 13, 30, 39, 186, 188; felt sense 9, 13, 64, 86; felt-thought 8–9; lived body 3, 12, 13, 40, 62–63; mind-body parallelism 13; physical understanding 13; relationship to creative work 76

emotion: connection to body 11; different types of responses in brain 11; emotional reaction 6–7, 31; James-Lange theory 39
empathy: Action Observation Network (AON) 124; affective empathy 114; cognitive empathy 114; defined 114; neuroscience and empathy 122–123, 124–125; relationship to dance 117; relationship to Social Emotional Learning 117–119; relationship to the arts 115; sympathetic modeling 29; teaching empathy 115, 119
environment 6, 13, 21, 27, 33, 37, 54, 58, 72, 94, 117, 119, 125, 127, 130, 140, 151, 154, 161, 163, 165, 167, 171, 182, 197, 208; relationship to movers 15, 74, 79, 126

Faber, Rima 23, 168–170
Ferrari, Michel 13, 64, **210**
Feuillet, Raoul-Auger 139
Fisher, Vicky 79, 83, 96, 180
Fitt, Sally 22
Fontana, David 130
Foster, Susan Leigh 114, 120, 126–127
Fraleigh, Sondra 35
Franklin, Eric 77, *80*, 80–81, 86–87, 89

Gardner, Howard 140, **152**, 159–161
Gendlin, Eugene 9, 64
George, Doran 8, 14, 15, 57
Gestalt therapy 64
Gibson, James 127
Giguere, Miriam 69, 154, 165, 180, 189
Gilbert, Anne Green 161, 170–171; BrainDance 170–171; suggested activities based on brain development 171
Gingrasso, Susan 185
Gottschild, Brenda Dixon 57
Grandin, Temple 177
Guest, Ann Hutchinson 139–140
Guss-West, Clare 32–36, 44, 70–71, 74–75, 158

Halprin, Anna 31
Hammond, Zaretta 113, 167
Hanna, Judith Lynne 180
Hardiman, Mariale 212
Hawkins, Alma xiii–xiv
H'Doubler, Margaret 14
Heiland, Teresa 89–90, 141
Hellison, Don 117

Henley, Matthew 21–22, 24, 26, 31, 33–34, 37, 39, 40, 68
Horst, Louis 186; pre-classic dance forms 186
Hubbard Street Dance 119

imagery studies: anatomy based 89; body image as basis 93–95; posture and turn-out as basis 90; psychological skills as basis 92–93; somatics based 91; specific dance movements as basis 89–90
imagery types: anatomical 80, **82**, 90–91; auditory **82**, 88; body image **82**, 93–95; direct 79–80, **82**; external 79, **82**, 87–88, 103; global 89; indirect or metaphoric 79–80, **82**, 87–88; internal 79, **82**; kinesthetic 77–78, 79, 86, 88–89, 179; lines-of-movement 80; mental practice 79, **82**; motor 77–78, **82**, 84, 87; tactile-kinesthetic 77; visual 77–78, 79, 83, 88
imagery uses: comparison of 87–88; general uses 87; somatics uses 84–86; teaching dance technique 86–88; theoretical basis for use 81–83
Immordino-Yang, Mary Helen 212
improvisation 69–70, 76; uses for 75
inspiration 76, 93, 96, 103, 121–122, 132, 139, 169–170, 172, 174, 177, 179, 180–181, 182, 185, 208, 209
International Baccalaureate Dance Program 165, 190; curriculum 190
intuition 4, 9, 22, 76, 77, 167, 209
Irish step dancing 34

James, William 70
Jeannerod, Marc 83–84
Johnston, Dale 154–155
Jung, Carl 131, 162

Kaku, Michio 11, **12**, 170
Kandel, Eric 11, **12**, 67, 170
Kant, Imanuel 3–4, **210**
Kaplan, Bernard 6, **12**, 140
Keller, Helen 177
kinesthesia 13, 22–23, 36, 127, 129
knowledge: declarative 154; explicit 63; procedural 154, 184–185; tacit 63
Knust, Albrecht 139
Kosslyn, Stephen 77

Laban, Rudolf 14–15, 130, 139, 141, 169, 194; efforts 14–15, 130, 169

learning movement and dance 31–40; role of proprioception 36–39
learning theories: active learning 151; Brain-Based Learning 151, **153**, 166–167; connections between learning theories 172–173; constructivist learning 162, 194; cooperative learning 151, **153**, 163–165; dance, relationship to learning theories154–155; experiential learning 151, 162; Index of Learning Styles (ILS) 156; Kolb Experiential Learning Theory 162; learning styles 151, **152**, 155–158; Multiple Intelligences 151, **152**, 159–160; socially shared regulation in cooperative learning (SSRL) 164–165; Zone of Proximal Development (ZPD) 151–154
Leibniz, Gottfried 2
Lewin, Kurt 8, 154, 162
literacy 29, 63, 118, 132, 175, 189
Locke, John **152**, 162

McGregor, Wayne 97–98
Martin, John 125, 126; kinesthetic sympathy 125
Matsumoto, David 126, 128
memory: as anatomical process 63; cognitive markers 172; encoding of 135; long-term 11, 170, 172; short-term 170
Merleau-Ponty, Maurice 12–13, 63, **210**
metaphor 79–80, 87–88, 131, 133, 167, 180
mind-body: Cartesian duality 2; eastern perspective 3–4; mind-body dichotomy 1–18, 63, 64–65, 113, 132; mind-body integration 30–31; summary of mind-body information 11–12; western perspective xiii, 2–3
mindfulness 15, 21, 25, 30–31, 58, 60–61, 72, 83, 116, 192, 207
Minton, Sandra 23, 36–37, 45, 46, 76, 80, 88, 90, 96, 131, 151, 155, 165, 166, 168–170, 175, 179–180, 182, 186, 190–191, 197
mirror neurons 10, 65, 66–67, 122–125, 168–169; mimicry 122–123, 135; studies related to movement 123–124
Moradian, Ann 207–208, 211
Mulder, Theo 84

Nadel, Myron 185–186
neuroscience 33, 73; cognitive neuroscience 67; educational neuroscience 167, 170, 212; research on xiv, 77, 122, 124

Newton, Isaac 177
nonverbal communication 125–130; cultural differences 127–129; dance as a form of 129–130; facial expressions 125, 130; gestures 125, 128; learning 129, 130; Mudras 136

Oliver, Wendy 93, 95
organizations: Centre for Educational Research and Innovation (CERI) 187; National Dance Education Organization (NDEO) 187
Ornstein, Robert 9–10, **12**
Overby, Lynette Young 78, 86–89, 185, 197

Paivio, Allan 78
perception 27, 30, 38–39, 54–55, 69; emotional relationship to 28; haptic 28; visual 28, 33
phenomenology 12, 63
Piaget, Jean 13, 64, 162
Pinker, Steven 132–133
Plato 2
Polanyi, Michael 63
Posner, Michael 169
post-diaster psychological symptoms (PTSD) 58
private speech 154–155
proprioceptors: golgi tendon organ 23, *25*; joint receptors 23; muscle spindles 23, *24*; skin receptors 23, 27, *28*

Radell, Sally 93–94
Ramachandran, V. S. 9–10, **12**
Rapaport, David 6–7, 8
Ratey, John 169, 188
Reedy, Patricia 212–213
Reich, Steve 26, 181
Rolf, Ida 56
Root-Bernstein, Robert and Michèle 132, 175–179
Rosett, Joshua 7–8, **12**
Rugg, Harold 8–9, **12**

Sacks, Oliver 10, **12**
Saint Augustine 2
Saint Thomas Aquinas 2–3
Schilder, Paul 6, **12**, 80–81
Schunk, Dale 153–154, 156, 162, 164, 166, 173–174
Schupp, Karen 165
Scott, Gladys 22–23
sensation 26–31; connection to action 26–27; integration 25–26

sensory motor 6
sensory systems: audition or hearing 26; dominance of vision 32–35; early sensory and motor patterns 6; exteroception 21; interoception 23–25; nociception 23; proprioception 21–23; smell 21, 83; tactile/touch 21, 26, 31–32, 35–36; taste 21, 22, 83, 177; vestibular 21–22, 26, 31, 171; vision 21, 27, 32–35
Sheets-Johnstone, Maxine 12–13, 62–63
Shlain, Leonard 131–133
Siedentop, Daryl 117
Smith-Autard, Jacqueline 76, 96
Social Emotional Learning (SEL); arts connections 115–116; Collaborative of Academic, Social and Emotional Learning (CASEL) 116; connections to dance 117–119; improving SEL 116–117; intelligence connections 118
somatics: applications 57–58; cultural connections 57, 64; dance applications 58–62; somatic experiencing (SE) 58; student teachers' use 58
somatic systems: The Alexander Technique 14, 35, 56, 59, 86; The Aston Paradigm 57; Bartenieff Fundamentals of Movement 14, 72; Body-Mind Centering 31, 48, 49, 72; Feldenkrais Awareness through Movement 86; The Feldenkrais Method 15, 35, 56, 62, 72, 86; Gerda Alexander's Eutony (GAE) 56; Ideokinesis 15, 58, 59; Pilates 59–60
Sousa, David 170, 212
Spinoza, Baruch 3, 10
Stebbins, Genevieve 126, *127*
stimulus 7–8, 11, 22, 29–30, 38, 66, 70, 77, 175, 208
Stinson, Susan 187–188
Sweigard, Lulu 84–85, *85*, 90
symbols: abstractions 131–132; communication 130–131; eastern versus western use 133–134; dance notation 139–142; language as symbols 132–133; Language of Dance ® (LOD) 139; literal symbol 131–132; right and left-brain connections 131, 132; signs 131; visual symbols, increased use of 132, 134

teaching: arts integration 186, 195; auditory teaching cues 34–35; chunking 172; cuing 21, 32, 34–37, 74; dance integration 186; distributed practice 62, 166; interdisciplinary teaching 197; mnemonic device 178; novice learners 32, 69, 74, 124, 141, 154, 172; Pattern Play 181, 182; related to dance 87, 191; research, teaching through dance 197; student-centered 62, 65, 151, 165; tactile teaching cues 35–36; teacher-centered 62, 65; teaching blind students 36; teaching special needs or exceptional students 32–33, 189; teaching through the arts 31; visual teaching cues 32–34
technology used to explore mind-body connection: functional magnetic resonance imaging (fMRI) 77; positron emission tomography (PET) 77
theories: based on meaning 27; Neuromatrix theory 39
thinking: abstract thought 159–160; connection to electrical energy in brain 11, 83; connection to movement 6, 13, 68, 69; synesthesia 179; thirteen creative thinking tools 175
Titchener, Edward 126
Todd, Mabel Elsworth 15, 84

unconscious 22, 67, 76, 126, 129, 131, 166, 172, 209; connection to physiology 15

vision 6, 21, 23, 27, 32–34, 40–41, 135, 156; shapes, contours and boundaries 10
Vygotsky, Lev 140, 151–152, 155

Warburton, Edward 35, 129, 140
Washburn, Margaret Floy 5–8, *5*
Watson, James 178
Werner, Heinze 6
Wilder, Penfield 10
Williams, Diane 212
Willis, Judy 212

Zull, James 10, 83, 122–123, 170

For Product Safety Concerns and Information please contact our EU
representative GPSR@taylorandfrancis.com
Taylor & Francis Verlag GmbH, Kaufingerstraße 24, 80331 München, Germany

www.ingramcontent.com/pod-product-compliance
Lightning Source LLC
Chambersburg PA
CBHW051355290426
44108CB00015B/2024